Wayne Jones
Editor

E-Serials
Publishers, Libraries, Users, and Standards
Second Edition

Pre-publication
REVIEW . . .

"**S**timulating, informative, and at times even humorous, this is an outstanding collection of articles on electronic serials. *E-Serials: Publishers, Libraries, Users, and Standards, Second Edition,* covers many of the most topical issues of interest to librarians working in the electronic publishing world today.

There is much to interest the reference librarian in this collection—from Gough's article about knowledge environments, to McCracken's article on Serials Solutions, to Hunter's article on ScienceDirect. Catalogers will enjoy Shadle's and Cole's articles on the difficulties of applying AACR2 cataloging rules to electronic serials, while archivists and historians will want to read Day's article on digital preservation. Regardless of their area of specialty, librarians will find this book enjoyable and well worth reading."

Lucy A. Barron, MLS
Head, Serial Cataloging Section II,
Serial Record Division,
Library of Congress;
CONSER Representative
for the Library of Congress

E-Serials
Publishers, Libraries, Users, and Standards
Second Edition

THE HAWORTH INFORMATION PRESS
Haworth Series in Serials and Continuing Resources
Jim Cole and Wayne Jones
Senior Editors

E-Serials
Publishers, Libraries, Users, and Standards
Second Edition

Wayne Jones
Editor

The Haworth Information Press®
An Imprint of The Haworth Press, Inc.
New York • London • Oxford

Published by

The Haworth Information Press®, an imprint of The Haworth Press, Inc. 10 Alice Street, Binghamton, NY 13904-1580.

PUBLISHER'S NOTE
Due to the ever-changing nature of the Internet, Web site names and addresses, though verified to the best of the publisher's ability, should not be accepted as accurate without independent verification.

Cover design by Jennifer M. Gaska.

Library of Congress Cataloging-in-Publication Data

E-serials : publishers, libraries, users, and standards / Wayne Jones, editor.—2nd ed.
    p. cm.
Includes bibliographical references and index.
   ISBN 0-7890-1229-4 (alk. paper)—ISBN 0-7890-1230-8 (pbk. : alk. paper)
   1. Libraries—Special collections—Electronic journals. 2. Libraries—United States—Special collections—Electronic journals. 3. Electronic journals—Publishing. 4. Acquisition of electronic journals. 5. Cataloging of electronic journals. I. Title: Electronic serials. II. Jones, Wayne, 1959-
   Z692.E43 E2 2002
   025.2'832—dc21
                           2002012842

CONTENTS

ACQUISITIONS AND COLLECTION DEVELOPMENT

Chapter 4. An Eclipse of the Sun: Acquisitions in the Digital Era

PRESERVATION AND ARCHIVING

PROJECTS AND INNOVATIONS

CITATION

ABOUT THE EDITOR

Wayne Jones, MLS, worked as a librarian for sixteen years, first as a subject indexer of the vertical file at the Royal Canadian Mounted Police, then as a monograph cataloger at the Ministry of the Solicitor General, a cataloger of serials and government documents at the National Library of Canada, and finally as head of serials cataloging at NLC and at MIT. He has edited or co-edited four other books about serials and e-resources, has published several articles and book reviews in professional journals, and currently serves as senior editor of *The Serials Librarian.* He has a BA (Honors) from Memorial University of Newfoundland, an MA from the Universisty of Toronto, and an MLS from the University of Western Ontario. He is a freelance editor in Toronto (wayne@canedit.ca).

CONTRIBUTORS

Margret Branschofsky, MSLS, is DSpace Project Faculty Liaison, MIT Libraries, Massachusetts Institute of Technology, Cambridge, Massachusetts (e-mail: margretb@mit.edu).

Eric Celeste, MLS, is Associate University Librarian for Information Technology at the University of Minnesota (Twin Cities) Libraries, Minneapolis, Minnesota (e-mail: efc@umn.edu).

Jim Cole is Principal Serials Cataloger at the Iowa State University Library, Ames, Iowa (e-mail: jecole@iastate.edu).

Leslie Daigle is Principal, Thinking Cat Enterprises (e-mail: leslie @thinkingcat.com).

Ron Daniel Jr. is a Standards Architect at Interwoven, Inc. (e-mail: rdaniel@interwoven.com).

Michael Day is Research Officer at the U.K. Office for Library and Information Networking (UKOLN), University of Bath, Bath, United Kingdom (e-mail: lismd@ukoln.ac.uk).

Ellen Finnie Duranceau is Digital Resources Acquisitions Librarian, Massachusetts Institute of Technology Libraries, Cambridge, Massachusetts (e-mail: efinnie@mit.edu).

Kristin H. Gerhard is Electronic Resources Coordinator and Catalog Librarian, Parks Library, Iowa State University, Ames, Iowa (e-mail: kgerhard@iastate.edu).

Nancy R. Gough, PhD, is Associate Editor, *Science*'s STKE, American Association for the Advancement of Science, Washington, DC (e-mail: ngough@aaas.org).

Kathlene Hanson is Electronic Resources Coordinator at California State University, Monterey Bay Library, Seaside, California (e-mail: kathlene_hanson@monterey.edu).

Karen Hunter is Senior Vice President, Strategy, Elsevier Science, New York City (e-mail: k.hunter@elsevier.com).

Mark Jacobs is Electronic Resources/Serials Cataloging Librarian at Washington State University, Pullman, Washington (e-mail: majacobs @wsu.edu).

Cindy Stewart Kaag is Head of the Science Libraries at Washington State University (WSU), Pullman, Washington (e-mail: kaag@wsu. edu).

Cheryl Kern-Simirenko is Associate Dean and Director of Public Services and Collections, Purdue University Libraries, West Lafayette, Indiana (e-mail: cks@purdue.edu).

Peter McCracken, MSLS, MA, is a Co-Founder of Serials Solutions, LLC (http://www.serialssolutions.com), and Coordinator of Reference in the Odegaard Undergraduate Library at the University of Washington (e-mail: peter@serialssolutions.com).

Cecilia Preston is a Partner at Preston & Lynch (e-mail: cecilia@ well.com).

Cathy Rentschler is Chair of the Library and Information Science Discussion Group of the Association of College and Research Libraries (e-mail: crentschler6066@aol.com).

Steven C. Shadle is Serials Cataloger, University of Washington Libraries, Seattle, Washington (e-mail: shadle@u.washington.edu).

Simon Buckingham Shum is Lecturer, Knowledge Media Institute, The Open University, Milton Keynes, United Kingdom (e-mail: sbs@acm.org).

Tamara Sumner is Assistant Professor, Center for LifeLong Learning and Design, University of Colorado, Boulder, Colorado (e-mail: sumner@ colorado.edu).

Janice R. Walker is Assistant Professor in the Department of Writing and Linguistics at Georgia Southern University (e-mail: jwalker@ gasou.edu).

Bonita Wilson, MSLS, is Managing Editor of *D-Lib Magazine* (e-mail: bwilson@cnri.reston.va.us).

Gregory Wool, MA, MLS, is Associate Professor, Monographs Cataloger, and Authorities Unit Supervisor at the Iowa State University Library, Ames, Iowa (e-mail: gwool@iastate.edu).

Simeon Yates is Senior Lecturer, School of Cultural Studies, Sheffield Hallam University, Sheffield, United Kingdom (e-mail: s.j.yates@simeon.org.uk).

Preface

This book is an update of the edition published in 1998. Most of the chapters from that first edition have been retained, but because so much has happened with e-serials in the last three years, the authors have often had to completely restructure their work in order to reflect the current situation: merely fiddling with details or doing a light rewrite have not been enough. There are new chapters in this book, too, exploring in more detail some topics which took up less room on the plate in the first edition—for example, experimentation by e-journal publishers and tracking titles in aggregator packages.

My goal in putting together this collection has been to provide a broad view of e-serials from various perspectives—the publisher, the librarian, the user—in a fairly compact volume. No doubt there are gaps, things I should have covered but didn't, but I take some consolation in the fact that it's pretty impossible now to produce a book about all-things-e-serial without it being the sizes of a James Michener novel.

I'd mostly like to thank the authors represented here for taking the time to write about their respective expertises. In addition, for keeping me up-to-date on a daily basis about the nitty-gritty details of serials cataloging and e-serials generally, I'd like to gratefully acknowledge the members of the Serials Cataloging Section at MIT, affectionately known as SerCat: Arnie, Craig, David, Jennifer, Lauren, and Walter.

PUBLISHING

Chapter 1

D-Lib Magazine: Incremental Evolution of an Electronic Magazine

Bonita Wilson

INTRODUCTION

D-Lib Magazine (http://www.dlib.org) is produced by the Corporation for National Research Initiatives (CNRI) in Reston, Virginia, with sponsorship from the U.S. Defense Advanced Research Projects Agency (DARPA).[1] The magazine is one part of the support provided by the D-Lib Forum to "the community of researchers and developers working to create and apply the technologies leading to the global digital library community."[2] Currently, *D-Lib Magazine* is available free of charge to anyone with an Internet connection. Eleven issues of the magazine are released each year, and the first issue appeared in July 1995.

Each issue of *D-Lib Magazine* is composed of articles, an editorial, a featured collection, and two columns: "In Brief" and "Clips and Pointers." The "In Brief" column is made up of contributed short items about new digital library projects, the launch of new discussion lists, scholarship and grant opportunities, and reports from conferences and meetings. Excerpts from news and press releases are also included in the "In Brief" column. The "Clips and Pointers" column lists, describes, and provides hyperlinks to new "print" resources (In Print), collections of links (Point to Point), calls for participation, and upcoming events (Goings On). In addition, calls for participation with imminent deadlines and events that will take place before the next issue of *D-Lib* is released are listed under the Deadline Reminders section of the "Clips and Pointers" column. In each issue, we feature a collection or Web site that serves as an excellent example of the possibilities for the dissemination of digital information. Occasionally, *D-Lib* includes book reviews, project briefings, and opinion pieces. The magazine welcomes letters to the editor, which are published along with the comments of the author of the original article, opinion, or other feature when possible.

Over the course of its publication history, *D-Lib Magazine* has sought to evolve and improve its service to the digital library community. Changes have been made incrementally, as we have kept in mind that our readership is international and that those who read the magazine come from many different environments, with different computer platforms and levels of technological skills.

DIGITAL LIBRARY RESEARCH

By 1995, digital library research in the United States had begun to be recognized as an important field in its own right as a result of the Computer Science Technical Reports project (1992-1995) and the Digital Libraries Initiative (1994-1998).[3] In 1998, a follow-up initiative, the Digital Libraries Initiative Phase 2, was launched, and in 1999 the National Science Foundation issued a solicitation for proposals for a program titled International Digital Libraries Collaborative Research. Early digital library projects and programs outside the United States included the Canadian Initiative on Digital Libraries; eLib: the Electronic Libraries Program in the United Kingdom; the European Research Consortium for Informatics and Mathematics (ERCIM); the Distributed Systems Technology Centre in Australia; the New Zealand Digital Library; and the Digital Library Network (DLNET) in Japan.

D-LIB MAGAZINE'S *MISSION*

In the first issue of *D-Lib Magazine,* Dr. Amy Friedlander, who was the magazine's editor at that time, wrote:

> Welcome to *D-Lib Magazine,* a magazine about digital library issues for researchers, developers, and the intellectually curious. . . . The magazine is itself an experiment in electronic publishing, which fulfills its communication function for the Digital Library Forum by testing the limits of writing in and for a wholly networked environment. We have no—and propose no—print analogue, and we will be most intrigued by substantive articles that take advantage of the power of hypermedia while retaining the strengths of traditional, print publishing.[4]

Six years after the launch of the magazine, the community of researchers in digital libraries has expanded greatly, but *D-Lib Magazine*'s aims remain much the same. We focus primarily on articles about innovation and research in digital libraries, but we also disseminate information on related topics, such as distance education, electronic publishing, virtual collection development, etc., and the magazine's audience has grown to include not just researchers, but also practitioners, those who are working "in the trenches" of digital libraries. Early on, a conscious decision was made to "help digital libraries be a broad interdisciplinary field, not a set of specialties that know little of each other."[5]

D-Lib's managing editor alerts the digital library community far and wide when new issues of the magazine are released, and uses various means to do so: sending announcements to library listservs, administering a subscriber mailing list, and coordinating the mirroring of the magazine at five sites on four continents. A discussion of the last two of these methods follows.

D-Lib *Subscriptions*

D-Lib maintains a list of subscribers to whom an announcement is sent upon the release of each new issue of the magazine. When *D-Lib Magazine* had a few hundred subscribers, each subscription activity, i.e., subscribing, unsubscribing, or changing e-mail addresses, was done by magazine staff who entered the subscription information onto a mailing list one by one. However, when the number of subscribers began to number in the thousands, it was no longer feasible to manage the subscriber list that way. An automated mailing list was established that allows subscribers to manage their own subscriptions. Also, the new mailing list program allows only the mailing list administrator to post messages; therefore, there is less opportunity for subscribers to be "spammed."

Mirror Policies and Procedures

The magazine's first mirror site was UKOLN, the U.K. Office for Library and Information Networking, in Bath, England. The Australian National University Sunsite, Canberra, Australia, became a mirror site for *D-Lib Magazine* shortly thereafter. As of April 2002, *D-Lib Magazine* has five mirror sites. In addition to the first two sites, the magazine is now mirrored by the State Library of Lower Saxony and the University Library of Goettingen, Goettingen, Germany; the Universidad de Belgrano, Buenos Aires, Argentina; and Academia Sinica, Taipei, Taiwan.

A policy and procedures document, "Mirror Policy for *D-Lib Magazine*," was written in 1999 to clarify the responsibilities of both the host mirror and *D-Lib Magazine*. The host mirror must agree to:

1. get the new issue (*D-Lib Magazine* should be pulled, not pushed, to the host mirror);
2. mirror the magazine in its entirety (including back issues);
3. mirror the magazine exactly;
4. provide the magazine free of charge, including back issues;
5. direct any requests for reuse of material to *D-Lib Magazine* so that the managing editor may forward them to the author(s), who retain copyright;
6. provide to *D-Lib Magazine*'s managing editor a point of contact, including the name, phone number, fax number, and e-mail address of the contact; and
7. notify the managing editor of *D-Lib Magazine* when the mirroring at the host site begins.

D-Lib Magazine's responsibilities to the host mirror are to:

1. notify the mirrors that the new issue is on its way;
2. notify the mirrors when changes are made to the current issue after the release date;
3. manage the *D-Lib Magazine* site in such a way that those parts that need to be mirrored can be mirrored simply, and those parts that should not be mirrored are easy to avoid;
4. identify and credit the mirror sites in the magazine in a prominent fashion; and
5. respond quickly to any problems.

Since January 1999, there have been two basic approaches in use for mirroring *D-Lib Magazine:* http and ftp. The http approach imposes no additional actions on the source side. The ftp approach, while a more efficient use of bandwidth, requires running an ftp service at the source. In order to control access, *D-Lib Magazine* has made the ftp site a password-protected site, as opposed to an anonymous ftp site. Maintaining the ftp site, even with password protection, increases the magazine's security risks; consequently, *D-Lib* is discouraging its future use. *D-Lib* enables the http approach in the sense of using relative links throughout the magazine so that the mirror sites can be self-contained. Full path links that would direct users out of the mirrors and back to the source are used sparingly. Currently, this is done only for the nonmagazine D-Lib Forum pages and for large executable files.

The mirror sites spread access to the magazine across multiple Web servers and offer readers in areas remote to the United States the opportunity for faster access from a site closer to their physical location. Although no formal evaluation has been made of the full impact of the mirrors on readership, as each mirror site has come on board, we have noticed an increase in the numbers of subscribers to the magazine from the geographical regions served by the new mirror site.

DESIGN AND STYLE

The look of *D-Lib Magazine* has changed over the years. The primary motivation behind the changes has been to keep the magazine in tune with advancing Web technology. Also considered were improved navigation and making the magazine more visually attractive. Some of the design experiments were short-lived. For example, the first issue employed a white background, but as Web design evolved and colored backgrounds became popular, a blue-gray background was added. When readers began to comment that they had trouble reading text on pages that used those backgrounds, a white background with spot color was introduced. You can see the evolution in design from 1995 to 1998 in Figures 1.1 through 1.3.

In 1999, we added a new monthly feature to "show rather than tell" readers about excellent digital collections. This resulted in a design change to the table of contents page, as shown in Figure 1.4.

In late 2000, another redesign was completed. The reasons behind the redesign this time were to:

- reduce the number of images on the table of contents page to enable the page to load faster;
- improve readability of the page by removing unnecessary text;
- reduce the need for scrolling;
- introduce simple style sheets to manage layout;
- improve compliance with HTML 4.01, the then-current World Wide Web Consortium (W3C) Recommendation; and
- begin to structure *D-Lib Magazine* for future viewing on handheld appliances such as PDAs.[6]

The resulting redesigned table of contents page is shown in Figure 1.5.

Page design and presentation continue to be important aspects of the magazine as a whole and will continue to be evaluated in light of future Web design developments. The main point to be made about Web design versus design in a print world is that while we may not *attract* readers with flashy design the way a print publication might, we may *keep* readers by employing good design.

PERSISTENT IDENTIFIERS

To ensure long-term accessibility of the magazine's articles and other features, beginning with the first issue of *D-Lib Magazine,* Web pages have been assigned persistent identifiers. The identifiers have

FIGURE 1.1. *D-Lib Magazine,* 1995.

been based on the Handle System architecture developed by CNRI.[7] The Handle System is a general purpose global name service that enables secure name resolution over the Internet. The initial handle assigned to the July 1995 table of contents page looked like this:

cnri.dlib/July95-contents

Beginning with the January 1999 issue, the persistent identifier assigned to *D-Lib Magazine* content has been the Digital Object Identifier (DOI) for which the Handle System is the underlying architecture. The DOI used for the *D-Lib Magazine* January 2001 table of contents page looks like this:

10.1045/january2001-contents

The Digital Object Identifier effort is evolving a framework for the management of intellectual property in the digital environment, including mandatory associated metadata and the ability to resolve a

FIGURE 1.2. *D-Lib Magazine,* 1996.

single identifier into multiple values, which could at a higher level be thought of as services associated with the identified object. These efforts are explained and can be tracked at the DOI Web site.[8]

Currently, *D-Lib Magazine* DOIs are registered with multiple uniform resource locators (URLs), so if you enter one, such as <http://dx.doi.org/10.1045/january2001-contents>, the page to which the DOI resolves may be the one located at the *D-Lib Magazine* originating site at CNRI in Reston, Virginia, or the DOI may resolve to a mirrored Web page from one of the magazine's mirror sites, e.g., in Argentina or Germany. As future developments are made to the DOI architecture, it will become possible for the user to select the Web site to which the DOI resolves.

One particularly relevant effort that has come out of the DOI is in the area of journal reference linking. The use of a persistent, location-independent identifier is particularly applicable to the long-term utility of references appearing within journal articles; consequently, a large number of publishers have joined the CrossRef effort.[9] *D-Lib*

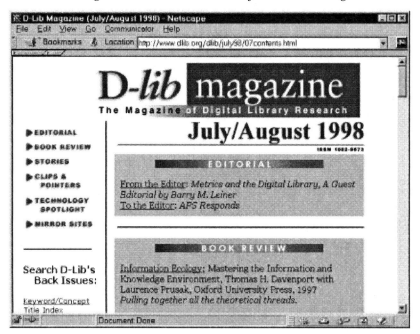

FIGURE 1.3. *D-Lib Magazine,* 1998.

Magazine will track this and similar efforts and join in or contribute to them as they evolve.

METADATA

Early in 1999, we began to explore the best way to create systematic metadata for *D-Lib Magazine* articles to facilitate information access and retrieval of the articles by future linking and resolution technologies. We looked for a metadata set that would satisfy several requirements:

- It should add only a small effort to the production of the magazine.
- It should be useful for information retrieval.
- It should be adequate for a variety of Web publications.
- It should be possible to extract the metadata using scripts.

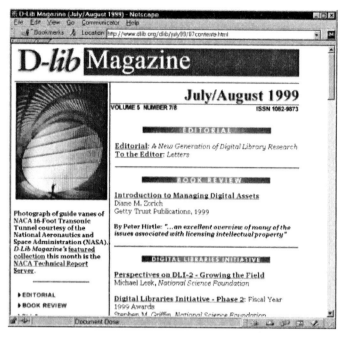

FIGURE 1.4. *D-Lib Magazine,* 1999.

In the end we decided to develop a Data Type Definition (DTD) to generate metadata in XML (Extensible Markup Language) using Dublin Core.[10]

Beginning in March 1999, *D-Lib* began to create metadata files for each of the magazine's articles. A link to the XML metadata file is put in the header of the source file. For example, in Eleanor Fink's article in the March 1999 issue of *D-Lib Magazine,* the header of the source file looks like this:

```
<head>
<LINK REL="metadata" HREF="03fink.meta.xml">
<meta http-equiv="Content-Type" content="text/html; charset=
iso-8859-1">
<meta NAME="DOI" CONTENT="10.1045/march99-fink">
<title>The Getty Information Institute: A Retrospective</title>
</head>
```

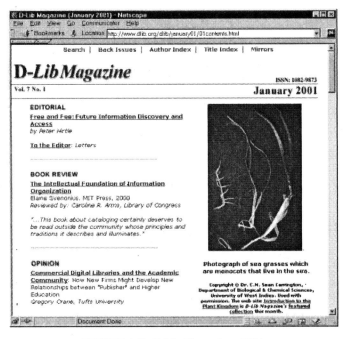

FIGURE 1.5. *D-Lib Magazine,* 2001.

The metadata file for the article looks like this:

```
<dlib-meta0.1>
    <title>The Getty Information Institute: A Retrospective</
    title>
    <creator>Eleanor E. Fink</creator>
    <publisher>Corporation for National Research Initiatives</
    publisher>
    <date date-type="publication">March 1999</date>
    <type resource-type="work">article</type>
    <identifier uri-type="DOI">10.1045/march99-fink</identifier>
    <identifier uri-type="URL">http://www.dlib.org/dlib/march99/
    fink/03fink.html</identifier>
    <language>English</language>
    <relation rel-type="InSerial">
    <serial-name>D-Lib Magazine</serial-name>
```

<issn>1082-9873</issn>
<volume>5</volume>
<issue>3</issue>
</relation>
<rights>Copyright (c) 1999 Eleanor E. Fink</rights> </dlib-meta0.1>

EDITING

In an article written for the first edition of *E-Serials: Publishers, Libraries, Users, and Standards*, Dr. Friedlander wrote:

> Editing . . . has been seen as an eternal war between the author and editor, where "writers write primarily to advance themselves, and editors edit to satisfy readers." We beg to differ. At least in the world of research, good stories will attract both readers and writers, and the role of the editor is to help the writer tell the story he or she wishes to tell. . . . Thus, we pursue an "author-centric" policy, inviting our writers to experiment with the capabilities of the digital medium within a very few limits . . . [11]

This *D-Lib* policy has not changed. The magazine remains "author-centric" and articles are carefully but lightly edited. In 2000, the document "*D-Lib Magazine* Guidelines for Authors" was finalized and made available on the Web. The guidelines are meant to be helpful, not restrictive. They end with a note to prospective authors that states, "The above guidelines are suggestions only, and they are open for further dialogue. The most important thing is to write the article you want to write in the way that you want it to appear!"[12]

The first year of publication, the author of every article that appeared in the magazine had been invited by the editor or publisher to submit the article. As *D-Lib Magazine* became better known, unsolicited articles and article proposals began to arrive. By the end of 2000, 39 percent of the articles published were submitted rather than invited, and the number of contributed, unsolicited articles continues to grow. In editorials and by other means, we have encouraged authors to send us proposals for articles. Today, we rely on the information that comes to us, because as the digital library community has grown, it is no longer possible to know all the creative activities that are taking place internationally.

From 1995 to 1998, *D-Lib Magazine* experimented with forms-based interactive messages to the editor using HyperNews software developed by Daniel LaLiberte, which had been made freely available by the National Center for Supercomputing Applications. Forms-based interactive messaging never really caught on as anticipated with readers, who only sporadically sent their comments to *D-Lib,* and its use was discontinued. A "Letters to the Editor" Web page replaced interactive messaging as a vehicle for reader comments. Readers are encouraged to send their comments for publication in a future issue; however, letters to the editor in response to articles have been few. Perhaps because we provide authors' e-mail addresses in the bylines of articles, readers who have comments about articles write directly to authors. On the other hand, in 1999 we began to accept occasional opinion pieces for publication, and the opinion pieces have been generating an increased number of letters to the editor.

In 1999, we created a new column, "In Brief," for the type of short pieces that used to appear at the beginning of the "Clips and Pointers" column. We search for and invite items for "In Brief" to provide current awareness services for readers wishing to be kept abreast of new projects, listservs, and grant and scholarship opportunities, among other things. At the same time, we added a new section—Deadline Reminders—to the "Clips" column. Our motivation for creating the new column for current awareness and for making the "Clips" column function more like an expanded monthly calendar of events was to make it easy for our readers, most of whom have very busy schedules, to focus quickly on those parts of the magazine that are of most value to them.

In October 1998, Dr. Amy Friedlander, who had been *D-Lib Magazine*'s editor from its inception, left the magazine to pursue new opportunities. During her tenure with *D-Lib,* she was instrumental in helping the magazine to "become a model for a new type of scholarly publication: consistent, reliable, and entirely on-line, with open access, author-retained copyright, and high production values."[13] The transition to a new editorial team was made easier by the sound editorial and production decisions made in the magazine's first two years. From the start, Dr. Friedlander scrupulously documented the magazine's mission, policies and procedures, editorial practices, and production work flow. She kept archives of correspondence between the editor and authors, and she made time for mentoring and cross-training. Her efforts in these matters assured a smooth transition to the new editorial team.

D-Lib's founding publisher, Dr. William Arms, left CNRI in May 1999 to return to academia at Cornell University. The magazine staff again adapted to fit the situation: Dr. Arms became the magazine's editor-in-chief; an associate editor, Peter Hirtle (also at Cornell University), was added to the editorial team; and I became the magazine's managing editor. Though the three of us are not co-located, meetings via teleconference, an editors' mailing list—hyperarchived so as to be available to each of us simultaneously or asynchronously—and an occasional face-to-face meeting have allowed us to continue production of *D-Lib Magazine* without pause.

Without doubt, there will be many changes in *D-Lib Magazine*'s future, but we are confident that those who produce the magazine will continue to adapt, and the magazine will continue to incrementally evolve to serve the digital library community.

NOTES

1. *D-Lib* is funded by the U.S. Defense Advanced Research Projects Agency (DARPA) on behalf of the Digital Libraries Initiative under Grant No. N66001-98-8908. The views and opinions expressed herein are those of the author and do not necessarily reflect those of the Corporation for National Research Initiatives (CNRI) or the government. The CNRI home page is available at: <http://www.cnri.reston.va.us/>, and the DARPA home page is available at: <http://www.darpa.mil/>.

2. Barry Leiner, "D-Lib Forum Charter," September 1999. Available at: <http://www.dlib.org/forum/D-Lib-forum-charter.html>.

3. The Digital Libraries Initiative (DLI) (http://www.cise.nsf.gov/iris/DLHome.html) was a four-year program supported by three agencies of the federal government: the National Science Foundation (NSF), the Defense Advanced Research Projects Agency (DARPA), and the National Aeronautic and Space Administration (NASA). The original DLI program expired in 1998 and was superceded by the Digital Libraries Initiative Phase 2, sponsored by the following agencies of the federal government: NSF, DARPA, NASA, the National Library of Medicine (NLM), the Library of Congress (LOC), and the National Endowment for the Humanities (NEH).

4. Amy Friedlander, "From the Editor: A Word or Two of Welcome," *D-Lib Magazine,* July 1995. Available at: <http://www.dlib.org/dlib/July95/07editorial. html>.

5. William Y. Arms, "What's in D-Lib Magazine?" *D-Lib Magazine,* June 1999. Available at: <http://www.dlib.org/dlib/june99/06editorial.html>.

6. Bonita Wilson, "Editorial: A Matter of Style," *D-Lib Magazine,* September 2000. Available at: <http://www.dlib.org/dlib/september00/09editorial-2.html>.

7. The Handle System Web site is available at: <http://www.handle.net/ index.html>.

8. The DOI Web site is available at: <http://www.doi.org/>.

9. The CrossRef Web site is available at: <http://www.crossref.org/>.

10. The Dublin Core Metadata Initiative Web site is available at: <http:// dublincore.org/>.

11. Amy Friedlander, "*D-Lib Magazine*: Publishing as the Honest Broker," in *E-Serials: Publishers, Libraries, Users, and Standards,* ed. Wayne Jones (Binghamton, NY: The Haworth Press, 1998): 3.

12. "D-Lib Magazine Author Guidelines," revised April 16, 2001. Available at: <http://www.dlib.org/dlib/author-guidelines.html>.

13. William Y. Arms, "From the Publisher: A Change of Editor," *D-Lib Magazine,* October 1998. Available at: <http://www.dlib.org/dlib/october98/10publisher. html>.

Chapter 2

ScienceDirect

Karen Hunter

A BRIEF HISTORY

Elsevier Science began to think seriously about using electronic distribution technologies for its journals in the late 1970s. We approached a number of other scientific, technical, and medical publishers to form a cooperative venture to scan journals and store them electronically. ADONIS was the name given to the consortium. The goal was to encourage article supply services such as the British Library's to use these electronic archives locally as their source for articles, rather than photocopying from the paper originals. If the electronic system was more efficient than using paper, then a royalty could be paid to the publishers for the copy made—royalties that were not otherwise being paid.

The notion was a valid one, but it took several years for technology costs to catch up with the theory. The technology of the late 1970s was large optical disks, with $40,000 readers. The technology that ultimately worked was a turnkey CD-ROM system for use with low-cost PCs. ADONIS found its niche in providing weekly CD-ROM delivery of hundreds of biomedical journals to an international group of libraries, which continue to use them for local access and document supply services. What we heard repeatedly, however, was a desire for local networked access, to get the journals to the desktops of the users.

The second major initiative for Elsevier Science was intended to provide this networked access, again consistent with the technology then available. From 1991 to 1995, Elsevier and nine universities participated in an experiment to mount a database of materials science

journals for local network access. This experiment was known as
TULIP (The University Licensing Program). As with ADONIS, the
electronic journals were delivered to each site. However, in this instance the electronic files for the journals were not accessed through
publisher-supplied software (as exists on ADONIS), but rather each
university integrated the journals into its own local area network services. The database was large (11 gigabytes per year) and the universities and Elsevier each found unexpected problems, most of which
are documented in the experiment's final report.[1] Nevertheless, from
a production and user perspective, the database was a viable technology, and there was increased demand for this level of networked access, particularly once the Web took hold and removed the need to
customize the access software for different client operating systems
on the desktop.

From TULIP came a program called Elsevier Electronic Subscriptions (EES), now ScienceDirect Onsite (SDOS), which is the commercial extension of the TULIP concept. Nearly 1,100 Elsevier journals have been available in electronic form since 1995 through SDOS.
The files are delivered to the subscribing institution, where they are
stored and delivered over the local network. An Elsevier-endorsed
Web server is available for implementation, if desired. End-user delivery can also be over wide-area networks if the files are licensed for
sharing among institutions, as in the case of consortia. This service
can be tailored to local needs and integrated with other information
relevant to the subscribing institution. At present an estimated 3.5 million users worldwide have desktop access to SDOS files.

WHAT IS SCIENCEDIRECT?

ScienceDirect is a logical extension of and complement to the
ADONIS, TULIP, and EES/SDOS experiences. It is also a reflection
of the potential of the World Wide Web environment to facilitate access to complicated large databases from remote locations. Certainly,
remote hosting is not a new phenomenon. Dialog, Data Star, Lexis-
Nexis, and others have been in this business for more than two decades. But the ability to handle color and complex graphics, which
are critical to the delivery of scientific material, has been pushed for-

ward by Web developments and, perhaps more significantly, by the enormous increase in computing power and sophistication of the desktop.

ScienceDirect was first introduced on a fully commercial basis in 1998. It is a Web-based service that delivers Elsevier Science journals and the journals of other participating publishers via the Internet. At the time of writing (April 2002), ScienceDirect included over 1,200 journals and over 2 million articles covering a broad range of scientific disciplines. The bulk of the journals are from physical, biomedical, and engineering disciplines with a good representation of titles from social, economic, business, and management fields. So far, experience on ScienceDirect has shown that usage continues to rise dramatically, with over 30 million page hits per month in mid-2002, resulting in nearly 5.4 million article requests and 1.9 million abbreviated full-text (SummaryPlus) requests each month.

ScienceDirect (http://www.sciencedirect.com) offers a sophisticated service for browsing, searching, and printing from the journals database. The service is designed to store both SGML and PDF files for the journals. HTML displays are generated on the fly, and PDF is available for both viewing and printing. The service can also accommodate journals for which the full text is only available in PDF, but not all features will be implementable in those files.

One feature that requires SGML is SummaryPlus, a unique element that provides a capsule of the article for quicker scanning. SummaryPlus includes the full bibliographic information, abstract, index terms, all tables and graphics, and all cited references. The references (both in SummaryPlus and in the full text article) are, in turn, linked to abstracts of the referenced articles and, when available, the full text of the referenced article. Users can store searches to rerun on demand and create SDIs (selective dissemination of information profiles) for automatic alerting of new material on demand.

Among the things learned in the TULIP experiment was that the value of the full-text article was greatly increased if one means of access was through the normal method of searching in a more comprehensive abstracting and indexing file. Within ScienceDirect, this is done primarily by providing options to the customer to add various abstract and indexing databases to the platform. Currently there are nine databases from Elsevier Science, including the well-established brands Embase and Compendex, and four from third-party providers: Medline, Inspec, EconLit, and Biosis. In addition to existing abstracting and indexing (A&I) databases, an additional unique database of abstracts from all scientific disciplines has been created to act as a simple, easy to use disclosure layer for the wide range of journals included in ScienceDirect.

In addition to the basic disclosure service, the user also has access to "power searches" that provide searching via an individually tailored interface for each A&I database. In each of these cases—searching within the ScienceDirect layer or searching the full A&I database—there is an option to purchase via a document delivery service any article that is not available in the online collection.

Just as it is important to place the full-text information within a broader context for searching purposes, it is also important to try to provide as much full text in one location as possible. One of the underlying premises of ScienceDirect is that it is more efficient to have a large corpus of information in one location than to have to go to hundreds or thousands of individual Web sites for each title or small cluster of titles.

For that reason, Elsevier Science has invited other publishers to make their material available to ScienceDirect subscribers. There are two ways this can be done: loading the other publishers' materials within ScienceDirect or providing gateways to that material. Although more functionality is possible in the first option, both methods are being pursued. Again, the goal is to provide as comprehensive an environment as possible and to permit users to move from one environment or server to another with a minimum of disruption.

In this context, Elsevier Science has had discussions on participation in or links to ScienceDirect with a large number of journal publishers. Over twenty participating small- to medium-sized publishers and scientific societies now have their journals available through online subscription on ScienceDirect, and many more are in active discussion concerning getting their titles loaded.

Most larger publishers, whether society or commercial, prefer a link to their Web sites. Through its "gateway" facility, ScienceDirect has established linking agreements with several partners, including ISI Web of Science, Silver Platter, Cambridge Scientific Abstracts, and MathSciNet. Gateway agreements facilitate one-to-one linking between ScienceDirect and each partner. However, an important way that scientists use information is to look for articles cited in the reference lists of the article being viewed. There has been increasing interest from both librarians and publishers in creating "seamless" linking between article references and the cited article itself—regardless of publisher platform. To do this effectively requires cross-linking agreements involving several parties at once.

As a result, a new cross-reference service was established in 1999 to provide a common protocol for cross-publisher linking based on Digital Object Identifier technology. The service, called CrossRef, is run by the not-for-profit Publishers International Linking Association (PILA), and in the last three years has grown to over seventy primary publisher members and is still increasing. More recently, affiliate members have included vendors of A&I databases and other secondary providers of information. CrossRef provides the linking protocol and the primary publisher determines the full text access entitlements.

When ScienceDirect was built jointly by Elsevier Science and its sister company, Lexis-Nexis, it was built with the institutional library subscriber in mind. Librarians can customize the terms of access to their users (e.g., enabling or disallowing transactional activities) and track (and charge users) on a departmental level. There are also features which will enable "turning off" of a graduating class, for example, or otherwise putting time restrictions (expiration dates) on user access.

ACCESS TERMS

Access is licensed to institutions based primarily upon subscriptions to the journal titles. ScienceDirect is not intended for a document delivery-type positioning where anyone interested comes into the Web site, browses or searches, and then pays for the individual article. The user must be affiliated with a subscribing institution. Access is restricted to a defined Authorized User Community, usually synonymous in an academic institution with the faculty, staff, and students whose primary affiliation is with that institution. A subscription entitles the institution's end users to unlimited access to the database and unlimited personal printing or downloading.

One has to say "unlimited" with a small caveat, as this is still a somewhat unknown area for both librarians and publishers and there must be an opportunity to judge from still greater experience whether "unlimited" works. So far experience on ScienceDirect has shown that usage continues to rise dramatically, with over 18 million page hits per month in mid-2001, resulting in nearly 4.5 million article requests each month. Fortunately, ScienceDirect has the benefit of the experience of the Lexis-Nexis operations staff, but as a Web service in science, this is still relatively new territory. Obviously, it is not a question of whether demand can be satisfied, for that is a matter of adding boxes on the floor and telephone lines. But in the happy event that usage continues to rise at the present rate, the costs associated with providing those services will need to be reviewed in the context of the overall access terms.

Each publisher participating in ScienceDirect establishes its own subscription price for each of its journals and receives all of the income from that subscription. The libraries decide which journals to subscribe to. ScienceDirect is also paid by each publisher for certain loading and storage costs.

If permitted by the journals' publishers, a library may also purchase articles on a transactional basis for journals to which they do not have a subscription. The cost for these articles has two components: the fee that the publisher of the journal sets for its content (e.g., an equivalent of the Copyright Clearance Center fee), and a ScienceDirect handling charge to cover infrastructure and direct-billing costs. This is consistent with other commercial document delivery services.

Pricing for electronic journals is, in general, a difficult issue for most journal publishers. One of the things Elsevier did to learn more about this issue was to work with the University of Michigan on an experimental project completed in 1998 to test six different pricing variations for remotely hosted journals. Called the PEAK (Pricing for Electronic Access to Knowledge) Project, this experiment was managed at Michigan by a librarian (Wendy Lougee) and an economist associated with the University's School of Information (Jeffrey MacKie-Mason). While PEAK did not directly test access to ScienceDirect (because Michigan was locally hosting the journals), the results provided valuable input for the basis of pricing and product options within ScienceDirect today.

BACK FILES, ARCHIVING, AND ACCESS
AFTER CANCELLATION

One of the regular questions of those who offer electronic access is: What is the policy on archival access? Some publishers say that as long as they are also publishing a paper version, that is the answer: If you want an archive, buy the paper. In the Elsevier Science SDOS program, the archiving question is moot, as the library takes physical possession of the files. In a remote environment, it is not that simple.

Traditionally, online host services were (and still are) limited to current subscribers and current files. There is no promise of access, for example, to an outdated file that has been removed from Dialog. If you had an account in 2000 and dropped it in 2001, you are not given some type of limited access to the 2000 records. But when one moves into the world of online journals, the paper paradigm and notion of what is meant by a subscription seem to continue to prevail. There is an expectation that, having paid "a subscription," one has permanent access.

Within ScienceDirect a current year's subscription gives an institution access to that year plus a number of prior years. A new subscriber at present starts with a four-year back file and the current year, adding years as the subscription progresses. All older back files are available for a separate fee. Elsevier Science has embarked on a major investment program to load the back files of its entire journal list, estimated at some 40 million pages, for all titles going back to Volume 1, Number 1. The files will be scanned to create "wrapped" PDF, but the abstracts and reference lists will be re-keyed to provide HTML files and enable reference linking. The program is scheduled for completion in 2004. In mid-2001, some one million pages of titles in the field of chemistry and chemical engineering were available through ScienceDirect, with some titles going back to 1947. Each back file subject collection will be available to libraries for a one-time license fee.

Subscribers have a permanent contractual right to the years for which they have purchased a subscription. Should they cease being ScienceDirect subscribers, the current policy is that the library can acquire a copy of the file at the cost of duplication.

As an ever-increasing amount of information is available electronically, the issues of how the digital archive is managed and by whom have become of central concern to many in the industry. Considerable work is being done in consultation with libraries to determine the best archival policy and to investigate infrastructural matters, such as how to build and maintain the archive and what the metadata should be to describe and manage the archive. Elsevier Science has embarked on several projects to explore the creation of permanent archives with trusted third parties. One of these is in collaboration with Yale University under funding from the Mellon Foundation. In addition, at the very least, Elsevier guarantees that it will maintain a permanent archive of its journals.

In this context it is worth noting that by 2000 there were a significant number of libraries were choosing to cancel print versions and receive electronic journals only. Although some countries have moved more quickly than others (notably libraries in Sweden and Australia), there are e-only ScienceDirect customers in many parts of the world, increasing the need for permanent, safe digital archives.

SCIENCEDIRECT AS A PUBLISHING ENVIRONMENT

In deciding to build this database, Elsevier Science had in mind more than just the services described previously. ScienceDirect is also an environment or resource upon which other discipline- or industry-tailored services can be built. Traditional publishing is market-driven, and scholarly publishing is no different. Publishing staff focus on a specific discipline or subdiscipline in order to understand the scientific and information needs of that community. Historically, that has resulted in books and journals tailored to those communities. In the future, one can also expect community-specific electronic services to be common.

The Elsevier Science journals (and the journals of other participating publishers) that are available within ScienceDirect and the software infrastructure offer the opportunity to create niche services for specific disciplines. These community services include a selection of journals and other related publications and services. There may be special services for authors, enhanced multimedia features, access to related Web sites, advertising, and moderated forums. These services are targeted in the first instance at individual scientists and their departments and are meant to be complementary, not competitive, to the basic ScienceDirect service. An example is the BioMedNet community Web site, which was acquired by Elsevier Science in 1997. Built for biomedical research scientists, the site offers linking access to ScienceDirect journals in addition to its own specific news and information services.

Another example of the synergies that are possible are the links that are planned between ScienceDirect and the ISIS service of MDL, the chemical software and information company that joined Elsevier Science in 1997. MDL has specialized software systems, databases, and services in the areas of chemical, biological, and genomic information management, high-throughput synthesis and screening, materials science, chemical sourcing, and environmental health and safety. New functionality will be introduced in ScienceDirect that allows the user to link through from the full text of the referenced articles to, for example, the chemical structure in the Beilstein database or view the structure on 2-D or 3-D using MDL proprietary software. The intent is to develop, over time, sophisticated cross-database access for customers of both services.

FUTURE RELATIONSHIP OF SDOS AND SCIENCEDIRECT

ScienceDirect Onsite is a local service limited to full-text articles and, in theory, to Elsevier journals. In fact, we make our standards fully open and accessible and that permits other publishers to link into the same implementations on their own terms and conditions. We encourage other publishers to work with us, and we also encourage SDOS library customers to use the SDOS standards to make the loading of other journals easier. ScienceDirect is a sophisticated remote service, with integrated abstracting and indexing services and integrated access to other publishers' journals. As a remotely hosted service, ScienceDirect removes the local need to store and maintain the data or access software. Those who *choose* to locally host, however, have the ability to customize their service. Both services have the option to be linked to locally mounted A&I services. SDOS will continue as long as customers want the local, customized option (and a significant number of our customers have confirmed that they have this desire).

There have been many enhancements to the ScienceDirect OnSite offering, including a hybrid solution that links onsite and remote access. There is continued evolution of SDOS underway to provide smooth integration with ENCompass, Endeavor's total digital management system.

FUTURE TECHNICAL DEVELOPMENT OF SCIENCEDIRECT

The goal is to work with the library and scientific community to learn how to improve the service in ways that provide better efficiency and effectiveness. Work on enhancements—whether for back office and administrative features or user functionality—continues steadily, with essentially the same level of technical staffing as went into the first release (which was designed over a one-year period and brought online over a second one-year period). The level of investment is high but consistent with providing a distribution system to change a total publishing program from a paper-only to a paper and electronic environment (and anticipating the day when there may be electronic only). It is not intended that the cost of the investment will be recouped solely on added electronic income.

The development has not been without difficulties, as it is a sophisticated undertaking. As most publishers who have tried it have learned, creating data based journal files in SGML is a tricky process. However, as more and more material is available in this format, the services that ScienceDirect (and others tuned to using SGML) offer should have a significant impact on the links and access mechanisms that can be provided for the scientific literature.

IN SUMMARY

ScienceDirect is a major initiative intended to provide a sophisticated set of services and options to our library customers, to our scientist end users and authors, and to our publishing staff. Its goal is to provide broad access to as many quality scientific journals as possible. In that context, Elsevier Science is pursuing a range of options for linking to other publishers' servers. There is much to learn as online full-text services grow in experience and it is that market experience that will shape the future of ScienceDirect.

NOTE

1. The TULIP *Final Report* is available at <http://www.elsevier.com/locate/tulip>.

PRICING

Chapter 3

Electronic Serials Costs: Sales and Acquisitions Practices in Transition

Kathlene Hanson

In their 1999 article "Serials Publishing in Flux," Lee Ketcham-Van Orsdel and Kathleen Born write that the

> Web and the electronic journal are deconstructing the serials landscape. Scholars can now publish without publishers, publishers can distribute without vendors, and end users can get access to the scholarly literature without going to the library. From a technological perspective much is possible. From a business perspective, what is possible may not prove to be profitable or affordable.[1]

It is certainly true that the serials landscape has changed significantly over the past decade and that much is now technologically possible. Traditional acquisitions and collection development practices are being reexamined in light of the ways electronic serials are being made available. Publishers, vendors, and librarians are having to reassess who will take the lead and how they will proceed in archiving electronic purchases. All have their own interests to protect. Publishers and vendors want to be able to continue to produce revenue through the services they offer, and librarians want to be able to get greater access to the information their patrons need at less cost. Although some believe that electronic publishing should cost less, others talk about the added costs of converting publishing systems from print to electronic and of sustaining electronic availability.

What almost all players in this game seem to agree upon is that we are in a state of change as a result of the possibilities of full-text electronic access to the content of serials. One of the central impacts of this state of change is the difficulty of ascertaining specific costs associated with electronic serials, particularly for aggregated content. Bill Robnett states (in a personal conversation around April 2001) that when he wrote the chapter on online journals pricing for the first edition of this book, there seemed to be more availability of list prices. His bibliography and content reflect some of this information.[2] However, due to shifts in the marketing strategies of publishers and vendors, many of the sources of information he used in his article are no longer available today. Currently, the real cost of electronic serials, particularly for aggregated content, seems to be a moving target. Cost information is most readily gathered directly from the vendor, and comparisons of cost are best made by talking with those at similar institutions who have paid for access to the same product or service. Although some useful comparisons for individual electronic serial titles are beginning to appear in the literature, similar comparisons for aggregator and bundled products are largely absent. (Though in some cases they can be much the same, aggregator products consist of serials from various publishers with the full-text content negotiated by the aggregator or vendor, while bundled products consist of a number of serials, from one publisher, bundled together.)

As specific prices are often not freely available in the current literature, this chapter focuses on some of the emerging cost and packaging trends and on some of the views of librarians, scholars, vendors, and publishers impacting and being impacted by these trends. Examples of some of the trends are provided and average price projections for individual serials are presented. Some strategies and plans being developed to push toward more affordable access to electronic resources are highlighted, and the possible benefits and drawbacks of some existing trends are discussed.

COST OF ELECTRONIC VERSUS PRINT PUBLISHING

In the first edition of this book, Bill Robnett states that although all players in the industry thought that online journals might be a panacea for the pricing crisis, it has become clear that capital is required for experiments in online publishing.[3] Since Robnett's words in 1998, much has remained the same in that publishers who are investing in migrating from print to electronic state that the cost of this migration offsets the possible savings from printing and delivery. Whether this will change in the long term remains to be seen. Some people in the industry argue that it is possible to curtail these costs now, and some venture that once migrations to electronic publishing processes have been completed, the cost should come down. Others state that the true costs of electronic serials and the inflation of serials prices in general are tied to new features being requested by those acquiring and using electronic serials. Still others are working on ways to circumvent traditional commercial publishers for lower cost alternatives.

At this time it may be premature to speculate whether electronic serials will ultimately be more cost effective than print serials since most publishers continue to rely on print subscriptions to maintain revenue streams. Ketcham-Van Orsdel and Born state that electronic serials are so tightly associated with print that "a mere half of the 5,000 e-journals in EBSCO's database can be purchased without the print counterpart."[4] They go on to say that no major commercial publishers have discontinued the print version of an online journal. While true e-journals are available either freely through the Internet or through small or large commercial publishers, it is indeed the case that what most publishers seem to be doing is presenting the print journal electronically, rather than creating a unique electronic resource. Although the conversion of print to electronic content does provide greater access, the value-added potential of electronic media which end users desire really has yet to be fully explored by many traditional commercial publishers. However, some publishers are certainly becoming more aware that online publishing is "a means of publication in its own right, with its own strengths and weaknesses, and its own necessary logic" and are beginning to use the medium for what it is best suited for.[5] Another factor in the shift from print to electronic content is the move some libraries are making toward implementing online-only subscriptions. Libraries are feeling more at ease about the usability, reliability, and linkability of online serials and are trying to influence publishers who bundle online content as part of a print subscription to cease doing so.[6] As a result of this move, those publishers linking print with electronic subscriptions may need to reconsider their marketing and production strategies.

Despite library demand for electronic serials separate from print, it is difficult to average the cost of the individual electronic journal without looking at the cost of print. This is because many electronic publications continue to be offered as an ostensibly free addition to the print subscription. How much the annual increase in print subscriptions is attributable to the cost of producing the electronic version is hard to gauge; often no specific figures are available to the public about publishers' production costs, although society publishers such as the American Chemical Society have indicated that first-copy costs of a high-quality electronic journal represent 82 to 86 percent of total journal production cost.[7]

Another model for e-serials pricing is to add a cost onto the print subscription base for addition of the electronic version. The argument for this model is that the cost of producing the electronic version is passed on directly to those interested in purchasing this version and not to those who want only the print.[8] In 1998, the average added cost for the electronic version of a print title was 10 to 20 percent.[9]

Although some individual e-journals are emerging in the market that are less expensive than some of the average costs for serials publications presented in *Library Journal*'s *(LJ)* Periodicals Price Surveys, many e-journals on the market have a cost comparable to that of print. Thus, *LJ*'s price surveys remain one of the most useful indicators of the rising cost of both electronic and print serials publishing for unbundled content. They compile data on serials represented in three Institute for Scientific Information databases: Arts and Humanities Citation Index, Social Sciences Citation Index, and Science Citation Index. For smaller academic libraries, the surveys provide an analysis of a subset of titles represented in EBSCO's Academic Search. According to the authors of these surveys, the cost of commercial publishing in the electronic environment is often comparable to the cost of print publications, and inflation trends for print are also being applied to electronic publications. Whether you choose to go through a subscription service such as EBSCO or to go directly to the publisher, the average costs represented in the surveys by subject area are a useful indicator of what you can expect to spend for electronic titles. Inflation rates over the past few years have shown some slight fluctuation both downward and upward but are tending to remain steady at about 9 to 11 percent for the sciences and social sciences and about 7 to 9 percent for the humanities.

PURCHASING INDIVIDUAL ELECTRONIC SERIAL TITLES

One of the ways to gain access to electronic serials is by purchasing individual titles either through a subscription service or direct from publishers. The advantages of purchasing individual titles are the ability of libraries both to select only those titles that they feel will be of high use to patrons and to gauge what each title costs. Another advantage of purchasing titles individually is the ability to avoid duplication of titles. Libraries that subscribe to a number of aggregator services have certainly seen significant overlap in their electronic titles. Some of the issues in purchasing individual titles are how to present the titles to patrons, how the publishers' prices vary according to the amount of simultaneous users of the serial, whether the publisher will allow for fair use of the item, whether the library selecting the item has the technology needed to support access to these journals, and whether a search interface will be provided. Costs to libraries for institutional subscriptions to individual serials titles are directly impacted by the kinds of licensing arrangements that are made with the publisher regarding the issues mentioned above. Most publishers will not disclose their list prices for institutional subscriptions on their Web sites or in any public forum unless they have information from the subscribing library as to how the serial will be used and how many users will have access. They state that these arrangements are so variable as to significantly affect list prices from institution to institution. Ovid's Web site, for example, allows the user to see prices only after setting up a journal quoting account.[10] The potential subscriber can set up this account online by answering some questions about the institution. Even then, Ovid states that the quotes are merely indicators of price and that a sales representative will provide the final quote.

SEARCH INTERFACE PROVIDERS

To address the issue of providing a way for users to access all their electronic serials, many libraries have invested in providing their own search interfaces for electronic content. However, as not all libraries have either the expertise or the resources to build their own search interfaces, a number of vendors have also established services aimed at providing a common search interface for individual subscriptions. Some examples of these are OCLC's Electronic Collections Online and Blackwell's Electronic Journal Navigator. These services provide the convenience of a common interface to individual titles for users.

Of course, both "home-grown" search interfaces and those built by vendors and publishers have their own added costs. In addition, the search interfaces provided by vendors are not a template libraries can use to provide access to individual electronic serials with which the services have not made an agreement. David Majka says that these services "have negotiated access agreements with a limited number of publishers to carry indexing and full text of certain titles."[11]

"BUNDLING" OR PACKAGING
OF ELECTRONIC SERIALS

The current trend of many publishers seems to be away from offering individual titles and toward bundling and offering them through aggregators. Hal Varian outlined a scenario in 1996 that is still one of the concerns for many publishers today:

> But what happens if the library subscribes to an electronic version of the journal that it mounts on the campus network? It is then no longer as inconvenient to access the library copy, and some members will no doubt decide to cancel their memberships or subscriptions, thereby reducing the revenue for the publisher.[12]

Varian goes on to say that there are some possible solutions that might keep individuals subscribing, such as providing individual subscribers with services they would not receive in an institutional subscription. One such service might be offering the individual subscriber more current content, while delaying the content to institutional subscribers. In one recent response to such a scenario, a large number of research libraries declined to sign site license agreements because of an embargo on content for institutions not imposed on personal subscribers.[13]

Some publishers bundle content either through their own proprietary gateway, such as Elsevier ScienceDirect and Wiley Interscience, and others through contracts with aggregators such as EbscoHost Academic Search, Expanded Academic Index, and ProQuest Direct. Publishers indicate that bundling models help to maintain revenue because the cost associated with billing, marketing, and user gateways is streamlined.[14] Another reason that publishers bundle content is to attempt to increase use of less popular titles by providing them alongside the more frequently used titles. Publishers who work through aggregators also reason that this transfers to the aggregator vendor the costs associated with the conversion of print to electronic format and the creation of user gateways, thus removing the cost to the publisher.

Purchasing aggregated electronic serials has some advantages for libraries. One of these is that the cost of the bundles is theoretically substantially less than that of each individual title. Many aggregators aim to collect a wide breadth of titles in numerous subject areas. This amount of increased subject access expands information access for many libraries and their users, particularly smaller institutions that might never be able to purchase each individual title. Some aggregators focus on particular subject areas and on developing depth of full-text offerings in these areas. This can also be advantageous to libraries.

However, there are also some disadvantages to buying aggregate products, most notably the lack of control over the long-term archiving of titles (because the aggregator and publisher determine what remains in the database and what is removed), the lack of ability to deselect titles, and the cumulative effect of overlap in serials titles. For example, in our library here at California State University (CSU), Monterey Bay, our systems librarian has created a journals list that can be searched to determine whether a title is held in our print collection or through one of the many vendor and publisher aggregator products we subscribe to. It is not unusual for a serial title to be contained in two or more aggregators. Why does our library purchase so many aggregators when the overlap is apparent? The central reason is that we are interested enough in the unique titles each of the aggregators offers, yet we do not have the option of purchasing those unique titles unbundled because they are not offered that way. When does the cost of purchasing the overlap, even if the titles are individually less expensive, become greater than that of the value added by each individual title we could purchase? This is something our librarians have not been able to quantify under current electronic serial pricing models. Low usage statistics can be helpful in making decisions against individual titles. However, decisions become more difficult when the title is offered as part of a package containing other titles that are frequently used. For now, the advantages of providing expanded information access through aggregator products seem to outweigh the disadvantages of having to change our view of collection development. We still seem to be getting more for our money than we would be if we had the ability to purchase each title separately, particularly since we are currently a small institution and the library's buying power is limited.

A number of articles have recently been written questioning the cost effectiveness of aggregators for libraries. Kenneth Frazier argues that to purchase bundled products is to weaken the collection with serials that are neither wanted or needed and that purchasing in this way increases our dependence on large publishers.[15] To some extent he is correct. Even small institutions probably prefer to be able to choose their electronic serials title by title and to have assurance that they will have access to a consistent archive of these items. However, as is indicated in a response posted to the International Coalition of Library Consortia (ICOLC) mailing list by the OhioLINK Library Advisory Committee, "by negotiating and carefully fashioning business contracts that involve the aggregation of publisher's content . . . dramatic increases can be achieved in cost containment, economies of scale, market penetration, and most importantly widespread access to scholarly and scientific information."[16] In other words, while aggregator databases have obvious advantages for the publishers and vendors, there is also potential for libraries to work with aggregators to libraries' advantage.

How much do aggregators really cost? Again, it is difficult to find public data provided by vendors and publishers about the cost of building and maintaining these products. List prices are often established internal to these organizations based on production and marketing costs, plus revenue. However, these rates are highly variable depending on the size of the institution subscribing to the product and what the terms of the license are. Although pricing schemes are not made public by most vendors and publishers, it is possible to do some research about the added value of aggregator products by gathering estimates from vendors directly, by talking with other institutional representatives from similar institutions about their costs, and by evaluating the potential cost of the individual content within the aggregate product.

CONSORTIA: BUYING IN BULK

A growing trend in attempting to bring down the prices of electronic products and services is consortial buying. One representative of a major academic consortium states that consortial buying is saving participating institutions up to 25 percent over the cost of subscribing individually. However, for consortia to be effective, it is important that the consortial partners have a common need for packages of electronic serials so that publishers will be motivated to work with them on reducing the price because of the bulk of new markets they can tap. Consortia can also having an overall impact on current trends in electronic serials pricing by working with vendors to try to establish new purchasing models. One project that has created momentum in this area is the Journal Access Core Collection (JACC) project of the California State University Software and Electronic Resources Group (SEIR). The goal of this project was to allow the CSU libraries to be able to choose a common subset of journals from vendors and to be able to deselect titles that are currently being bundled with those titles. Although not all phases of this project were successful, the participants in the project were able to convey to publishers some of their concerns with current pricing models and some of the areas of concern for libraries that purchase electronic content. These concerns include the provision of complete and current content, proper management and usage data, permanent and perpetual rights to archival access of the e-journals acquired, and the right to exercise fair use in fulfilling interlibrary loan requests for nonsubscribers.[17] These concerns also reflect those outlined in ICOLC's "Statement of Current, Prospective and Preferred Practices for the Selection and Purchase of Electronic Information."[18]

COST OF ARCHIVING

One of the major issues for publishers, vendors, and libraries is perpetual access to serials provided in electronic formats. In traditional acquisitions of print materials, libraries essentially purchased the physical item and could then archive it for its users even after ending current subscriptions. The physical item is owned and can be used by the libraries' patrons and for fair use in interlibrary loan. Most electronic serials subscriptions, however, are really leasing rather than owning arrangements. Certainly, some libraries do work with publishers to load electronic content locally so that they can provide archival access to items. However, many of the trends discussed above, particularly aggregator databases provided by publishers and vendors, focus on allowing use of electronic serials for only as long as the library subscribes to the product. Some well-established projects, such as JSTOR, offer archiving services for electronic serials. For the most part, publishers and librarians alike are grappling with who should be responsible for archiving electronic content and for the associated costs. Ketcham-Van Orsdel and Born assert that "until the archiving issue is resolved, there is little reason to believe that librarians will force publishers to explore with much enthusiasm the possibilities of life without print."[19] For librarians it is important to reflect upon the importance of archiving issues before deciding on electronic serials and to either reexamine the importance of archiving electronic content or at least to assess the cost of the possibility of creating archival access in-house.

POSSIBLE SCHOLARLY PUBLISHING ALTERNATIVES

Many of the issues librarians are facing regarding the prices of electronic serials are associated with the increase of costs of scholarly serials in general. Rather than try to influence publishers to bring down the prices of these traditional commercial scholarly journals, some librarians and scholars, such as journal publishers that are part of the Scholarly Publishing and Academic Resources Coalition (SPARC) of the Association of Research Libraries and HighWire Press, are trying to create a critical mass of more affordable electronic scholarly journals: the idea is to offset the cost of the larger commercial scientific, technical, and medical (STM) publishers and to establish the fact that full-featured electronic journals do not have to come from commercial publishers. Whether these efforts can be sustained in the long term depends on a number of factors—including the willingness of scholars to publish in these alternative journals though they may not be as well known, the willingness of libraries to forgo purchasing some of the more established commercial scholarly journals in favor of these journals, and the sustainability of smaller society publishers in a market where larger publishers seem to be buying up more and more smaller ones.

THE FUTURE OF ELECTRONIC SERIALS PRICING

How will trends in the pricing and packaging of electronic serials develop over the coming years? What influence will librarians and scholars have over vendors and publishers to change some of the ways in which electronic serials are sold? These questions remain to be answered. What is clear is that all parties concerned have their views about what is most useful and cost effective for them. There are still many issues to be resolved to the mutual satisfaction of electronic serials providers and the libraries that will continue to acquire electronic serials to better serve their patrons. It is the hope of this author that more useful data on the specific prices of aggregated databases will become available for comparison as publishers and vendors begin to settle into their electronic content marketing strategies. In the meantime, it is as much the buyer's responsibility to decide whether and when it is valuable to purchase electronic products in the way they are currently provided as it is the seller's to create a product or service that buyers will continue to want. After all, as Ketcham-Van Orsdel and Born state, "one might say that we are in a learning market, which makes for risky, interesting times" for all parties concerned.[20]

NOTES

1. Lee Ketcham-Van Orsdel and Kathleen Born, "Serials Publishing in Flux," *Library Journal* 124(7) (April 15, 1999): 48.

2. Bill Robnett, "Online Journal Pricing," in *E-Serials: Publishers, Libraries, Users, and Standards,* ed. Wayne Jones (Binghamton, NY: The Haworth Press, 1998), 55-69.

3. Ibid., 56.

4. Lee Ketcham-Van Orsdel and Kathleen Born, "Pushing Toward More Affordable Access," *Library Journal* 125(7) (April 15, 2000): 49.

5. Michael Jensen, "Developing the Appropriateness Matrix," *Journal of Electronic Publishing* 4(1) (September 1998), <http://www.press.umich.edu/jep/04-01/jensen.html>.

6. Ketcham-Van Orsdel and Born, "Searching for Serials Utopia," *Library Journal* 126(7) (April 15, 2001): 54.

7. Robert H. Marks, "The Economic Challenges of Publishing Electronic Journals," *Serials Review* 21(1) (spring 1995): 86.

8. Ketcham-Van Orsdel and Kathleen Born, "Pushing," 49.

9. Lee Ketcham-Van Orsdel and Kathleen Born, "E-Journals Come of Age," *Library Journal* 123(7) (April 15, 1998): 42.

10. Ovid, "Ovid Pricing," <http://www.ovid.com/sales/pricing.cfm>.

11. David R. Majka, "The Seven Deadly Sins of Digitization," *Online* 23(2) (March/April 1999): 44.

12. Hal R.Varian, "Pricing Electronic Journals," *D-Lib Magazine* (June 1996), <http://www.dlib.org/dlib/june96/06varian.html>.

13. Ketcham-Van Orsdel and Born, "Searching," 56, 58.

14. Ketcham-Van Orsdel and Born, "Serials Publishing," 50.

15. Kenneth Frazier, "The Librarian's Dilemma: Contemplating the Costs of the 'Big Deal,'" *D-Lib Magazine* 7(3) (March 2001), <http://www.dlib.org/dlib/march01/frazier/03frazier.html>.

16. Tom Sanville, letter on behalf of the OhioLINK Library Advisory Committee in response to Frazier, "The Librarians' Dilemma," March 30, 2001, *D-Lib Magazine* 7(4) (April 2001), <http://www.dlib.org/dlib/april01/04letters.html#SANVILLE>.

17. Christa Easton, "The California State University Journal Access Core Collection," *Serials Review* 26(2) (summer 2000): 44.

18. International Coalition of Library Consortia, "Statement of Current Perspective and Preferred Practices for the Selection and Purchase of Electronic Information," <http://www.library.yale.edu/consortia/statement.html>.

19. Ketcham-Van Orsdel and Born, "Pushing," 49, 50, 209.

20. Ketcham-Van Orsdel and "Serials Publishing," 21.

ACQUISITIONS AND COLLECTION DEVELOPMENT

Chapter 4

An Eclipse of the Sun: Acquisitions in the Digital Era

Ellen Finnie Duranceau

INTRODUCTION

Serials acquisitions work has been utterly transformed in the past seven years by the advent of the World Wide Web. The issues acquisitions librarians face, the work they do, and the skills required to do it—all have shifted focus. We work in an environment with pricing models that require teams to analyze them, licenses that require legal expertise to evaluate and negotiate, and products whose massive, fluctuating content challenges our ability to provide information about what is being purchased and appropriate, accurate access from our catalogs. We work in an environment in which the very definitions of "serial" and "monograph" have become outdated at best, arbitrary at worst; an environment in which assumptions must be challenged and challenged again. It is an interesting time to be buying library materials.

This "interesting time" can be exciting and invigorating, but also very confusing and overwhelming. Carl Lagoze, a research associate in Cornell's Department of Computer Science, has described our marketplace as a "disruptive context." Building on, and quoting from, language originated by management writer Clayton Christensen, Lagoze says: "Whereas a *sustaining* technology improves the performance of an established product, and therefore appeals to an existing customer base, a disruptive technology brings 'to a market a very different value proposition than had been available previously.'"[1] For example, an electronic typewriter could be seen as a sustaining technology in relation to the manual typewriter, while the advent of the personal computer (PC) could be seen as a disruptive technology, one that entirely redefined the market for text preparation and changed "typing" into "word processing." The companies making typewriters were not necessarily the ones who ultimately succeeded in the PC market.

Disruptive technologies transform a marketplace so much that old players are pushed out and new ones have a chance to stake a claim. Disruptive technologies that confront libraries include, according to Lagoze, low-cost computers, broadband networking at home and office, and the World Wide Web. All of these technologies, along with a shift to a purchase system based on license agreements, have transformed our service context. As Lagoze explains:

> Research libraries are unquestionably confronted with a suite of disruptive technologies, so numerous that they can be described as a *disruptive context*. . . . In combination, these factors seriously undermine the practices, and in fact the raison d'être, on which the research library has relied for over a century.[2]

It is not surprising, then, that this is a turbulent time; librarians are literally fighting for their position as information intermediaries in a world where the means of delivering information are being reinvented on a nearly monthly basis. Our universe of information delivery has expanded, even exploded, with the advent of the Internet and the Web. Every planet in our universe, including the twin suns of the catalog and the traditional collection methods that were used to populate that catalog, are being realigned into new orbits, in relation to a new center.[3] Part of the difficulty of this realignment is that the new center—the new mainstay of information management and control—has yet to be fully redefined and identified.

In this new swirling chaos of re-creation, the very processes of negotiating for content and purchasing Web-based information—both acquisitions roles—have taken on new and highly charged significance, even as traditional selection methods and the primacy of the OPAC as *the* access tool are challenged.

The breadth and depth of the change in purchase patterns is clear from the Massachusetts Institute of Technology (MIT)'s experience. Purchase patterns at MIT indicate that the print portion of the new serials pie is shrinking at a rapid rate. Although MIT may differ somewhat from other research libraries given its emphasis on science and engineering, the facts are nevertheless telling: of the total number of serial orders for paid titles placed by the MIT Libraries during the six months from January through June 1997, 23 percent, or a little under one quarter, were for electronic serials. Electronic serials represented 85 percent of the dollars expended for *new* serial orders in the same period. However, of the entire list of MIT's committed serials, in June 1997, only 0.7 percent of the titles, or 4 percent of the serial dollars, were electronic. At roughly the same time of year in 2001, by contrast, more than 20 percent of MIT's titles were electronic, representing 25 percent of the total dollars committed. Eighty-two percent of the new titles ordered through April 2001 were electronic; 81 percent of the dollars spent on new titles were for electronic resources. Given the volume and significance of these purchases, we cannot afford to avoid the complex issues such purchases raise or the sweeping revolution represented by them.

THE DIGITAL RESOURCE PURCHASE PROCESS

Why Networked Electronic Serials Cannot Be Treated "Just Like the Print"

Networked, Web-based electronic serials break the mold. Procedures designed to order, receive, and check in print serials worked—with some awkwardness—for serials arriving on floppy disks or CD-ROMs, but there is simply no way to use a print-based acquisitions model for Web-based serials. The two formats place entirely different demands on the system and present entirely different problems to solve.

The work flow in the print universe, which seemed challenging while it was our only model, looked (and still looks) something like Figure 4.1 at MIT.[4] The basic characteristics of this process are that an order is passed along a linear path of six steps, with one person working independently on it at any given time. An order is requested, placed, and entered into our databases; then a piece is received, cataloged, and shelved.

For a Web-based serial, the work flow bears little, if any, resemblance to the print process (see Figure 4.2). In the case of a networked serial, the process is considerably more complicated, involves an entirely different set of players, and is not a linear process. Unlike the print serial order, which is handled by one person at a time, the networked serial requires a team-based approach from the outset. Because many Web titles are very costly or interdisciplinary, it is no longer appropriate for one subject specialist to decide whether or not to order these titles.

Subject specialist chooses title
(one person)
↓
Order initialled by head of preservation and collections management
(one person)
↓
Order number assigned and entered into online databases
(one person)
↓
Order placed with vendor via e-mail
(one person)
↓
First piece of order received, sent to cataloging
(one person receives, one catalogs)
↓
Piece shelved
(one person)

FIGURE 4.1. Work Flow: Print Serial Acquisition

Subject specialist and/or sponsor proposes title for review in meeting of NERD
(twelve people involved)

↓

Acquisitions establishes and announces trial
Sponsor and NERD test product for up to two months
(twelve or more people involved;
may often include notification to faculty and other groups

↓

Acquisitions requests license and pricing information
(one person)

↓

Pricing negotiated
(one person coordinating with two or more others)

↓

Meeting of NERD, title weighed against other products, general discussion,
consensus to purchase (twelve people)

↓

Order initialled by head of preservation and collections
(one person)

↓   ↓

License negotiated   Systems notified of access method
License review team meets   (two) people
Acquisitions acts as negotiator
(three people, over several weeks)

↓   ↓

License prepared, signed, mailed, copied,   IP addresses and/or passwords sorted out
distributed   (one or two people)
(three people)   (may involve I/S)

↓ →   ↓

Order number assigned and entered into   Authentication script writing may begin;
online databases   links worked out on Web
(one person)   (one person communicating with up to ten)

↓

Order officially placed
(one person)

↓   ↓

Access tested
(one person required; others usually try out)

↓

Access announced
(one person)
(NERD, selector, other interested parties, cataloging)

↓

Title cataloged (or not)

FIGURE 4.2. Work Flow: Networked Serial Acquisition

At MIT, a subject specialist proposes a title for review in a larger standing committee, created expressly as a result of the demands of purchasing digital resources. This committee, the Networked Electronic Resources Discussion Group (NERD), consists of the collection managers and reference coordinators from each divisional library, the Head of Acquisitions, and the Digital Resources Acquisitions Librarian. This group of twelve librarians, one of whom is a department head, and all of whom are in positions above entry level, reviews products and makes collective decisions about what to buy.

Early in its existence, NERD's main quandary was finding out what was on the market and deciding if it was something we wanted. In recent years, the explosion of products available has forced the group to analyze, define, and document its decision-making process in much more depth. The decisions have grown vastly more complex and vastly more difficult as both the number of products and the number of features available electronically grows. Typical of the kind of analysis that must go on, for just one type of product, an aggregated group of e-journals, is determining how well the search interface and indexing work, how the content in various e-journal packages differs, how often that content changes, whether journals are offered in complete runs, whether any content is "embargoed," whether the content overlaps with other packages purchased, whether unique Uniform Resource Locators (URLs) for titles within the package are available, whether nonsubscribed material will show to users (and if so, what error message will appear), whether the images are of high quality and usability, and whether printing can be done with ease and clarity.

Given this array of issues, combined with a growing group of competing products, it becomes critical to have a sense of direction as well as a set of criteria for purchases. Without this grounding, the decision process begins to feel arbitrary, superficial, or both. At MIT, NERD recently used a decision matrix to categorize what matters most to MIT in deciding to buy an electronic product.[5]

The method may be of some interest to other libraries, as it helps to rank various criteria for purchase (or for any other library activity). First, we brainstormed the criteria we use, digested the list, and then entered each element on the list into a grid that forced us to compare each element or criteria against all the others, defining a more important and less important criterion in each pair compared. After summing up the number of times a particular criterion was deemed the more important of a pair, a weighted list of criteria emerged. For NERD, the final list included eleven ranked criteria (see Figure 4.3). The first nine of these were as follows:

- Critical to an MIT discipline or constituency
- Institutional commitment (Does MIT have a particular philosophical or administrative reason to purchase a product?)
- Offers full text
- Good cost-benefit ratio
- Good access model
- Consortial benefits or obligations
- Offers remote access
- Good business model
- Good archival policy

Having these criteria in place helps provide a solid underpinning for our discussions of products: we know what is important to us and why, and how each element ranks in importance compared to others. We can also use this ranking scheme to assist in a difficult choice between two products, by assigning numerical values to each according to their performance on these measures. This gives us a more objective assessment of a product's value to us, and helps ground group discussion.

Once NERD has used these evaluative criteria and decided to pursue a given product, the digital resources librarian obtains a copy of the license, and begins to negotiate price. When the trial is complete and the pricing information stabilized, NERD makes a final purchase decision. The order request is prepared and initialed (in the only step that mirrors the print world) and then the license review process begins. (Note that the order is not placed at this stage, since we cannot commit to a purchase before determining that we can agree with the vendor on license terms.)

License review at MIT involves another expensive team, this time a group of three librarians, including one department head and one associate director. This team currently meets weekly to review licenses and discuss licensing issues. The digital resources acquisitions librarian begins the negotiation, and then, based on the informa-

	A. Good Business Model (Licensing & Pricing)	B. Good Access Model	C. Technical Support	D. Offers Full Text	E. Critical to an MIT Discipline/Constituency	F. Serves Lincoln Lab	G. Consortial Benefits	H. Institutional Commitment	I. Good Archival Policy	J. Offers Remote Access	K. Good Cost-Benefit Ratio
A. Good Business Model (Licensing & Pricing)	X	**B**	**A**	**D**	**E**	**A**	**A**	**H**	**I**	**J**	**K**
B. Good Access Model	X	X	**B**	**D**	**E**	**B**	**B**	**H**	**B**	**B**	**K**
C. Technical Support	X	X	X	**D**	**E**	**F**	**G**	**H**	**I**	**J**	**K**
D. Offers Full Text	X	X	X	X	**E**	**D**	**D**	**H**	**D**	**D**	**D**
E. Critical to an MIT Discipline/Constituency	X	X	X	X	X	**E**	**E**	**E/H**	**E**	**E**	**E**
F. Serves Lincoln Lab	X	X	X	X	X	X	**G**	**H**	**F**	**J**	**K**
G. Consortial Benefits	X	X	X	X	X	X	X	**H**	**G**	**G**	**K**
H. Institutional Commitment	X	X	X	X	X	X	X	X	**H**	**H**	**H**
I. Good Archival Policy	X	X	X	X	X	X	X	X	X	**J**	**K**
J. Offers Remote Access	X	X	X	X	X	X	X	X	X	X	**K**
K. Good Cost-Benefit Ratio	X	X	X	X	X	X	X	X	X	X	X

A = 3; B = 6; C = 0; D = 8; E = 9.5; F = 2; G = 4; H = 9.5; I = 2; J = 4; K = 7

1. Critical to an MIT Discipline/Constituency (9.5)
2. Institutional Commitment (9.5)
3. Offers Full Text (8)
4. Good Cost-Benefit Ratio (7)
5. Good Access Model (6)
6. Consortial Benefits (4)
7. Offers Remote Access (4)
8. Good Business Model (3)
9. Good Archival Policy (2)
10. Serves Lincoln Lab (2)
11. Technical Support (0)

FIGURE 4.3. NERD Purchasing Criteria Matrix

tion provider's response, the team may have to revisit the terms of the license several times during the negotiation. It can take anywhere from five hours in one round of discussion, to several weeks or months with four or five rounds of discussion, to achieve resolution.

Simultaneously with license negotiation, systems assessment and implementation begin. The systems office is notified of the impending arrival of the product, and access methods, whether IP- or password-based, are discussed and worked out. Communication with

MIT's Information Systems (I/S) office and/or the vendor may be necessary. Authentication script writing to ensure that only MIT community members can access the product occurs (if needed) just as, and after, the order is being placed. The proxy server is configured for remote access, if the product's license allows for this.

Once access is available, it is tested, and the product is announced to most of the libraries' staff. The title is then cataloged, unless it is part of an aggregated database, in which case a review of cataloging and access options takes place before any decision to catalog is made. In a recent review of our cataloging policy, we concluded that since each product is still so different and presents very different challenges and options (including issues such as: Are records available from the information provider? From OCLC? From a peer institution? How stable is the content? What parts have we already cataloged in print? How will this resource and its component parts be used? Are materials we have considered monographs mixed with materials we have considered serials?), we need to assess each product individually to determine the best cataloging approach.

It is clear from comparing these work flows that the purchase of a networked serial requires an entirely different level of staff-wide commitment and involvement. The characteristics of the two processes, far from being comparable, are almost diametrically opposed. Table 4.1 summarizes the differences in the two work flows.[6]

The print world is linear and involves a mix of low- and higher-level staff; the process is standardized, and rarely varies. In six steps, the work is done. Little, if any, communication or coordination is needed. Most of the time delay is in waiting for the first piece to appear. The print purchase process is a short, straight garden path.

The digital world is cyclical, and involves high-level staff almost exclusively; the process is different each time and is completely unstandardized. Communication, coordination, and team effort are required at almost every stage. More than twice as many players are involved, and nonlibrary staff may be involved. In a minimum of fifteen steps, many involving extensive documentation, the purchase process is a long, complex, winding dirt road filled with potholes.

The MIT Libraries have felt the need to create a new role of "sponsor" to accommodate the large number of expensive, interdisciplinary digital resources. Our print purchase model allocated a certain

TABLE 4.1. Comparison of Characteristics: Print versus Networked Serial Acquisition Process

Print	Networked
Characteristics of process	*Characteristics of process*
One person at a time works on each step	Team-based
Requires mix of support and librarian staff	Requires high-level librarian staff
Little coordination is needed	High demand for communication and coordination
Linear process	Cyclical, not linear, process
Documentation limited (copy of purchase order)	Documentation intensive (lots of paper!)
Little variation	Great variation
Total number of individuals involved	*Total number of individuals involved*
Six	Fifteen for an "average" networked title
Two are support staff whose operations take only a few minutes	All are high-level staff; director must sign each license
No staff outside libraries involved	I/S staff needed at times
	MIT legal counsel may need to be consulted
Total number of steps	*Total number of steps*
Six	Fifteen, some repeated
Time frame	*Time frame*
Order request to order: one week or less	Order request to order: weeks or months
Order to receipt: weeks or months	Order to receipt: one day to one week

budget figure to each of hundreds of funds in ten decentralized public service locations, with a subject specialist in charge of purchases for each fund. High-cost interdisciplinary titles do not lend themselves to this model, since the subject funds are inadequate and a broader constituency needs to review a product that covers many disciplines.

Adding the sponsor and the standing committee (NERD) has slowed and complicated the purchase process. The same could be said for the increased number of consortial purchases, driven by lower prices available to groups and the new format's ability to avoid the question that has plagued the print world: "But who will get to house it?" These consortial purchases further complicate the picture by adding players, constraints, and time lags (as well as added time pressure in some cases) to the process. Although the team-based model has lengthened, complicated, and increased the scope of the collections decision and purchase process, it has fostered wise decisions and productive new relationships both inside and outside the MIT Libraries. It has provided a funding model that allows for more power and flexibility in purchasing. We have learned a great deal about group process and complex decision making, not always without pain along the way.

STAFFING

Clearly these dramatic differences in work flow have broad and deep implications for staffing in libraries and in serials acquisitions. Broad, because many roles and jobs are affected; deep, because the changes required are profound.

In the MIT Libraries, we responded to the demands of the digital world by carving out a new position from an existing vacancy in another department. In late 1997, we created a position to manage the acquisition of digital resources. This position was charged to perform the following tasks:

- Maintain an awareness of the development of electronic products
- Act as a resource for staff on trends in product development

- Facilitate the acquisition process, including defining access options, equipment requirements, and arranging tests and demo sessions
- Manage license review, negotiation, and compliance
- Collaborate with subject specialists and systems office staff
- Contribute to ongoing planning for the management of digital resources in the MIT Libraries

We perceived a need for this position because the demands of the digital products were so great that we did not feel that they could be met by an "ad-on" to another position. In addition, an integrated work flow seemed impossible at this stage, given the drastically different characteristics of the print and digital purchase processes. Clearly, however, it was costly to create this position; in times of downsizing and fiscal constraint, creating a new position is extremely costly to *any* organization.

In fall 2000, we added a half-time support position to the digital resources unit, also carved out of existing vacancies, in recognition of the tremendous growth in the volume of digital resources. This position was intended to support the acquisition of digital resources at MIT by entering and maintaining library database records; investigating electronic journal and database access problems; establishing access to new electronic journals; preparing contracts for scanning; gathering and recording product usage statistics; and assisting with other projects.

An early trend in 1997 and 1998 toward creating positions to support digital resources has evolved into a fairly standard offering seen regularly over listservs. Many libraries are adding support staff to newly created positions, as was recently done at Yale and Harvard. A newer trend toward the creation of associate-level positions for digital resources seems to be developing, as evidenced by positions at this level advertised in 2000 at several universities, including Princeton. This trend is most pronounced at larger academic research libraries, such as Association of Research Libraries (ARL) institutions, but will inevitably become more widespread as electronic resource collections grow relative to print.

Digital resources have driven the creation of new roles while causing the traditional lines between public and technical service, and subdivisions within technical services between acquisitions and cataloging, to blur. In this new digital world, the lines between acquisitions, cataloging, collections, and systems work seem particularly fluid and unclear. If someone needs to worry about implementation, access, copyright, and quality control, it is not always clear who. This blurring of roles means confusion, ambiguity, and the potential for turf wars, but also opportunity. Different institutions have chosen different places to add a position; yet they all seem to address a similar demand and achieve similar goals: getting *someone* to focus on the unique demands of digital material. Acquisitions and serials librarians are well-positioned to take on many of the key tasks involved in bringing these resources to the library managing records related to them, and making them accessible.

Acquisitions staff understand what the product is that has been purchased. For example, they can readily distinguish between a "package" that was bought—such as Blackwell Science—and a group of titles set up independently under the same interface, but not as a package—such as titles available through a gateway like Ingenta. These are essential distinctions to make in creating access records and understanding what to expect to be available at the site.

As the systems we use to offer digital resources proliferate outside the traditional OPAC, the need for URL maintenance grows, and the questions of who should create and maintain access records that do not belong in a traditional OPAC, but instead in separate databases or Web pages, becomes unclear. In many new systems the acquisitions record itself acts as an access point and serves as a catalog record. Staff that traditionally worked solely in acquisitions or solely in cataloging may need to be trained to work flexibly across many systems, with varying standards and rule sets, to offer the services needed in libraries today.

QUALITY CONTROL IN THE DIGITAL WORLD

Although the traditional staffing breakdowns are clearly in question, there is no doubt that the concepts of "check-in" and "claiming" are obsolete, except as metaphors, in our new world. Check-in and claiming work flows were built on the concept of a physical object being received, and are not applicable to digital resources. However, the fundamental goal of providing quality control remains the same: acquisitions needs to be able to ensure that we get what we pay for and that we are making resources that have been chosen for our collections available to our community in a timely and effective manner.

In the digital world, this means link checking and maintenance, and checking holdings of remote sites. In the print world, we do not have to continually verify that something we received several years prior is still available. In the digital world, we have to monitor Web sites to be sure that they are live, are being added to on schedule, and that the entire run of holdings we expect access to is still present. We also need to check for any added holdings.

This sounds simple, but actually is one of the more vexing and complex problems presented by the digital format, and requires a substantial commitment of labor. Given that we live in a highly evolved capitalist economy, however, it is not surprising that various companies have jumped into the market to offer services to meet libraries' need to track changes in what they have purchased. At least three such companies exist at the time of this writing: Serials Solutions, TDNet, and Journal Web Cite LLC. These companies offer digital content update services for an annual subscription fee. Serials Solutions offers several products (printed lists, html lists of links, spreadsheet data) that tell libraries what changes have occurred in the packages they subscribe to (see http://www.serialssolutions.com/Home. asp). A competitor to Serials Solutions, Journal Web Cite's JournalList. com, offers a similar service, providing an alphabetical list of the journals a particular library receives, a link to the provider's site, and the years the journals cover. They offer a range of data formats, including MARC for cutting and pasting, XML, and others, and other services such as financial and usage data reports (see http://199.234.242.79/ main.asp). TDNet offers a broader service for managing e-resources, including weekly updating of all the URLs contained in the TDNet database. TDNet is also positioning itself to obtain access rights for e-journals to which a library subscribes (see http://www.tdnet.com/). (In addition, Ex Libris's SFX product, a fairly recent entry into the market, offers an alternative kind of solution in that the SFX Knowledgebase contains customizable information about which electronic journals are available in which e-journal packages. Because SFX is primarily a context-sensitive linking tool and not a content-tracking tool, it is not discussed in full here, but it represents an important innovationin e-journal management and control.)

An alternative to for-profit services such as those mentioned above, the Jointly Administered Knowledge Environment (jake), offers an open-source option for libraries hoping to control access to titles within aggregated packages. Jake, which is hosted by the Cushing/Whitney Medical Library at the Yale University School of Medicine, and is maintained by Daniel Chudnov, allows users to identify which packages contain a particular full-text electronic journal. Local implementations can involve customizations of the software so that it is possible to see search results reflecting the purchases of the local library, rather than the publishing market at large (see http://jake.med.yale.edu/).

The information providers themselves (for example, EBSCO and Bell and Howell) have also jumped into the market gap, offering MARC records and updates to them along with their products. There are also creative third-party based options for link maintenance. Web tools such as Mind-It (ceased as of July 1, 2002) and OCLC's CORC (see http://corc.oclc.org/) software can be leveraged to help with content management.[7] Link-checking software, such as the shareware product Linklint (see http://www.goldwarp.com/bowlin/ linklint/), also exists and is in use in the MIT Libraries. (MIT has also signed with Serials Solutions.)

These new services are a very positive market development. Such services, in tracking changes once, can then offer the information to many customers, using economies of scale to reduce the cost of maintaining so much detailed information. For each library to do such tracking on its own would be extremely inefficient and uneconomical. This market trend, however, pushes libraries in the direction of outsourcing the capturing of the kind of access and control information they used to create themselves. This may feel like a threat to our base business, and it *is* sobering to note that functions libraries used to manage entirely, or at least largely, on their own in the past—such as keeping records about what was in their collections—seem to need the support of outside services to be managed efficiently in our new world. Many of the aspects of access control that libraries "owned" in the past (checking serials in, cataloging them, withdrawing them) seem to be blurring into what are now sold as product features or enhancements in our new marketplace. However, it is also true that our cataloging processes have depended on a shared bibliographic utility—OCLC—for decades, and the new URL maintenance services are, in effect, simply the development of a similar kind of tool, a tool newly needed in the digital marketplace. It is true that many of these new tools are being offered on a for-profit basis, which distinguishes them from OCLC. But libraries have also been relying on for-profit companies for a range of services, such as authority control and table of contents services for our OPACs. If we define our base business as providing needed information (wherever we obtain it) to our users, and remember that we have always relied on outsourcing in one form or another, these new support services for e-resources can be seen not as threats, but rather as enhancements to our role, by allowing us to provide more accurate information faster and cheaper.

This new market for record sets and record update services is a natural part of a marketplace in which big packages have become a key method of acquiring digital resources, replacing title-by-title selection. There is a strong user demand for libraries to purchase, provide access to, and then track and link accurately to components of large aggregated packages. This demand will continue for the intermediate future. Some librarians have spoken out against the entire notion of purchasing large aggregated packages—railing against what Kenneth Frazier has dubbed the "Big Deal."[8] Robert Michaelson, writing among others in support of Frazier, has stated, "It is imperative, in my view, that libraries reject the attempt by these for-profit organizations to abrogate our role as selectors."[9]

Yet the Big Deal does not have to be a bad deal for libraries. The digital era has tended to highlight the value of acquiring large bodies of full text over individual title selection. Recent studies are demonstrating the dramatic power and positive user impact of purchasing large volumes of electronic journals.

Recognizing this, some librarians are emphasizing the strengths of the new bulk, high-volume purchasing model. Kent Mulliner, Collection Development Coordinator at the Ohio University Libraries, has commented, "As a gatekeeper, I think a librarian's job is to open the gate as widely as possible, not to restrict access to far fewer titles."[10]

Rick Anderson, Electronic Resources and Serials Coordinator at the University of Nevada, Reno, also supports the concept of the Big Deal, noting, "The library is not supposed to be a monument to our skill and insight as librarians, but a tool for research."[11]

OhioLINK's experience offers strong evidence that indeed, most libraries "have had a rationing problem first and a selection problem second."[12] OhioLINK has found that there is a huge unmet demand for a wide range of titles that libraries have not been able to afford to subscribe to given the price pressures inherent in the contemporary title-by-title purchase market. David Kohl, Dean and University Librarian at the University of Cincinnati, in a talk aptly titled "What If What We Know Isn't True," reported that the OhioLINK libraries were "astonished" by the data they gathered on the use of their newly acquired e-journal aggregated packages: 58 percent of the articles downloaded were downloaded from titles not previously held by the user's library. There was actually *more* use from the titles that had not been selected for print collections.[13]

Rather than interpreting this data as an indicator that selection methods were poor, Kohl sees this it as evidence of "huge pent-up demand for access to more e-journals."[14] Thus, Kohl believes that libraries in a title-by-title purchase model simply could not select enough titles to meet demand. Larger libraries were doing better at meeting content needs, because they could buy a larger portion of the overall market of titles available, not because their selection methods were better than those at the smaller libraries.

OhioLINK's analysis of the impact of the Big Deal in Ohio suggests that we have entered the era of acquisitions: an era in which we do our best to negotiate and purchase the best deals possible, for the largest amount of relevant material, and let our users determine what is of value to them. This feels natural to acquisitions staff; we have always focused on bringing material in quickly, efficiently, and at the lowest cost possible. Our goals have always been to streamline purchase methods and access. The Big Deal suits this worldview. Usage statistics give us the power to renegotiate deals; we are not reduced to being supplicants at the feet of large commercial publishers. It may be that the new collection development model will be heavily driven by usage statistics, and that acquisitions will play a larger role in getting the best deal for the library. Driven by market forces, acquisitions work seems to be merging into collection development, and collection development into acquisitions. When we had to choose title by title, and titles were purchased as physical objects, it was sensible to select on that basis. Our new market offers us a new, and powerful, paradigm. The Big Deal offers us a chance to truly see what users will need and then verify exactly what they use. Single-publisher aggregations price on the print holdings of what a given library has selected in the past, but providing access to all the titles available online offers a new, positive method of acquiring access for users and testing the use of e-resources in a completely new environment, where the use of information will not be limited in the same ways it was with print publication. In our new universe, the rising star—the acquisition of material in large volume with the best tools to find and use this volume, whether through SFX or other licensed resource databases such as MIT's Vera—is described in the next section.

LICENSING

Whether through a Big Deal or a small deal, digital resources are generally sold under license agreements. Our landscape has therefore changed from a copyright-based environment to a license-based environment. Of the many challenges facing libraries buying digital resources today, negotiating a contract that meets the library's users needs, and being able to manage the resource in relation to the terms agreed to, is one of the most significant.

First, libraries have to understand that a license trumps copyright law; libraries can—and do—sign away rights that were afforded to them under the fair use provisions of U.S. copyright law. As Rob Richards has explained: "contracts in which licensees waive their rights under copyright law are enforceable. These arguments . . . privilege the notion of freedom of contract over the sovereignty of federal statutory law."[15]

It is essential that librarians understand this, and that they become familiar enough with licenses for library material that they can confidently negotiate a contract that maximizes the benefits of a given product for a given library. Fortunately, many standard licenses have emerged over the past few years, along with licensing principles.[16]

Such standards can jumpstart a library's entry into the world of license negotiation.

In addition to standards, other helpful documentation to help libraries understand the legal terminology in licenses is offered by the outstanding Web resource "Liblicense" (see http://www.library.yale.edu/~llicense). Created by a team of library and legal professionals, Liblicense describes itself (much too modestly) as "a useful starting point toward providing librarians with a better understanding of the issues raised by licensing agreements in the digital age."[17] This resource offers definitions of the major legal terms used in licenses, explains the key licensing issues, and, most importantly, presents clauses from actual licenses in each key licensing area with a discussion of the issues raised by the clauses.[18]

The key licensing issues for any campus tend to be characterized by the standard journalistic elements of who, how, where, and what: that is, the definition of the user population, how the product can be used, where the product can be used, and what is being purchased.

All of these issues can present problems in one guise or another, and yet—despite helpful standards and documentation—there is no single checklist to follow that will ensure success in negotiating a license. First, each institution needs to develop its own principles from which to negotiate because values and priorities vary. Second, what is acceptable in one contract may not be acceptable in another: Every purchase amounts to a business decision in which the value of the particular product is weighed against whatever risk is entailed in signing off on a particular set of terms. At MIT, we pay particular attention to the following issues during our reviews of licenses (this is not a complete list of issues we negotiate; it is rather a list of key issues we must commonly address).

Who

The definition of the user population for the site is an essential element of any license negotiation. Licenses arrive describing the users as "employees" only, or restricting access to anyone called a "consultant." In many cases, the definition of "authorized user" does not include patrons physically present in the library (walk-ins who have no affiliation with MIT). We almost invariably need to request that one or more of these user categories be added to the definition of "user."

Because this issue is common to almost every license, MIT has created a template user definition that we ask to have in every license. This defines our users very explicitly and specifically, so that the information provider knows exactly what groups will have access to the product. Such a definition can take weeks to create: in MIT's case, it involved discussions with Human Resources, Systems, Benefits, and Network Accounts to obtain all the necessary information to create an accurate definition. The definition now reads:

> Authorized users shall consist of: 1) persons officially registered as full or part-time students of MIT including those participating in distance education programs; its faculty (including some retired faculty) and other members of the teaching staff; administrators; employed staff;* 2) authorized affiliates (including, e.g., some House Masters and Chaplains; the President's spouse; and Members of the MIT Corporation); affiliated or visiting scholars or researchers; and consultants under contract with MIT; 3) other individual authorized users sponsored by senior MIT faculty or staff with guest accounts to complete academic or administrative work; and 4) patrons physically present in the MIT Libraries.

> *Please note that there may be approximately six months' lag time during which those no longer associated with MIT retain access to their campus network accounts.

How

Licenses define authorized uses of information (including quotations, copying, and printing); we have tried to ensure that something approximating fair use as defined for materials in Section 107 of the U.S. copyright law (P.L. 94-553) applies to our digital products. We ask for revisions to language that prohibits all copying, downloading, and sharing, asking that such activities in support of education and research be considered acceptable, as long as they are not systematic.

Perhaps our most important issue in negotiations is avoiding responsibility for the actions of individual members of our user community. Many—if not most—licenses will ask that the licensee (the MIT Libraries) ensure that there will be no unauthorized use or unauthorized users on the system. We always request a rewording to suggest that the limit of our abilities is to make "reasonable efforts" to inform users of the rules of use, since we cannot control individual users.

Where

A primary consideration in each contract is the question of the location from which users will want to access the information. Access from faculty homes and student apartments is increasingly an expected feature of digital resources, rather than an extra. We try to negotiate this access into our licenses. We also need to negotiate the inclusion of two research laboratories that are not located in Cambridge, along with the rest of MIT. We have developed a computing and site definition document that we share with information providers. This helps to move the negotiation forward more quickly, although it does not guarantee the results we hope for in every case.

What

It is imperative that the license and order form be checked and re-checked to be sure everyone involved in the purchase understands exactly what is being bought. It is impossible to be too explicit in asking questions about this. Through painful experience, the MIT Libraries have learned to ask most or all of the questions during every negotiation:

1. How many simultaneous users are covered by this price quote? Is this for unlimited access?
2. Is this price a special first-year or incentive price? Or have we received a standard price quote?
3. Will users see the site exactly as we saw it in the trial? If not, how will it be different?
4. Will the entire site be accessible to our users?
5. If not, what error message will appear to users if they attempt to access material at the site that is not part of our purchase?
6. Do you offer unique URLs for titles within your product?
7. How often is the site updated?
8. How often does content change, and how are we notified of changes?

Asking these questions, and others like them, can help avoid some of the ugly surprises that are inevitable in a market that is still changing rapidly.

There are also some other key issues that continue to be important for most libraries, including MIT.

Venue/Governing Law

Our legal counsel has advised us to avoid clauses that would cause a lawsuit to be carried out in another state or under another state's laws. In addition, we try to add a statement about UCITA, the Uniform Computer Transactions Act, so that pre-UCITA law will apply should UCITA become part of our state's law. This is because the provisions of UCITA are anticonsumer and antilibrary in many cases. This legislation applies to a library only if the library's state has adopted it as law. In 2000, several states, including Maryland and Virginia, adopted it, but since then no others have done so (as of April 2002). One possible effect of UCITA is to strengthen "shrinkwrap" or unsigned and/or clickable licenses, which is not a positive development for libraries. Other unwanted outcomes could include, according to Rob Richards, the fact that "UCITA does not require licensors to make conspicuous many restrictive terms of a license," and permits "license terms that 'restrict uses of information that are now protected by copyright law,'" such as "fair use, first sale doctrine, and library reproduction rights."[19]

Indemnification and Liability

We try to be sure that the providers are not asking us to indemnify them (that is, to "take financial responsibility for damages that the [information provider] may suffer"[20]) and guarantee that they have not infringed intellectual property rights in creating their product. We also attempt to negotiate an exception to any cap on damages for cases involving intellectual property infringement.

Performance Warranty

Although we are not often successful in enumerating the details of acceptable service levels, we do try to be sure we can obtain a prorated refund if the product fails to meet our needs.

GROWING PAINS: THE NEGOTIATION PROCESS

After scaling the learning curve related to these myriad licensing issues, one of the biggest challenges is shepherding a license through the process in a marketplace that seems chaotic and unformed. A fairly typical case at MIT will stand to demonstrate a very general problem. In this case, MIT wanted to buy the electronic versions of journals we already owned in print, which were published by a society. The acquisition process went roughly like this:

Librarian contacts society to ask for license (January 2, 2001)

Society says they will send the license (January 2)

License not received; Librarian contacts society to ask for license

No response

Librarian contacts society to ask for license, again

License received (mid-February)

Librarian reviews license, prepares comments, and submits to society (March 1)

Librarian asks if comments received

Society indicates all requested changes will be made and license sent to librarian (March 13)

Revised license not received; librarian calls, cannot reach society contact (mid-March)

Librarian gives up waiting for revised version from society and instead makes changes in own version of license, faxes to society (about March 19)

Hearing nothing, librarian calls society; society has not seen the fax (March 21-22)

Librarian contacts print vendor to upgrade order and pay society for online, since have agreement, in principle, on license terms (March 15)

Society e-mails librarian, fax was lost, is now found (March 22)

Librarian asks for quote to add one off-site lab to access (March 26) [no response as of May 31]

Online provider indicates online access is working for all but one title (March 27) [it has now been three months since the license was originally requested]

However, society says order still not received

Librarian contacts print vendor to ask about upgrade, again
Society says order not received (March 22)
Librarian contacts print vendor to ask about upgrade, again
Print vendor confirms orders upgraded (April 6)
Library still waiting to hear final title is working and for requested price quote on second site (May 31)
Library confirms payment from print vendor has still not reached society (June 18)

If this is tedious and frustrating to read, that represents a small portion of the tedium and frustration felt by the staff involved. Yet, this labor-intensive undertaking appeared at the outset to be a "best-case scenario" involving a motivated nonprofit publisher, a motivated buyer, and a very reasonable base license to work from.

Clearly the entire market is feeling the strains of growth. It is difficult to be efficient and move nimbly when each deal is different and all the players are continuously sorting out their procedures and roles. It is difficult to explain to those outside the process why it all takes so long; it is important for us to take the time out, as hard as it is to find the time, to educate our staff and user communities about what is involved in buying digital resources. Managing expectations while striving for excellent service has always been part of our game plan; it is even more important now.

MANAGING LICENSES AND RESOURCES IN RELATION TO LICENSE TERMS

Since negotiating licenses is relatively new for most serials librarians, managing license compliance is perhaps the least developed aspect in the revolutionized serials chain. We have simply not been through many cycles of negotiating, signing, and renewing contracts, and managing compliance with them.

Many libraries are developing tools to manage their licensed electronic resources, given the demands that we offer these resources in relation to the terms of the contract. This is, in fact, a key development since 2000, and one that will allow libraries to regain the efficiencies in internal procedures that they had for exclusively print-based collections.

Timothy Jewell of the University of Washington has been researching and codifying the data points that libraries across the United States track for their e-resources. He has developed a spreadsheet showing all the data types gathered, and written a paper about his findings.[21] Jewell sees two possible and productive outcomes of his research: working with integrated library system (ILS) vendors to create functionality within the ILS framework that meets the needs he has recorded; and/or pursuing an open-source model for creating and modifying shared software to control e-resources. Both avenues have already shown significant promise: Jewell has begun discussion about the open-source model with two ILS vendors.

Meanwhile, seemingly independent of Jewell's work, Pennsylvania State University Libraries have developed a shareware version of their Microsoft access system for controlling e-resources. Their system, called ERLIC (Electronic Resources License and Information System), was developed by the Penn State Libraries staff. It offers, among other data: the URL for the resource; a scanned license agreement; access and authentication information for remote users; an indication of whether the title is part of a package; and an indicator of usage statistics availability.[22]

The MIT Libraries have developed a similar tool, launching Vera—our presentation, organization, and management system for electronic journals and databases—in January 2000. Vera, which is an acronym for Virtual Electronic Resource Access, is a FileMakerPro database, with custom scripting and a Web interface for the public. It allows us to create records for electronic resources that both track the licensing terms and offer services in relation to those terms. It also offers users the quickest means to identify and locate e-journals and databases purchased by the MIT Libraries.

For the users, Vera allows searching by title keyword or broad subject area, or browsing through an alphabetical listing of e-journals or databases.[23] Vera also shows users where and how they can use a resource, and where they can learn more about a resource (see Figure 4.4).

For staff, Vera allows links to nonstandard terms through a red "L" (for license) icon; includes provider contact information to use when a product is not functioning; creates rule-driven systems based on the logical relationship between fields, such as the rule allowing for re-

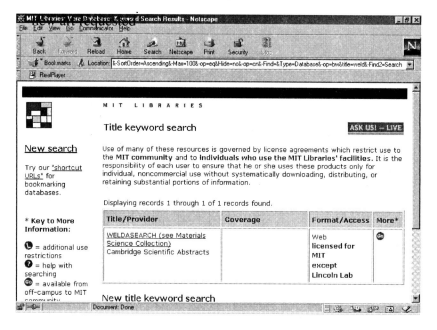

FIGURE 4.4. Vera: User Display

mote access; flags "broken" resources; displays simultaneous user limits; provides interlibrary loan information; shows renewal dates; offers access to scanned licenses; shows donor information; and allows quick updates and record entry.

Vera's power lies in its ability to do all of these things (and more) from a single record for each resource (see Figure 4.5). For example, the "Go" service, offering off-campus or remote access, is driven by the logical relationship between fields describing the license terms (such as whether remote access is allowable under the terms of the license), and fields describing whether the proxy server has been configured for the product. Scripting allows the green Go symbol to appear when all necessary conditions for allowing remote access have been met. Users then have a quick visual indicator of whether a particular resource will work off campus.

Since we have committed to making reasonable efforts to inform users of the rules of use for each product in most of our licenses, an important feature of any e-resource management tool we use is the

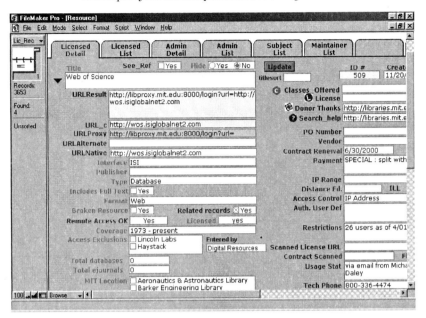

FIGURE 4.5. Vera: Staff Display

ability to display such rules at point of use. Vera does this for us in two ways: First, by displaying our generic statement of rules of use, which covers the terms we have negotiated in 80 to 90 percent of our contracts. This "generic" wording appears at the top of every results screen in Vera:

> Use of many of these resources is governed by license agreements which restrict use to the MIT community and to individuals who use the MIT Libraries' facilities. It is the responsibility of each user to ensure that he or she uses these products only for individual, noncommercial use without systematically downloading, distributing, or retaining substantial portions of information.

Second, for resources with more restrictive or explicit rules for use, we offer the red "L" button, which appears in the "more" column for users. Clicking on the L button for *SciFinder Scholar*, for example, the user would see the screen shown in Figure 4.6. This allows us

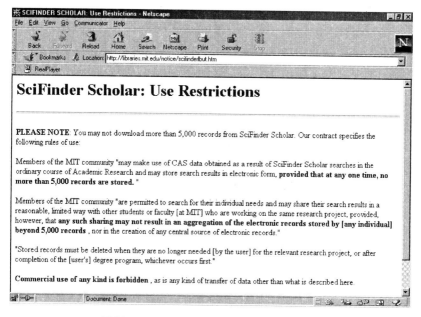

FIGURE 4.6. Sample Restrictions Screen

to create customized language for products as needed. While our goal is to have most of our licenses' rules of use described by our generic language, which essentially reflects fair use, Vera also allows us a quick and simple method of displaying more information as needed.

The information that was formerly captured and laboriously maintained in many Web pages we had created to keep up with the staff's need for information about electronic resources is now available from reports generated on the fly from the Vera database. Thus, Web pages covering interlibrary loan (ILL) privileges and restrictions, remote access, expiration dates, vendor phone numbers, and lists of scanned licenses are all now available as Vera reports, based on a single database record for each resource. Figures 4.7 through 4.10 contrast the old and new methods.

The beauty and power of Vera is that it fully leverages the time involved in creating the initial database record, because it not only tracks license terms, it also offers resources in relation to those terms, and offers an access tool for users as well.

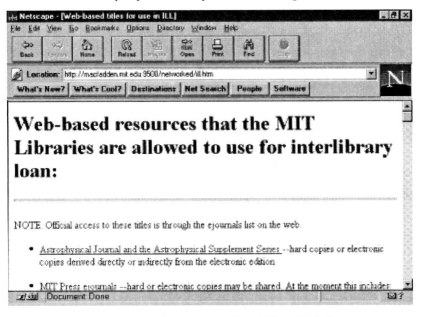

FIGURE 4.7. Old ILL Method—Stand-Alone Web Page

Vera allows us to readily display information for users regarding which resources they have access to, and which they do not. At MIT, as at many institutions, we are not always able to include every part of our MIT community in every license. Our off-site laboratory, the Lincoln Laboratory, for example, has been excluded from some of our licenses. Now users can see that, for example, a particular resource is accessible to all MIT departments except Lincoln Laboratory, as shown in Figure 4.4. This avoids the confusion that we had before Vera, when it was not clear to these users whether there was a technical or a licensing problem keeping them from access.

Our users and our staff are extremely happy with Vera. We believe that the functionality we have come to rely on in Vera will be needed in whatever the next generation of e-resource and license management systems offers us. Yet, while we are thrilled with the efficiency we have found through Vera, we are also hopeful that Timothy Jewell's efforts will pay off. It makes sense in the long run for libraries to have the opportunity to use a widely available system, rather than be forced to invent, invest in, and maintain such systems on their own.

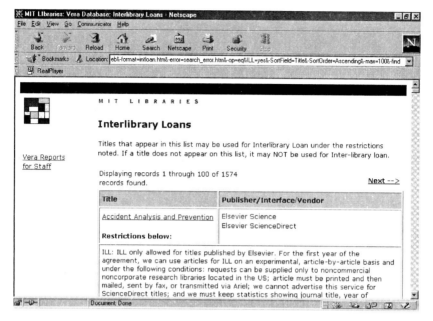

FIGURE 4.8. New ILL Method—Vera Report

THE ROLE OF THE TRADITIONAL SERIALS VENDOR

Another major shift in focus that has resulted from the growth in digital resources is that the vast majority of interactions for digital products are direct with publishers or information providers, not with serial vendors. In the print world, a majority of orders are placed with vendors, and a large portion of our problem-solving occurs through major vendors. In the print model, managing vendor relationships and managing allocation of titles among vendors is a big feature on the map of serials acquisitions. In the digital world, vendors are only beginning to find a role in purchase and implementation; significant barriers to a third-party role still exist. Because license agreements are nonstandard and complex and raise issues that are specific to a given institution, discussions of these issues must take place between the library and the provider if the process is to be as efficient as possible.

However, vendors have recently begun to create their own new roles in the digital environment. For example, in the spring of 2001,

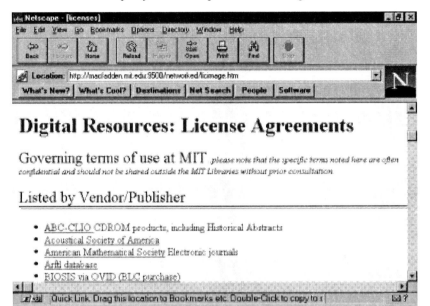

FIGURE 4.9. Old Scanned License Method—Stand-Alone Web Page

Mike Markwith announced the development of a new product that tracks e-resources: TDNet has entered the library market as a tool to help libraries with all aspects of e-resource management. Faxon offers "License Depot," a license negotiation service, which provides libraries with "access to information about e-journal licensing, pricing, access and ordering details."[24]

Such products may ultimately change the way libraries access electronic serials, but as they are still emerging and evolving, they have not been a significant transformative force in the market to date. At least at MIT, we continue to find we need direct communication with the provider to purchase and implement Web-based resources. Our needs are for support in tracking content changes and providing up-to-date URLs for what we have purchased, as well as in notification of which e-journals are available electronically and what steps must be taken to establish that access. There seems to be unmet demand for more third-party services of this kind, which could well be offered by the present serials vendors, should they choose to do so.

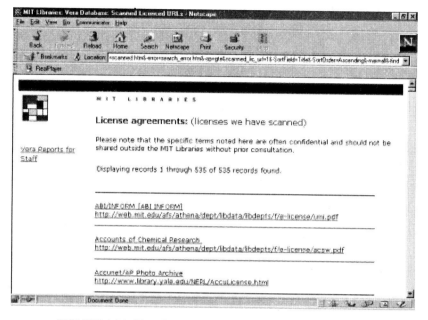

FIGURE 4.10. New Scanned License Method—Vera Report

ARCHIVING

Libraries, at least research libraries, seem to have come to agree that they do not want to abdicate their historical archiving role to a commercial entity such as a vendor. Libraries and publishers are taking significant steps toward the creation of archiving models that will provide a safeguard for future scholars.

A significant development in 2001 was the Mellon Foundation's issuing of seven grants to support libraries' investigation of archiving e-journals. Each university receiving a grant has taken on a different aspect of the problem. At MIT, the focus is on archiving "dynamic e-journals," the kind of scholarly community created through MIT Press's CogNet; at Harvard, the focus is on working with three major publishers of scholarly journals—Blackwell Publishing, John Wiley and Sons, and the University of Chicago Press to "develop an experimental archive for electronic journals."[25] Projects at Yale and Cornell focus on other publishers and other aspects of archiving. Yale's grant focuses on creating an archive for Elsevier titles. According to Yale's press release, "The plan for a library-based archive of the digital publications of Elsevier Science will include the business arrangements necessary for maintaining the archive over time." Yale hopes that a digital archive could be "in place by 2003" and that as time goes on, Yale Library "might be able to offer model archival services to publishers other than Elsevier Science."[26]

Cornell's project, called Project Harvest, focuses on agriculture journals. It is described as "a $150,000, one-year planning grant . . . [that] will allow Cornell University Library to explore the idea of creating permanent digital archives for scholarly journals, with the goal of setting up a pilot archive of agricultural journals."[27]

These efforts coincide with the beginnings of a trend toward publishers allowing for archiving rights in contracts. At least one major STM publisher has recently offered such rights in its contract. These dual efforts—in working out archiving models and allowing for archiving in licenses—suggest a direction that will ameliorate the archiving problem that exists in the digital arena now. Our current paradox is that we care deeply about long-term archival access to electronic products, and we want to negotiate clauses that allow for this, but most libraries do not have the infrastructure to deal with any archival output that a provider might, in the best current case, offer. Mounting a group of PDF images and creating a workable search interface, and refreshing both the data and the search software over time, require skills and systems that are not fully developed as yet in most libraries. These Mellon grants are a first step—a giant step—in developing models and systems for archiving, so that every library is not required to archive all of its titles itself. We are coming closer to the goal of achieving cooperative arrangements, and sufficiently—but not excessively—redundant systems.

RELATIONSHIP OF SERIALS ACQUISITIONS TO CATALOGING

Web-based e-journals and databases challenge our cataloging philosophy and practice. Although the particulars of cataloging issues, like those of archiving, lie outside the scope of this discussion, cataloging issues do affect serials acquisitions as well. The last line of the digital serial work flow diagram (Figure 4.2) shows the path to cataloging after acquisition of a remotely accessed title as a single step. This step glosses over many complicated issues and policy questions, including:

- a lack of prescribed or standard relationships between what is bought and what is cataloged;
- burdensome demands for tracking components of aggregated packages, which lead to
- significant pressures to purchase record sets from publishers and other third-party suppliers, and creating loaders or designing separate database schemes to store such records; and
- the emerging model of the catalog as one of many tools, not *the* tool.

Karen Calhoun, Assistant University Librarian for Technical Services at Cornell University, has reinforced this final point with an apt metaphor, a metaphor I have borrowed and shaped to my own purposes here. Reviewing trends in "our changing information space," she recently noted that the current view of the catalog is that "the catalog is the sun"; but that the emerging view is "the catalog is a planet."[28] This is a very useful way of picturing the revolution in libraries: our OPACs have been our key tool for describing and providing access to our collections. Acquisitions' job was to bring resources in so that they could be moved to cataloging. In the new world we inhabit, the OPAC will be just one planet; the new "sun" is likely to be an SFX-like server, or a piece of software acting like a highly sophisticated gateway.

CONCLUSION

Digital resources have placed research libraries, including acquisitions departments, in a "disruptive context" that has, in half a decade, swept away all of the accepted understandings and shared assumptions about how our services work. What it means to buy something for the library, how to identify that object, what it means to catalog it, and how these processes take place have all changed radically. The systems we need to track and control our digital resources make ILS systems obsolete; our access to large fluctuating collections strains the boundaries of what can be accomplished through title-by-title, intensive in-house descriptive cataloging. Our systems are creaking and groaning under the strain of this new type of library resource. Our universe is being reborn around us, and we are both shaping it and being shaped by it.

In this reconfiguring of the information universe, the acquisitions role has become a rising star. As we have learned from the massive OhioLINK experiment, buying more is basically, in the broadest sense, better. The process of the purchase itself—the contract negotiation, the pricing negotiation, the offering of resources in relation to the license terms—all of these parameters have risen in significance and importance with the advent of the Big Deal. The time has come when libraries can have their biggest impact and provide their best service by buying in volume, and letting the users decide what has worth. The time has come for libraries to begin to manage access by importing and exporting large data sets, most of which will be provided by third parties.

These changes can seem overwhelming, and daily life in libraries can feel like little more than crisis management. However, as the respected family psychologist and writer Judith Wallerstein has said, "Every crisis carries within it the seeds of destruction as well as the possibility of renewed strength."[29] Libraries have shown that, while still spinning from the tornado of change that is sweeping through our doors, we have already begun to emerge with new models and new ideas that are consistent with this new era. We are designing database systems to control licensed resources and are already working cooperatively to share them; we are finding new ways to provide access to the mega-resources we are buying; we have begun to build archiving models and partnerships to prepare for the future; we have rethought our tools, our processes, and our purpose. The resilience of our profession—the new ideas and tools that continue to rise to the surface after each digital tsunami—is both inspirational and hopeful.

NOTES

1. Carl Lagoze, "Business Unusual: How 'Event-Awareness' May Breathe Life into the Catalog?" in *Bicentennial Conference on Bibliographic Control for the New Millennium: Confronting the Challenges of Networked Resources and the Web*, November 15-17, 2000, <http://lcWeb.loc.gov/catdir/bibcontrol/lagoze_paper.html>.

2. Ibid.

3. I want to acknowledge my appreciation and thanks to Karen Calhoun for originating the sun/planet metaphor that has given shape to this chapter, when she used it in relation to the OPAC and access methods in "Aggregators and the Catalog: Where Will It End?" (presentation at NELINET Conference on E-Books and E-Journals, Amherst, Massachusetts, May 22, 2001). Here at MIT, we have been grappling with the proper metaphor for the reshaping of our access methods and information management systems; we have been thinking of "donuts" and "wheels" and "hubs" and even worked for a while with water metaphors. Karen Calhoun's choice of metaphor seems to crystallize both the concept of the change, and its significance, in a particularly apt way. I have reshaped her idea in my own way, and hope it is not a distortion of her original image.

4. Figures 4.1 and 4.2 were developed originally for a presentation: Ellen Duranceau, "Buying a Used Car Every Day: The Implications of the Digital Revolution for Serials Acquisitions at MIT" (ACRL New England Chapter Serials Interest Group Panel Discussion: "From Overdrive to Cyberdrive: The Impact of Technology on Technical Services," Gutman Library, Harvard University Graduate School of Education, Cambridge, Massachusetts, May 7, 1997).

5. See George L. Morrisey, *Morrisey on Planning: A Guide to Strategic Thinking* (San Francisco: Jossey-Bass Publishers, 1995).

6. Table 4.1 was also initially developed for "Buying a Used Car Every Day."

7. For more detail, see Ellen Duranceau, "Ejournal Forum: Tracking Content Changes at Aggregated Websites for Serials," *Serials Review* 27(1) (2001): 51-57.

8. Kenneth Frazier, "The Librarian's Dilemma: Contemplating the Costs of the 'Big Deal,'" *D-Lib Magazine* 7(3) (March 2001), <http://www.dlib.org/dlib/march01/march01/frazier/03frazier.html>.

9. Robert Michaelson, "The Big Issue: The Future of Electronic Publications" *Newsletter on Serials Pricing Issues* 254 (December 19, 2000), <http://www.mathdoc.ujf-grenoble.fr/NSPI/Numeros/2000-254.html#2>.

10. Kent Mulliner, "Response to 'The Big Issue: The Future of Electronic Publications,' by Robert Michaelson," *Newsletter on Serials Pricing Issues* 255 (February 1, 2001), <http://www-mathdoc.ujf-grenoble.fr/NSPI/Numeros/2001-255.html#4>.

11. Rick Anderson, posting to Reedelsecustomers discussion list, January 10, 2001.

12. Tom Sanville, letter on behalf of the OhioLINK Library Advisory Committee in response to Frazier, "The Librarians' Dilemma," March 30, 2001, *D-Lib Magazine* 7(4) (April 2001), <http://www.dlib.org/dlib/april01/04letters.html#SANVILLE>.

13. David Kohl, "What If What We Know Isn't True: Selection, Collection Development, and Usage" (presentation at NELINET Conference on E-Books and E-Journals, Amherst, Massachusetts, May 22, 2001).

14. Ibid.

15. Rob Richards, "Licensing Agreements: Contracts, the Eclipse of Copyright, and the Promise of Cooperation" (unpublished update of article in *The Acquisitions Librarian* 26 [2001]).

16. See, for example, John Cox Associates model licenses at <http://www.licensingmodels.com/>; models put together by the Digital Library Federation and the Council on Library and Information Resources at <http://www.library.yale.edu/

~llicense/modlic.shtml>; and principles agreed to by ARL, ALA, and SLA at <http://www.arl.org/scomm/licensing/principles.html>.

17. <http://www.library.yale.edu/~llicense/intro.shtml>.

18. Liblicense: Licensing Digital Information, http://www.library.yale.edu/~Llicense/index.shtml>.

19. Richards, "Licensing Agreements."

20. Okerson et al., "Liblicense," example clause 8, "Warranties, Indemnities and Limitations of Liability,"<http://www.library.yale.edu/~llicense/warrcls.shtml>.

21. Timothy Jewell, "Selection and Presentation of Commercially Available Electronic Resources: Issues and Practices," <http://www.clir.org/diglib/forums/spr2001/commforum.htm>; see Jewell's surveys and other work at "A Web Hub for Developing Administrative Metadata for Electronic Resource Management," <http://www.library.cornell.edu/cts/elicensestudy/>.

22. For information on ERLIC, see <http://www.libraries.psu.edu/iasWeb/fiscal_data/ERLIC_SHARE/Publish/index.html>.

23. For an overview of Vera, see Nicole Hennig, "Improving Access to E-Journals and Databases at the MIT Libraries: Building a Database-Backed Web Site Called 'Vera,'" *The Serials Librarian* (forthcoming 2002), <http://www.hennigWeb.com/publications/vera.html>.

24. Faxon Library Services, "License Depot," <http://www/faxon.com/Id/default.htm>.

25. "Harvard University Library and Key Publishers Join Forces for Electronic Journal Archive," May 16, 2001, posting to Liblicense-l discussion list, <http://www.library.yale.edu/~llicense/ListArchives/0105/msg00096.html>; for a description of all seven Mellon archiving grants, see Digital Library Federation, "Preservation of Electronic Scholarly Journals," <http://www.diglib.org/preserve/presjour.htm>.

26. "Yale Library to Plan Digital Archives with Elsevier Science," February 2001, *Yale University Library News Releases*, <http://www.library.yale.edu/Administration/newsreleases/elsevier_release.html>.

27. "Preserving Scholarly Journals in Digital Form Raises Questions Cornell University Library Will Try to Answer," January 2001, *Cornell University News Service Releases*, http://www.news.cornell.edu/releases/Jan01/ProjectHarvest.ws.html>.

28. Calhoun, "Aggregators and the Catalog."

29. Judith Wallerstein and Sandra Blakeslee, *The Good Marriage* (New York: Warner Books, 1995): 332.

Chapter 5

Perspectives on the Library
As E-Journal Customer, Intermediary,
and Negotiator in a Time of Chaos

Cheryl Kern-Simirenko

INTRODUCTION

The role of academic libraries as content providers has always placed librarians in a unique situation relative to their role as selectors and purchasers of content. Libraries and librarians are the customers but not the primary consumers. Their role as customer is an intermediary role, executed on behalf of their particular community of consumers. As has been noted in numerous discussions of the serials/scholarly communication crisis, these consumers are also creators of the content being purchased. When purchasing traditional print containers (books and journal subscriptions), the library customer has, for all intents and purposes, always dealt with a monopoly marketplace. Unlike the domestic customer, faced with a bewildering range of choices in home electronics, or a business customer, able to choose among multiple manufacturers as the supplier of widget X, libraries have had to buy content from sole sources and function in a seller's market. Society all-pubs offerings, focused on a subject area and advantageously priced, and some limited bundling (Part C offered only in conjunction with subscriptions to Part A or B), have not been unusual. If more than one publisher offers content in the same subject area, the typical result has been consumer pressure on the library to purchase multiple containers of similar content—an outcome consistent both with the exponential growth of research and publication and with the desired goal of making all the relevant literature readily available to the researcher/consumer. It is in the context of finite or scarce resources that choices between journal offerings are made; collection development or selection is an exercise in the allocation of resources as well as an exercise in providing content.

Fast forward to the age of rapid growth in e-journal availability and an environment in which simple subscription purchases have been replaced by licensing and contract law. Models for delivering online full-text content are in a state of flux. Publishers undoubtedly have legitimate concerns about revenue streams. Librarians have equally legitimate concerns about responsive and responsible resource allocation. Foundational moments such as these call for careful attention to the long-term consequences of entering into agreements that will likely have the effect of limiting or reducing the range of options available in the future.

TOWARD SYSTEMIC THINKING
AND OUTCOMES ORIENTATION

Margaret Landesman and Johann Van Reenen have highlighted some of the potentially divergent and conflicting outcomes for libraries in the simultaneous pursuit of consortial purchasing and reform of the system of scholarly communication. The long-term impact of an increasing portion of an acquisitions budget being devoted to a few large publishers is one of the issues being raised.[1] Kenneth Frazier has elucidated the potential pitfalls of licensing bundled products through the application of game theory, specifically "The Prisoners' Dilemma" and "The Tragedy of the Commons." [2] Self-evident, rational strategies individually employed actually lead to outcomes that are less than optimal for the participants.[3] Dietrich Dorner's *The Logic of Failure* also offers a useful conceptual framework when considering the impact of signing a contract for an individual publisher's entire e-journal output. Dorner's work emphasizes systemic thinking and key factors such as: the importance of anticipating the side effects and the long-term repercussions that can result from an action (or a linear series of actions); the danger of assuming that the absence of immediate and obvious negative consequences signifies that the correct actions have been taken; and the disastrous long-term consequences that can result when decision-makers focus on isolated cause-and-effect relationships. [4]

Consider also the current environment for higher education. The focus is increasingly on evaluation and assessment; on accountability; on outcomes; on what has actually been accomplished rather than simply on inputs and/or outputs. Strategic planning is likewise a hallmark of the changes taking place in higher education, as institutions refocus their missions, set priorities for achieving excellence, and establish budgets that support those goals and priorities. The need for nimble responses to new challenges and opportunities is emphasized. Expectations for budgeting to support institutional priorities and accountability for outcomes cut across the entire institution, and academic librarians are called upon to manage collections and services within these institutional norms. Given the importance of journal literature to the learning and discovery (formerly teaching and research) missions of the parent institution and the relatively large portion of the materials budget devoted to making this literature available, it seems reasonable to expect that management of these resources should reflect, and change along with, the priorities of the institution.

TOWARD ACTIVE NEGOTIATING STRATEGIES

Although the move to licensing and contract law raises concerns about losing fair use under copyright law, contracting for content and services also opens up opportunities for negotiating terms that offer benefits to both signatories. Admittedly, it may be difficult for librarians, under pressures from their consumer community and/or their consortial partners, to view themselves as being in a position to negotiate for terms that are balanced rather than one-sided. Publishers are likely to be surprised when confronted with librarians who refuse "standard" terms, that is, terms set by the publishers in the same "take-it-or-leave-it" mode as the traditional print market. However, negotiating mutually beneficial contracts is the norm in the business world, and it behooves librarians to sharpen their negotiating skills. Consider for a moment the businessperson seeking a supply of widget X. Is it likely that he or she will sign a contract requiring the acceptance of a manufacturer's entire output of widget X, or to also buy widget Y and widget Z in order to obtain widget X, in excess of his or her actual needs? The analogy to trade in other products has its limitations. Nonetheless, if librarians are going to operate successfully in a context of accountability, arranging for delivery of e-journal content will need to take place in a context of judicious choices that support institutional priorities.

Contracts for publishers' print/electronic bundles may include features such as limitations on the ability to cancel print subscriptions; access to e-content through a proprietary front-end; direct payment to the publisher for e-access fees, and a cap on annual price increases over multiyear contracts, expressed as a percentage of print costs; and a paid document-delivery model when users access titles not held in print. Consortial contracts are likely to provide e-access to all the print holdings of the consortium for all members.

OPTIMIZING VERSUS MAXIMIZING

Data on e-journal content use, whether the library has a single-institution license or is part of a consortial agreement, indicate that viewing of articles includes the active use of titles not owned by the particular library. These usage patterns are often cited as evidence of success in meeting user needs, on the one hand, and lack of success in predicting and meeting user needs through selection of core collections, on the other. The expansion of e-content established under these contracts is thus seen as achieving a positive impact, and the strategy for creating this impact is regarded as a successful one. Yet librarians know that the presence of content online correlates highly with use. Visibility in the supermarket correlates with sales (hence the purchase of display space by suppliers), and online visibility of e-journal content virtually guarantees that the content will be looked at, regardless of its quality or its ratio of relevance relative to other published works. "By selling packages to libraries," Landesman and Van Reenen note, "vendors ensure the visibility of their electronic journals and limit the visibility of other titles."[5] This perspective suggests real parallels with the world of the supermarket. The issue of use behaviors in response to visibility also raises a significant question about the extent to which more online content and more use of that content actually correlate with successful outcomes for the consumers of that content. The correlation, it seems, is not automatic. Although the provision of seamless access to both higher- and lower-use e-journal content is an attractive goal, consideration needs to be given to outcomes in relation to both short- and long-term costs and to potential constraints on achieving other priorities of equal or greater value. Optimizing strategies frequently trump maximizing strategies.

ANALYZING IMPACTS

Librarians (and university administrators) have long been frustrated with the lack of stability and predictability in serials costs. They have made efforts to obtain firm pricing in advance of invoicing and to maintain expenditures within funded levels by canceling titles from a particular publisher in order to keep payments at the previous year's level or at a level adjusted to increases in the Consumer Price Index. Thus, a multiyear agreement with a cap on inflationary increases may be attractive. These inflation caps are usually combined with limits on cancellations, a quid pro quo giving stability and predictability to both sides. Achieving the library's goal of stability and predictability for a portion of serials costs may conflict with the goal of maintaining flexibility in managing serials holdings. One may also wonder just how much risk a publisher is actually taking in setting caps. Purdue University's library experienced an overall 43 percent price increase for titles from one large scientific, technical, and medical (STM) publisher over a three-year period. Subsequently, this same publisher offered a multiyear contract with a 6 percent-per-year cap. A 70 percent increase over six years would seem to suggest that the profit margin has been afforded a comfortable measure of protection.

Librarians have long lamented the impact of currency exchange rates on serials budgets, when, for example, 40 percent of titles may account for 60 percent of the expenditures. Bundled publisher packages of e-journal content could yield similar, and possibly even more constricting, results. Purdue University's library already has some 25 percent of the serials budget committed to a single STM publisher, accounting for less than 10 percent of titles held. The University of New

Mexico has reported that an analysis of the budgetary impact of this same publisher's e-only access package showed that acceptance of this contract would have moved the library's commitment of 35 percent of the serials budget for that single publisher to more than 50 percent of the budget in just two years.[6] Contemplating potential long-term repercussions for serials budget management tied to the acceptance of bundled access suggests the need for extreme caution. Might core materials from other publishers need to be sacrificed? Might higher-use materials in some disciplines be sacrificed to the maintenance of access for lower-use materials in other disciplines? Might the acquisition of content from small publishers in emerging disciplines be sacrificed? Might access to information for the university community as a whole be reduced? How would such conditions match the strategic planning priorities and the outcome measures of the parent institution?

OUTCOMES AND ACCOUNTABILITY

In the final analysis, collection development is as much about effective and efficient budgeting to meet institutional priorities as it is about selection per se. In the best of all possible worlds, every one of our consumers would have immediate and effortless access to all relevant information for his or her learning and discovery needs. In the real world, fiscal realities limit every institution's ability to deliver that content Shangri-La.

The need to maintain flexibility and options for managing materials budgets seems a key goal, particularly when institutions of higher education are undergoing rapid change. This need clearly conflicts with the concept of committing a majority portion of such budgets to the total output of large publishers, some of whose titles (quality considerations aside) are likely to be marginal to the programs of a particular institution. Commitments to maintain subscriptions may also create constraints that limit the opportunities for engaging in strategies that better match consumer needs.

A.B.A. Schippers has reported on the history of subscription management over some twenty years at the Physics and Astronomy Library of Utrecht University. Despite a significant reduction in serials subscriptions in 1994, a 1997 survey showed that some 85 percent of the respondents' reading needs could be met by titles representing 40 percent of expenditures.[7] In this example, unbundling, or customization, clearly represents a rational allocation of institutional resources.

Many libraries have incorporated assessment of document delivery options into the access equation. In the latest serials cancellation project, Purdue University's library gave special attention to high-priced journals for which reliable current awareness tools were already available. Titles that met these criteria and also showed a high cost-per-use ratio were specifically discussed with faculty consumers as candidates for document delivery (at no cost to the requestor) in lieu of subscription. In the case of a $15,000 STM subscription that was canceled as a result, monitoring of both rising subscription costs and document delivery requests and costs over three years indicates that this approach remains cost effective. Meanwhile, retention of a greater number of valued titles with lower cost-per-use ratios is regarded as a reasonable trade-off for the less-convenient access to one exceedingly costly title.

The circumstances surrounding the creation of a new journal, *Theory and Practice of Logic Programming* (TPLP), are another case in point. The editorial board (fifty people) of the *Journal of Logic Programming* (JLP), with the full support of the Association for Logic Programming, resigned from the JLP to found the TPLP, which has a projected price per page some 55 percent below that of JLP.[8] Purdue University, consumer demand for cancellation of JLP coupled with acquisition of the new title was immediate, with the expectation that the library would be responsive to a situation wherein quality content for the logic programming community was going to be made available at a more reasonable price.

Aggregated databases of full-text e-journals present particular challenges for libraries since there is an additional level of uncertainty associated with unpredictable changes in content. Access to full text depends upon contractual relationships between the aggregator and third parties, leaving libraries vulnerable to both random loss and substitution of content and random increases in content duplicated in other library-publisher or library-aggregator contracts. It may be difficult to cancel such access even in the face of significant content loss, unsatisfactory content substitution, or redundancy if users have come to rely on the unique content available in the aggregated package. Since pricing is usually not adjusted to reflect content loss or less-than-satisfactory substitution, and since over the longer term multiple expenditures for significant content redundancy are incompatible with responsible fiscal management, librarians may quickly find themselves in an untenable position. Although aggregations may support very well the learning needs of undergraduates, functioning as a macro-level set of online reserve readings, researchers may be significantly underserved when the only access is through proprietary search engines. These situations again raise the question of whether decisions that maximize rather than optimize resource subsets may, over the long term, reduce congruence with overall institutional priorities.

The impact of contract terms, such as direct payment to the publisher, can be felt in areas beyond the library's materials budget. Use of a serials vendor for both print and e-journals has obvious advantages for libraries: avoiding the proliferation of invoices; maintaining a comprehensive record of all transactions, such as discounts applied to print subscriptions; the ability to load detailed financial data directly into the local integrated system; and greater stability in service fees as the print base shrinks in favor of e-access only. Stephen Bosch has elaborated on the challenges of losing vendor value-added services for e-journal-only packages.[9] Although real costs are associated with these vendor services, there are nonetheless economies of scale in outsourcing these activities rather than hiring additional staff to carry out the tasks. As decision making in universities becomes increasingly data driven and outcomes oriented, librarians need to be mindful of just how deleterious these seemingly peripheral impacts from an e-journal contract may be when the library is called upon to demonstrate accountability and support of institutional priorities.

The need to manage pathways for optimal access by consumers, through both OPACs and Web portals, adds another level of complexity to the challenge of dealing with e-journal content. Until technology can truly deliver cross-platform searching that is both successful and transparent, proprietary front ends for publisher-based subsets of e-journal content seem as constraining to the flow of information to consumers as the absence of standard-gauge railroad tracks were to the movement of freight in the early days of the railroads. The ability to conduct full-text searching across subsets of the knowledge universe is highly desirable, but direct browsing of that same content is no less desirable. For example, much consideration has already been given to the unique issues posed by e-journal titles held in aggregator databases when librarians strive to provide the information surrogates that answer "does-the-library-have?" queries.[10] Consumers also seek a ready answer to a broader question, expressed as "What e-journals does my library have?" Consideration of the pathway needs and expectations of consumers is yet another factor that merits attention in negotiating contracts for e-journal content.

CONCLUSION

The shift from the subscription to the licensing model offers librarians new opportunities to negotiate contracts that serve the needs of both parties and result in a configuration of resources that serve local needs over both the short and the long term. In an environment where e-commerce is moving to greater product/service customization based on customer profiling and preferences, "all-or-nothing" e-journal packages seem anachronistic. Active contract negotiation for optimal packets of e-content increases the likelihood of creating new models that can represent viable options for the future, for both buyers and sellers. It enables librarians to manage content provision on behalf of their consumer communities in ways that are both responsive and responsible in an era of accountability.

NOTES

1. Margaret Landesman and Johann Van Reenen, "Consortia vs. Reform: Creating Congruence," *The Journal of Electronic Publishing* 6(2) (December 2000), <http://www.press.umich.edu/jep/06-02/landesman.html> (viewed February 2, 2001).

2. Kenneth Frazier, "The Librarians' Dilemma: Contemplating the Costs of the 'Big Deal,'" *D-Lib Magazine* 7(3) (March 2001), <http://www.dlib.org/dlib/march01/frazier/03frazier.html> (viewed June 25, 2001).

3. For a brief introduction to game theory, see David K. Levine, "What Is Game Theory?" <http://levine.sscnet.ucla.edu/general/whatis.htm> (viewed January 1, 2001).

4. Dietrich Dorner, *The Logic of Failure: Why Things Go Wrong and What We Can Do to Make Them Right* (New York: Metropolitan Books, 1996), 18, 35, 198-199.

5. Landesman and Van Reenen.

6. Landesman and Van Reenen.

7. A.B.A. Schippers, "Tackling the Serials Crisis: Unbundling Journal Subscriptions," *Newsletter on Serials Pricing Issues* 253 (September 22, 2000), http://www-mathdoc.ujf-grenoble.fr/NSPI/Numeros/2000-253.html#4> (viewed June 25, 2001).

8. See *Theory and Practice of Logic Programming* for background, <http://www.cwi.nl/projects/alp/TPLP/index.html> (viewed June 25, 2001).

9. Stephen Bosch, "Impact of Electronic Aggregations at the University of Arizona," *SPARC E-News* (December 2000-January 2001), <http://www.arl.org/sparc/core/index.asp?page=g15#6> (viewed June 25, 2001).

10. Karen Calhoun and Bill Kara, "Aggregation or Aggravation? Optimizing Access to Full-Text Journals," *ACLTS Online Newsletter* 11(1) (spring 2000), <http://www.ala.org/alcts/alcts_news/v11n2/gateway_pap15.html> (March 30, 2000).

For an example of how one library provides information surrogates for e-journals and other electronic resources, see University of Michigan Library, "Access to Electronic Resources—Frequently Asked Questions," <http://www.lib.umich.edu/accesser/accessfaq.html> (June 25, 2000).

Chapter 6

Collection Development for Online Serials Redux: *Now* Who Needs to Do What, Why, and When

Mark Jacobs
Cindy Stewart Kaag

INTRODUCTION

This chapter provides a sample procedure detailing who in the library needs to be involved at which points in the selection/acquisition/cataloging process for electronic resources. Collection development is just one of the issues and questions pertaining to online serials. There is a considerable body of professional literature covering pricing, archiving, copyright, cataloging and bibliographic control, selection policies, etc.; a sampling of these is included in the bibliography. The following template is adaptable to your institutional needs to ensure the necessary people are involved at the right time.

WHO NEEDS TO BE INVOLVED IN GETTING ELECTRONIC PRODUCTS UP AND RUNNING?

Selections: they're not just for collection development librarians anymore. Before an online serial can be made available to users, a great deal of consultation and communication among library personnel have to take place. Leaving people out of the process, or not consulting key players at the right stage, can hold up access. Each library needs to determine *who* will be involved in making online serials available to users and at *what points* in the process they should be contacted.

Assume you are responsible for collection development and you are interested in adding the *Journal of Superfluous Research* to your collection. Depending on your local practice, you might normally:

- evaluate the product, make a decision, send the order to the acquisitions unit;
- evaluate the product, consult with colleagues in your unit, make a decision, send the order to the acquisitions unit;
- evaluate the product, consult with your head of collections, make a decision, send the order to the acquisitions unit; or
- some combination of these and/or other steps.

It's not that easy with online serials.

Suppose it is the online, not print, version of the *Journal of Superfluous Research* you want. Immediately new questions arise: Do you have the technology to make the online version available to users? Better check with your systems office. Do you have someone in your unit who can find out what the product requires and compare it to available hardware and software, or do you have to do that yourself? Are you talking about a locally loaded tape, or Internet access, or some other access permutation? If you choose Internet, will it be through your OPAC or some other interface? Will passwords be necessary, or will the user's IP address suffice for identification? If you have remote users, will you have to construct a remote access table on a proxy server? Will your license agreement allow you to fill interlibrary loan requests? Can your users download, print, and/or e-mail the text? Can they do it from office and home, or only from within the library? Can you get it wholesale, that is, through a consortium? How is the product priced: per capita, per station, per simultaneous user? It will not do you any good to send a purchase order to your acquisitions unit until these questions are answered.

Once an order has gone to the acquisitions unit, consultation and coordination are still needed. Acquisitions personnel may have to order a specific type of software, pay attention to back file restrictions and charges, specify the subscription period, and most especially make sure the licensing agreement is signed by both the vendor and the purchaser, and that a copy of it is received and filed by the library, whether that file is kept in the acquisitions unit or elsewhere. The order should specify that the signed license agreement be returned within a set time period. This is an area where vendors are notoriously lax; once they have your money and your signature, signing the license themselves and sending a copy back to you are not a high priority. If the vendor does not respond within whatever time frame you set, claim the license just as you would claim an unfilled order. The license file is just one of the new requirements of online serials, but it is one of the most important.

When the signed license agreement and passwords (if any) are received, the cataloging unit can take over, but here too there are questions to answer unique to online serials. Will your OPAC reflect the journal title only, and give its Internet address in lieu of a local location, or will the user be directed to a separate file of online journals, or will the record be hotlinked to the full text? Will you be using PURLS (persistent uniform resource locators)? Scripting for remote access? Will you list the title in your OPAC, in a separate list of online titles, or both? It is perfectly possible that all these options, and others, will be incorporated by your library for different titles with different license restrictions. Options need to be explored in consultation with the cataloging unit ahead of time, so clear instructions on what to do with the title in hand can be included with the original order.

Obviously, unless you are the sole collections-systems-acquisitions-cataloging librarian, you are going to have to talk to a number of people to determine the best process for your organization. It will undoubtedly be useful to find out what (if anything) has been done about handling online products in the past, talk to those who will be involved in the future, and draw up draft guidelines to circulate for comment. Because change can be scary, or at least bothersome, it is important to give everyone involved a chance to make suggestions about how to go about adding an online serial. It is especially important to make sure everyone understands that guidelines are not written in stone, that change is inevitable and improvement is expected, and that the important thing is to get a process in place and adapt that process as experience grows.

SETTING UP YOUR GUIDELINES

Possibly the most important factor in adding online serials to your collections smoothly is preventing panic. Library staff and users alike may feel overwhelmed by the newness of the approach and the changes it brings. The first step to helping your users is to help your staff realize that this is essentially no different from what they already do so ably: get the material to the user.

When you have drafted a set of guidelines for online serials, it will help if everybody gets to see the whole document, and not just a part of it. To that end, sending out a draft copy should serve two purposes: it will answer many questions, and it will generate many more! Even if you think you have covered all contingencies, someone will surely think of another. That is exactly the purpose of a draft—to refine, revise, rethink, and reforge.

Following is a sample cover letter sent along with the draft guidelines to library personnel; it was written to emphasize the malleable nature of the process.

> This is a draft of interim guidelines for obtaining and accessing electronic products, such as online serials. For the past few years library units have dealt with these issues piecemeal in response to questions as they arose. These guidelines bring together elements from individual unit practices into a cradle-to-grave overview of what needs to happen for the libraries to make an electronic product available to users. Keep in mind that:
>
> • Procedures will change over time.
> • Procedures will change as more efficient practices evolve.
> • Not all products will require all steps set forth in this draft.
> • Not all possible permutations are addressed by this draft.
> • Adjustments and exceptions are expected.
>
> If you have any additions or changes to suggest, please let us know.

DRAFT GUIDELINES FOR SELECTING, PROCESSING, AND ACCESSING ELECTRONIC RESOURCES

This is a guide for the decision-making process involved in acquiring electronic resources including online serials, CD-ROMs, database products, Internet sites, and software accessible to the public through public workstations or the online library catalog. This guide addresses who should participate at which stage in obtaining and handling electronic resources materials. There will *always* be exceptions to these guidelines.

I.   Selection

    A. Selection of materials, from the very beginning, must involve a collaboration between collection development and systems personnel. In order to make appropriate selections, collection development librarians must be aware of and incorporate into their thinking a host of issues (Box 6.1); a few samples:

- Is the title available electronically?
- Is it more cost-effective to purchase in print or electronic format?
- Is it more user-effective to purchase in print or electronic format?
- Is it part of an aggregation or is it purchased separately?
- Will it be linked through the OPAC or stand alone?
- What are the access restrictions? (There are always access restrictions!)
- Can it be purchased through a consortium?
- Will remote access have to go through a proxy server?
- Will access require a login or password?

    B. The selector checks reviews of electronic resources under consideration, based on the criteria listed in the "Guidelines for Electronic Resource Selection" (Box 6.2).

    C. The selector may check the usefulness of products by setting up a trial period. Arrangements should be made in collaboration with the electronic resources librarian and systems personnel. A trial period is a great opportunity for the selector to gather input from colleagues as to whether the resource is suitable for the library's collection before too much time and effort is invested in acquisitions. At the same time, while a product is being tested, groundwork for permanent acquisitions can be laid.

    D. The selector gathers necessary information on candidate products to facilitate decision making. Information may include system requirements, search engine, costs, network-

ing restrictions, dates of coverage, etc. An important consideration for selectors is whether the title is already available
in another format such as paper or microform, or whether it
is to be a digital resource only. Fewer and fewer electronic
versions are really "free with paper"; check costs carefully.

E. Selector submits this information to or consults with appropriate colleagues (electronic resources librarian, faculty,
systems personnel, branch campus personnel, collection
development head, etc.) and gathers needed signatures.

II. Purchasing

A. The electronic resources librarian's involvement is essential in determining whether:
- the resource is to be purchased based on simultaneous
users or on a head count;
- there are access restrictions;
- full coverage is available from one provider only; or
- recent electronic issues come from one provider, but
older issues from another.

B. The requesting unit fills in the Electronic Product Purchase
Request (Box 6.3) and forwards it to the acquisitions unit.
Acquisitions personnel then send requests for free resources that do not require licensing straight to cataloging
to be added to the OPAC, and to systems to be added to the
alphabetical list of resources or databases. Resources that
must be licensed are sent to the electronic resources librarian for license negotiations, approval, and signatures.

C. If the product requires systemwide access or a statewide consortium, appropriate personnel will need to coordinate solic-
iting the necessary information from other participants.

D. The electronic resources librarian determines in collaboration with systems personnel what is needed to make the
product work with the current configuration of the library
system and determines the best suitable access method/loca-
tion for the product (stand-alone workstation, LAN, loading
in the online catalog, etc.) after consulting with appropriate
public and technical service personnel (including other
units such as ILL).

E. Both the unit collection development head and the electronic resources librarian must sign off on purchase requests, except when the source of funding is outside of the unit, such as the university itself or a statewide consortium. In the latter case, the library director will sign along with the unit collection development head of the unit and/or the appropriate electronic resources librarian.

III. Licensing

A. When the person in charge of library systems receives licensing information, he or she will consult with appropriate librarians, including the selector, the electronic resources librarian, the head of interlibrary loans, and if necessary the library's legal counsel, on the terms of the license. He or she will send any proposed amendments to the vendor for approval.

B. After the library and the vendor agree to license terms, systems personnel make the amendments, add needed technical information relating to the local network, and send the document(s) to the acquisitions unit.

C. The electronic resources librarian forwards recommendations for the access location and licensing information (prices, number of users, etc.) to the acquisitions unit along with a purchase recommendation. The acquisitions unit then sends a notice of purchase to systems and/or cataloging. At this point a decision has to be made as to how the patron will access the resources—OPAC, alphabetical list, database, etc.

D. Purchase requests go to the acquisitions unit from the systems office, complete with payment information, signed license, address of vendor, and full user/location information in the order form.

IV. Acquisitions

A. Acquisitions personnel create an interim record and send the order with completed license, requesting return of countersigned license. All electronic products are ordered on a "rush" basis. Items (and signed licenses) will be claimed in thirty days if not received. Acquisitions personnel maintain the official license file for items in the collection (not for hardware and software) and send a copy of the completed license to the systems office with a list of the resources covered by the license.

B. Serials are shipped to appropriate unit. *Exception:* Subscription program software, e.g., Lexis-Nexis, is sent to the person designated on the purchase request.

C. Monographs are shipped to the acquisitions unit, which sends them on to the cataloging unit.

D. If the product is to be loaded into the online catalog, the selector(s) and/or the electronic resources librarian(s) forward the issue to the body in charge of the catalog for evaluation and approval. If access to the product is to be provided via a URL "hot link," the Cataloging Unit is notified by e-mail.

V. Cataloging

A. All electronic resources are cataloged on a "rush" basis.

B. Paperwork is sent to the cataloging unit from the acquisitions unit, along with the physical item, if any.

C. In collaboration with systems and acquisitions, the cataloging unit determines the appropriate URL or address to be used for access.

D. Cataloging personnel process the product and notify the systems office and the unit/electronic resources librarian as applicable when the item is available for public use.

VI. Postpurchase

A. If the license covers multiple titles, the selector notifies the acquisitions and systems office of any changes in titles covered. Systems personnel notify interlibrary loans and the Web master of the changes.

B. Systems personnel notify the interlibrary loan office of the titles and any license restrictions, and the Web master of any titles to be added to the library homepage.

C. Except in extraordinary circumstances, the process does not apply to single-user, stand-alone products with so-called shrink-wrap licenses. These usually do not require negotiation, and access is normally limited to the walk-in users of the library.

D. Products may be reviewed at any time, and should be reviewed for cost, usage, uniqueness, and importance at least yearly.

E. Terminations or changes in avenues of access need to be reported to the following:
- Web master
- Cataloging
- Unit head of collections
- Electronic resources librarian
- Subject specialist

Box 6.1. Policy for Selecting Online Resources

Following is an abbreviated guideline to serve as a starting point for developing your own policy.

Content

1. Content should be relevant to the information needs of the community served.
2. Coverage should be comparable or superior to other electronic or print products in the same subject.
3. Content should include a significant amount of material not already available in other locally accessible resources. If another version/format of the item is owned, cancellation should be considered.
4. Accuracy and completeness should be judged as for any other item under purchase consideration.
5. Bibliographic databases should be updated on a schedule reflecting the nature of the data and the needs of users.

Cost

1. Cost must be competitive with other electronic versions of the information, if any. Considerations include cost per use, back files to purchase, network fees, discounts for retaining or savings from canceling other formats, as well as costs of necessary new software and equipment.
2. Maintaining hard-copy and electronic versions of an item must be justified. *Considerations:* no archival coverage with electronic version; content differs between formats; license restricts printing, downloading, multiple users, etc.; graphics are not comparable.

Software

1. Software should be largely intuitive for the user. *Considerations:* appealing screen design, both free-text and indexed searching; Boolean and proximity searching; save search feature; speed; search engine appropriate for material; display modifications possible; printing and downloading capabilities; onscreen help that is really helpful; compatibility with existing systems and equipment; ease of maintenance.

(continued)

(continued)

Access

1. Resource should meet networking standards even if financial or legal constraints limit initial networking.
2. Resource should meet international data standards.
3. Multiple simultaneous use agreements are preferred.
4. If competing products have comparable costs, preference will go to the product with no added networking charges.
5. Preference will go to products which enhance access to materials currently unavailable or which maximize use of existing resources.

Additional Considerations

1. Cost should not be the overriding consideration for core resources. Non-core resources should meet one or more of the following criteria: unique access; inexpensive; improved service to users from improved staff efficiency.
2. Owning is preferable to leasing.
3. Staff resources should be considered.

A sample version or trial period before purchase is recommended. As with any other item, reviews are useful.

Box 6.2. Guidelines for Electronic Resource Selection

One of the best sources is the site developed by the Collection Development Policies Committee of the Collection Development and Evaluation Section (CODES) of the Reference and User Services Association (http://www.academic.uofs.edu/organization/codes/begin.html). This site includes Core Policy Elements for electronic formats in general, an annotated bibliography, and selected policy statements. Paper copies are available on interlibrary loan from ALA. Other good sites include the following:

- Acquisitions, Cataloging, and Collection Development Policies for Electronic Resources, <http://www.indiana.edu/~libsalc/policies/e-policies. html>
- Collection Development and the Internet: A Brief Handbook for Recommending Officers in the Humanities and Social Sciences Division at the Library of Congress: Collection Development Sites, <http://lcweb.loc. gov/acq/colldev/handbook.html#sites>
- Collection Development Policy for Electronic Journals, University of Oregon Libraries, <http://libweb.uoregon.edu/colldev/public_policies/ejour.html>
- Electronic Resources Collection Development Policy, University of Tennessee, Knoxville Libraries, <http://www.lib.utk.edu/~colldev/elrescd.html>
- Electronic Collections Development, <http://www.library.yale.edu/~okerson/ html>
- Sample Collection Development Policies for Electronic Resources, Reference and User Services Association 1997 President's Program, <http:// alexia.lis.uiuc.edu/~rrichard/RUSA/policies.html>

Box 6.3. Sample Electronic Product Purchase Request Form

Date _____

Title _____

Producer/publisher _____

Fund to be charged _____
Price _____
Order type (see list below) _____
Media _____
URL (if applicable)* _____

APPROVAL INFORMATION

Selector approval _____
Unit collection development head approval _____
Electronic resources librarian _____
Systems approval _____

ACCESS INFORMATION
Access method (Net, CD-ROM, etc.) _____
Location _____

Available to: ☐   Everyone
                ☐   Local campus
                ☐   Branch campus(es)
                ☐   Distance students
                ☐   ILL

Number of simultaneous users _____
Additional resources required for use _____
Passwords _____

TRACKING INFORMATION

Date license due from vendor _____
Date information/item sent to cataloging _____
Date Web master notified _____

Send availability notification to _____

Notes _____
_____
_____

CATALOGING INFORMATION

Include in OPAC? _____
Include in electronic serials list? _____
Link to record for paper version? _____
Link to record for earlier version? _____

(continued)

(continued)

Order Types	Media Types
MONO	CD-ROM
STO	DATATAPE
REPLACEMENT	MULTI
SERIAL SPECIAL	INTERNET
OTHER	OTHER

*URL information is mandatory for all Internet resources.

Unit approval needed for new purchases initiated from library units. Broad-based purchases (e.g., FirstSearch) or electronic versions of items for which there is a print counterpart (e.g., e-journals) would not normally require unit approval.

Systems approval normally required for multiuser CD-ROM and Internet licenses. (Single user, shrink-wrapped licenses do not need negotiation in most cases.)

License restrictions typically include access (who uses?); use (printing, downloading, interlibrary loan allowed); number of simultaneous users, and additional resources required for use (e.g., PDF files require Adobe Acrobat software).

Typically, when the license returns from the vendor, the item (or just the paperwork in the case of Internet resources) is given to cataloging at the same time that the Web master is notified. Thus, the license return date is an important date that must be noted.

When cataloging is finished, the unit will notify the name(s) listed on the form.

CONCLUSION

As convoluted as this procedure seems, you will find it better to be sure everybody is involved early on than to have access delayed because an essential step along the way was skipped. Once you have more experience in choosing and processing online serials, you will be able to simplify the process. Remember: you are still doing what librarians do best, bringing together the user and the information. The fundamental facts remain, as time goes by.

APPENDIX—SYNOPSIS OF KENNETH CREWS' "LICENSING FOR INFORMATION RESOURCES: CREATIVE CONTRACTS AND THE LIBRARY MISSION"

As a starting point, librarians must understand that a license is an enforceable contract that gives permission to one party to use the property of another party.* All parties involved in a license agreement have expectations. To come to a meeting of the minds and to identify binding contracts in the eyes of the law, three elements are generally required: offer, acceptance, and *consideration*. Of the three, *consideration* may be the hardest to understand. According to Crews, it is often defined as the "return benefit one receives for a promise," (p. 99) or it is the "detriment, or obligation incurred as the recipient of a promise" (p. 99).

The next important point for librarians to consider is who in the organization is to be responsible for negotiating license agreements. In the case of libraries, these contracts may be negotiated, approved, and signed by individuals acting on behalf of the organization by writ of the "proper authority" invested in them by the organization based upon the circumstances of their title or rank (p. 100). Librarians must also be prepared to "ascertain through direct questioning" just who in the other camp has the authority to negotiate, approve, and sign on their behalf (p. 100).

In order to make a responsible decision on behalf of the institution, librarians must be aware of the issues surrounding the acquisition and licensing of digital online resources. A library may find the fulfillment of its mission to optimize access to information hindered by a license agreement that "constrains the usefulness of resources" (p. 102). One hindrance lies in the difference between *purchase* and *license to use* agreements. Libraries are used to purchasing information resources for the use of their patrons and preserving this information for future generations. Now, increasingly, they enter into agreements with vendors and publishers giving them not ownership of resources, but a license to use them. The protection afforded them under the law when resources are licensed is different than that afforded when resources are purchased. Under a right of use agreement, subsequent disposition of the property, i.e., patron circulation or use, interlibrary loan, or de-accessioning, is "subject to the terms of the acquisition agreement or other approvals by the copyright owner" (p. 102).

On the other hand, librarians may also negotiate such agreements to expand patron access to these resources. There is an unlimited potential to de-

---

Virtually Yours: Models for Managing Electronic Resources is the published proceedings of the Joint Reference and User Services Association and the Association for Library Collections and Technical Services Institute, held October 23-25, 1997 in Chicago, and edited by Peggy Johnson and Bonnie MacEwan. This appendix contains a summary of an article in that publication by Kenneth Crews, titled "Licensing for Information Resources: Creative Contracts and the Library Mission" (pp. 98-110). This extensive summary is published with the author's permission, for which we thank him. This is a splendid examination of the exigencies of license agreements among libraries, vendors, and publishers, and can serve as a legal primer for librarians wrangling with this complex and complicated process.

fine the terms under which information resources may be deployed, thus enhancing the library's mission. After all, these contracts can be continually revised and renegotiated, based upon the agreement of the parties involved. It behooves librarians to accept this opportunity and negotiate earnestly for rights of use such as the following:

- Preservation and backup copies
- First-sale doctrine, *which allows libraries to circulate information resources to patrons and in which is implicit the right of transmission of information resources off campus*
- Displays and performance of works
- Classroom use and distance learning, *which may protect traditional rights of fair use as well as protecting the right to adopt "alternative and more practical conditions for the use of works in distance learning"* [emphasis added] (p. 104)
- Copies for interlibrary loans
- Fair use rights
- Preservation of the public domain, *which makes it essential that librarians "resist license agreements that constrain future benefit of materials in the public domain"* [emphasis added] (p. 104)

By remaining true to an advocacy of these fundamental rights, librarians can establish a firm foundation from which to enter into negotiations for the licensing of digital online information resources. A good starting point is essential as librarians will encounter an ever-changing assortment of licensing restrictions proposed by the enormous variety of information providers. Librarians should keep in mind five pertinent strategies for licensing information resources:

1. Identify the library's needs for the information resources
2. Identify rights granted under existing law
3. Develop baseline standards for contracts
4. Be prepared to reject offers and terminate negotiations
5. Participate in national policy development.

With these points in mind, you will be able to negotiate effective, efficient, and legal access to the resources your patrons need.

BIBLIOGRAPHY

"Acquiring electronic journals," *Library Technology Reports* 32(5) (1996): 636.

Amiran, Eyal, "The rhetoric of serials at the present time," *The Serials Librarian* 28(3-4) (1996): 209-221.

Anderson, William C. and Les Hawkins, "Development of CONSER cataloging policies for remote access computer file serials," *Public-Access Computer Systems Review* 7(1) (1995): 6-25.

Arnold, Stephen E., "The scholarly hothouse: Electronic STM journals," *Database* 22(1) (February/March 1999): 27-30+.

Banerjee, Kyle, "Challenges of using metadata in a library setting: The collection and management of electronic links (CAMEL) project at Oregon State University," *Library Collections, Acquisitions, and Technical Services* 24(2) (summer 2000): 217-227.

Barnes, John H., "One giant leap, one small step: Continuing the migration to electronic journals," *Library Trends* 45(3) (winter 1997): 404-415.

Bjornshauge, Lars, "Reengineering academic library services—The crucial steps towards the digital library; presented at the 1998 IFLA Conference" *DF-Revy* 22(2) (March 1999): 27-29.

Blake, Virgil L. P. and Thomas Terry Surprenant, "Navigating the parallel universe: Education for collection management in the electronic age," *Library Trends* 48(4) (spring 2000): 891-922.

Bordeianu, Sever Michael, Christina E. Carter, and Nancy K. Dennis, "Delivering electronic resources with Web OPACs and other Web-based tools: Needs of reference librarians at the University of New Mexico," *Reference Services Review* 28(2) (2000): 111-118.

Borgman, Christine, *From Gutenberg to the global information infrastructure: Access to information in the networked world* (Cambridge, MA: MIT Press, 2000).

Bullington, Jeffrey S., "Looking a gift horse in the mouth: Collection management following a statewide purchase of electronic resources: Impact of NC LIVE on serials usage at Western Carolina University: Report of a workshop at the 1999 NASIG Conference," *The Serials Librarian* 38(3/4) (2000): 305-311.

Burn, Margy, "Electronic journals: The issues for libraries," *LASIE* 26 (July/December 1995): 28-33.

Cameron, Robert D., "To link or to copy? Four principles for materials acquisition in Internet electronic libraries," <http://fas.sfu.ca/0/projects/ElectronicLibrary/project/papers/e-lib-links.html>.

Caplan, Priscilla L., "Electronic journals—Best practices: NISO/NFAIS workshop, February 20, 2000, Philadelphia," *Information Today* 17(5) (May 2000): 20-23.

Cargille, Karen, "Digital archiving: Whose responsibility is it? Special section," *Serials Review* 26(3) (2000): 50-68.

Case, Beau David, "Love's labour's lost: The failure of traditional selection practice in the acquisition of humanities electronic texts," *Library Trends* 48(4) (spring 2000): 729-747.

A bibliography containing what is now background information on electronic serials was included in the first edition of this book. This is an updated version of that bibliography.

Chu, Heting, "Electronic journals: Promises and challenges for academic libraries," <http://phoenix.liunet.edu/~hchu/ejournal.htm>.

Clendenning, Lynda Fuller, "E-commerce: Incorporating new options in library acquisitions: Report from the 1999 Charleston Conference," *Library Collections, Acquisitions, and Technical Services* 24(3) (fall 2000): 411.

Cochenour, Donnice, "CICNet's electronic journal collection," *Serials Review* 22 (spring 1996): 63-68.

Cochenour, Donnice, "How will they know? Libraries' responsibility to inform users of license restrictions for electronic resources," *Colorado Libraries* 26(4) (winter 2000): 45-46.

Cochenour, Donnice, "Taming the octopus: Getting a grip on electronic resources at Pennsylvania State University: Report of a workshop at the 1999 NASIG Conference," *The Serials Librarian* 38(3/4) (2000): 363-368.

Cochenour, Donnice and Elaine F. Jurries, "An idea whose time has come: The Alliance Electronic Journal Access Web site," *Colorado Libraries* 22 (summer 1996): 15-19.

Collins, Tim , "EBSCO's plans for handling electronic journals and document delivery," *Collection Management* 20(3-4) (1996): 15-18.

Coulter, Cynthia M., "Electronic journals: Acquisition and retention issues," *Technical Services Quarterly* 14(2) (1996): 75.

Crews, Kenneth D., "Licensing for information resources: Creative contracts and the library mission," in *Virtually yours: Models for managing electronic resources and services: Proceedings of the Joint Reference and User Services Association and Association for Library Collections and Technical Services Institute, Chicago, Illinois, October 23-25, 1997,* ed. Peggy Johnson and Bonnie MacEwan (Chicago: American Library Association, 1999): 98-110.

Crump, Michele J., "Acquiring and managing electronic journals: Integrated workload or special handling? A report of the ALCTS Automated Acquisitions/In-Process Control Systems Discussion Group meeting, American Library Association Conference, San Francisco, June 1997," *Technical Services Quarterly* 16(1) (1998): 57-60.

Davis, Susan A., "Nuts and bolts of aggregating journals: RUSA program at ALA Midwinter 2000," *Serials Review* 26(3) (2000): 77-79.

Duranceau, Ellen Finnie, "Beyond print: Revisioning serials acquisitions for the digital age," *The Serials Librarian* 33(1/2) (1998): 83-106.

Duranceau, Ellen Finnie, "Cataloging remote-access electronic serials: Rethinking the role of the OPAC," *Serials Review* 21 (winter 1995): 67-77.

Duranceau, Ellen Finnie, "The economics of electronic publishing," *Serials Review* 21(1) (1995): 77-90.

Duranceau, Ellen Finnie, "Electronic journals in the MIT libraries: Report of the 1995 e-journal subgroup," *Serials Review* 22 (spring 1996): 47-56+.

Duranceau, Ellen Finnie, "Examining the user registration model for e-journal access," *Serials Review* 25(3) (1999): 61-65.

Duranceau, Ellen Finnie, "Naming and describing networked electronic resources: The role of uniform resource identifiers," *Serials Review* 20(4) (1994): 31-44.

Duranceau, Ellen Finnie, "Old wine in new bottles? Defining electronic serials," *Serials Review* 22 (spring 1996): 69-79.

"Electronic journals: Trends in World Wide Web (WWW) Internet access," *Information Intelligence, Online Libraries, and Microcomputers* 14(4) (April 1, 1996): 1.

Ferguson, Anthony W. "I am beginning to hate commercial e-journals: Ten commandments for acquiring electronic journals," *Against the Grain* 8 (September 1996): 86.

Gardner, Susan, "The impact of electronic journals on library staff at ARL-member institutions," MSLS thesis, University of North Carolina at Chapel Hill, 2000.

Gibbs, Nancy J., "Using teams to evaluate and implement new services for electronic serials at North Carolina State University: Presented at the 1998 NASIG Conference," *The Serials Librarian* 36(3-4) (1999): 337-345.

Graham, Rebecca A., "Evolution of archiving in the digital age," *Serials Review* 26(3) (2000): 59-62.

Gregory, Vicki L., *Selecting and managing electronic resources: A how-to-do-it manual* (New York: Neil Schuman Publishing, 2000).

Harter, Stephen P. and Hak Joon Kim, "Accessing electronic journals and other e-publications: An empirical study," *College and Research Libraries* 57(5) (September 1996): 440-443, 446-456.

Hawkins, Les , "Network accessed scholarly serials," *The Serials Librarian* 29(3-4) (1996): 19-31.

Hickey, Thomas B., "Present and future capabilities of the online journal," *Library Trends* 43 (spring 1995): 528-543.

Holleman, Curt, "Electronic resources: Are basic criteria for the selection of materials changing?" *Library Trends* 48(4) (spring 2000): 694-710.

Hruska, Martha , "Remote Internet serials in the OPAC?" *Serials Review* 21 (winter 1995): 68-70.

Jaguszewski, Janice M. and Laura K. Proust, "The impact of electronic resources on serial cancellations and remote storage decisions in academic research libraries," *Library Trends* 48(4) (spring 2000): 799-820.

Johnson, Richard K., "A question of access: SPARC, Boone, and society-driven electronic publishing: Reprinted from *D-Lib Magazine,* May 2000," *ARL* Bimonthly Report, no. 211 (August 2000): 9-10.

Jones, Wayne, "E-packages: Problems of cataloging electronic serials presented in aggregated database format," *The Serials Librarian* 39(1) (2000): 15-18.

Jones, Wayne, "We need those e-serial records," *Serials Review* 21 (winter 1995): 74-75.

Jones, Wayne and Young-Hee Cannock, "Format integration and serials cataloging," *The Serials Librarian* 25(1-2) (1994): 83-95.

Kennan, Stella "Electronic publishing: A subversive proposal, and an even more subversive proposal, and a counter argument," *Online* 20(2) (April 1996): 93-94.

Kirkwood, Hal P., "Academic issues in e-journal selection and evaluation: Presented at the 1999 NASIG Conference," *The Serials Librarian* 38(1/2) (2000): 169-174.

Landesman, Margaret and Mary Radix, "New challenges for scholarly communication in the digital era—Changing roles and expectations in the academic community: A conference report, March 1999, Washington, DC," *Library Collections, Acquisitions, and Technical Services* 24(1) (spring 2000): 105-117.

Lee, Sun H., *Research collections and digital information* (Binghamton, NY: The Haworth Press, 2000).

Lewis, Marilyn P., "Unwrapping the serials package: California State University Journal Access Core Collection: ALCTS program at ALA Midwinter 2000," *Serials Review* 26(3) (2000): 79-80.

Loghry, Patricia A. and Amy W. Shannon, "Managing selection and implementation of electronic products: One tiny step in organization, one giant step for the University of Nevada, Reno," *Serials Review* 26(3) (2000): 32-44.

Lord, Jonathan, "Shoveling sand with a teaspoon: Managing electronic journals: Presented at the MLA Mid-Atlantic Chapter annual meeting, October 1999, Wilmington, North Carolina," *Virginia Libraries* 46(2) (April/May/June 2000): 17-18.

Luijendijk, Wim C., "Archiving electronic journals: The serial information providers perspective," *IFLA Journal* 22(3) (1996): 209-210.

Lynch, Clifford A., "Technology and its implications for serials acquisitions," *Against the Grain* 9 (February 1997): 34+.

MacEwan, Bonnie and Mira Geffner, "The CIC electronic journals collection project," *The Serials Librarian* 31(1-2) (1997): 191-203.

MacEwan, Bonnie and Mira Geffner, "The Committee on Institutional Cooperation electronic journals collection (CIC-EJC): A new model for library management of scholarly journals published on the Internet," *Public-Access Computer Systems Review* 7(4) (1995): 5-15.

Macklin, Lisa A., "The changing role of serials acquisitions librarians in the electronic environment: A report of the ALCTS Serials Section Research Libraries Discussion Group and Acquisitions Committee joint meeting, American Library Association Midwinter Meeting, Philadelphia, January 1999," *Technical Services Quarterly* 17(4) (2000): 63-65.

Manoff, Marlene, "Hybridity, mutability, multiplicity: Theorizing electronic library collections," *Library Trends* 48(4) (spring 2000): 857-876.

Marcum, Deanna, *Development of digital libraries: An American perspective* (Westport, CT: Greenwood Press, 2001).

McGinnis, Suzan D. *Electronic collection management* (Binghamton, NY: The Haworth Information Press, 2000).

McKay, Sharon Cline, "Accessing electronic journals," *Database* 22(2) (April/May 1999): 16-18+.

McKinney, Janet, "The development and use of a genre statement for electronic journals at Cornell University: Workshop at the 1998 NASIG Conference," *The Serials Librarian* 36(3-4) (1999): 429-434.

McKnight, Cliff, Liangzhi Yu, and Susan Harker, "Librarians in the delivery of electronic journals: Roles revisited: SuperJournal project," *Journal of Librarianship and Information Science* 32(3) (September 2000): 117-134.

McMillan, Gail, "Managing electronic theses and dissertations: The third International Symposium in St. Petersburg, Florida," *College and Research Libraries News* 61(5) (May 2000): 413-414.

McMillan, Gail, "Technical processing of electronic journals," *Library Resources and Technical Services* 36(4) (October 1992): 470-477.

Meadows, Jack, David Pullinger, and Peter Such, "The cost of implementing an electronic journal," *Journal of Scholarly Publishing* 26(4) (July 1995): 227-233.

Metz, Paul, "Principles of selection for electronic resources," *Library Trends* 48(4) (spring 2000): 711-278.

Montgomery, Carol Hansen and JoAnne L. Sparks, "The transition to an electronic journal collection: Managing the organizational changes at Drexel University," *Serials Review* 26(3) (2000): 4-18.

Montgomery, Jack G., "The changing structure of information in the electronic era: Report from the 1999 Charleston Conference," *Library Collections, Acquisitions, and Technical Services* 24(3) (fall 2000): 415-416.

Moothart, Thomas, "Providing access to e-journals through library home pages," *Serials Review* 22 (summer 1996): 71-77.

Morgan, Eric Lease, "Adding Internet resources to our OPACs," *Serials Review* 21 (winter 1995): 70-72.

Morgan, Eric Lease, "Mr. Serials revisits cataloging: Cataloging electronic serials and Internet resources," *The Serials Librarian* 28(3-4) (1996): 229-238.

Morris, Sally, "Archiving electronic publications: What are the problems and who should solve them?" *Serials Review* 26(3) (2000): 64-66.

NewJour: Electronic Journals and Newsletters, <http://gort.ucsd.edu/newjour/>.

Nisonger, Thomas E., "Are we still selecting?: Report of the Collection Development Librarians of Academic Libraries Discussion Group at ALA Midwinter 2000," *Library Collections, Acquisitions, and Technical Services* 24(4) (winter 2000): 479-482.

Nisonger, Thomas E., "Collection development in an electronic environment: Special issue," *Library Trends* 48(4) (spring 2000).

Nisonger, Thomas E., "Collection management issues for electronic journals," *IFLA Journal* 22(3) (1996): 233-239.

Norman, O. Gene, "The impact of electronic information sources on collection development: A survey of current practice," *Library Hi Tech* 15(1-2) (1997): 123-132.

Parang, Elizabeth, "The convergence of user needs, collection building, and the electronic publishing market place: Use studies of electronic resources at California State University, Fullerton and Lehigh University: Report of a workshop at the 1999 NASIG Conference," *The Serials Librarian* 38(3/4) (2000): 333-339.

Pavliscak, Pamela, "Trends in copyright practices of scholarly electronic journals," *Serials Review* 22 (fall 1996): 39-47.

Peek, Robin P., "Moving from theory into practice: Electronic journals," *Information Today* 16(5) (May 1999): 48.

Primich, Tracy, "Electronic collections in the age of the traditional library: Creative vision of electronic journals in college libraries," *Econtent* 23(2) (April/May 2000): 65-67.

Publicker, Stephanie and Kristin Stoklosa, "Reaching the researcher: How the National Institutes of Health Library selects and provides e-journals via the World Wide Web," *Serials Review* 25(3) (1999): 13-23.

Quinn, Marilyn, "Supporting e-journal integration through standards: The OCLC reference services experience and experiences from the field: Report of a workshop at the 1999 NASIG Conference," *The Serials Librarian* 38(3/4) (2000): 313-322.

Rich, Linda A. and Julie L. Rabine, "How libraries are providing access to electronic serials: A survey of academic library Web sites," *Serials Review* 25(2) (1999): 35-46.

Robnett, Bill, "Online Journal Pricing," *The Serials Librarian* 33(1/2)(1999): 55-69.

Rodgers, David R., "Eeee!-serials: Providing access to online serials at MIT: Workshop at the 1998 NASIG Conference," *The Serials Librarian* 36(3-4) (1999): 467-473.

Rogers, Michael, "Cal State proposes new e-journal buying model," *Library Journal* 124(3) (February 15, 1999): 107.

Rossignol, Lucien R., "Realistic licensing or licensing realities: Practical advice on license agreements: Report of a workshop at the 1999 NASIG Conference," *The Serials Librarian* 38(3/4) (2000): 357-361.

Rowland, J. F. B., "Electronic journals: Delivery, use and access," *IFLA Journal* 22(3) (1996): 226-228.

Schwartz, Marcia J., "Acquiring electronic journals: The role of vendors," *Library Acquisitions* 22(3) (fall 1998): 358-360.

Schwartzkopf, Rebecca B., "Building an electronic journal collection from the ground up at Skidmore College: Workshop at the 1998 NASIG Conference," *The Serials Librarian* 36(3-4) (1999): 421-428.

The Serials Librarian 30(3-4), entire issue and 31(1-2), entire issue. (These issues are devoted to the proceedings of NASIG's eleventh annual conference.)

Sigrist, Barbara and Andreas Heise, "Cataloging and retrieving e-journals in the Zeitschriftendatenbank, the German serials database," *The Serials Librarian* 39(1) (2000): 65-74.

Tenopir, Carol, "Managing scientific journals in the digital era," *Information Outlook* 1 (February 1997): 14-17.

Tenopir, Carol, "The states of online: Statewide licenses," *Library Journal* 125(20) (December 2000): 44-48.

Thornton, Glenda Ann, "Impact of electronic resources on collection development, the roles of librarians, and library consortia at Cleveland State University," *Library Trends* 48(4) (spring 2000): 842-856.

Tillett, Barbara B., "Problems and solutions in cataloging electronic resources: Presented at an international conference on cataloging, Russian State Library, April 1999," *International Cataloguing and Bibliographic Control* 29(1) (January/March 2000): 14-15.

von Ungern-Sternberg, Sara and Mats G. Lindquist, "The impact of electronic journals on library functions," *Journal of Information Science* 21(5) (1995): 396-401.

Weibel, Stuart W., "The World Wide Web and emerging Internet resource discovery standards for scholarly literature," *Library Trends* 43(4) (1995): 627-644.

Wood, Patricia A. and James H. Walther, "The future of academic libraries: Changing formats and changing delivery," *Bottom Line* 13(4) (2000): 173-181.

Woodward, Hazel, "Electronic journals in an academic library environment," *Serials* 10(1) (1997): 53.

Woodward, Hazel, "Electronic journals: Issues of access and bibliographic control," *Serials Review* 21(2) (summer 1995): 71-78.

Woodward, Hazel, Fytton Rowland, Cliff McKnight, Jack Meadows, and Carolyn Pritchett, "Electronic journals: Myths and realities," *Library Management* 18(3-4) (1997): 155.

Wusterman, Judith, "Electronic journal formats," *Program* 30 (October 1996): 319-343.

Chapter 7

Coordination and Collaboration: A Model for Electronic Resources Management

Kristin H. Gerhard

INTRODUCTION

In a 1997 article for *The Serials Librarian*, I described the cataloging of electronic resources (including serials) at Iowa State University, and suggested guidelines for libraries at the beginning of this process.[1] In this chapter, I focus more specifically on our local process, with the goal of providing information to other libraries wrestling with electronic resources (ERs). The model adopted at Iowa State is one of coordinated electronic resources management.

This chapter looks at the impact of ERs on academic libraries, describes the approach Iowa State has taken toward dealing with ER management, and identifies both advantages and disadvantages of this model. While this chapter is written by a technical services librarian and from the perspective of technical services work, the impact of ERs on libraries is broad enough that the principles have a wider application to the library organization as a whole.

THE IMPACT OF ELECTRONIC RESOURCES

There is no question that libraries must find ways to come to grips with electronic publications. In a survey conducted by the American Library Association and Ameritech Library Services, academic libraries were asked a series of questions about electronic services they provided. The result of the study, conducted in the spring of 1996, indicated that 71 percent of doctorate-granting institutions were providing access to original, free electronic journals. These are journals that have no print counterpart and are available to libraries at no cost. Original paid e-journals were provided by 57 percent of these institutions. A total of 81 percent of doctorate-granting institutions made full-text journals, whether free, paid, or a combination of both, available to their users. "Universally, the most likely method of access is from hard-wired terminals and/or PCs in the library."[2] The report concludes that

> [a]cademic librarians, especially those in the larger and more comprehensive institutions are already offering a wide variety of electronic services and planning to offer more. Also, academic librarians are expanding their traditional role by teaching students and faculty how to use these sources of information.[3]

Experimental data collected by ARL libraries over the past decade indicate that the portion of the library materials budget that is spent on electronic resources is indeed growing rapidly. Since the Supplementary Statistics were first reported, the percentage of the average library budget that is spent on electronic materials has increased almost fourfold, from an estimated 3.6 percent in 1992-1993 to 12.9 percent in 1999-2000.[4]

The boom in electronic resources has brought some important improvements to academic libraries. The number of resources available continues to increase at a rapid rate, with improving, albeit uneven, quality. The phenomenal growth in the Internet, particularly of the World Wide Web, continues. Publishers are increasingly taking steps to make their journals available electronically. Libraries are receiving printed materials in which URLs are noted.

Many electronic reference sources can be searched much more easily than their print counterparts. As Crawford and Gorman have pointed out, this is an ideal format for materials that do not require a linear reading, especially where sophisticated searching would be desirable.[5]

One result of this is that patron expectations have skyrocketed. Information can be delivered to patrons at library workstations, to faculty offices, to dormitories and homes. Not surprisingly, patrons like using electronic resources, sometimes to the point of resisting appropriate referrals to print sources. In order to hold the respect of our users, librarians must negotiate through present circumstances to provide increasing numbers of important electronic titles, which absorb a growing percentage of library acquisitions budgets. Libraries, and librarians, need to forge a positive, creative way to manage electronic resources.

ORGANIZATIONAL CHALLENGES

Electronic resources are here to stay, and we recognize the importance of what they contribute to our mission. Electronic resources are here to stay, as demonstrated by trends in library expenditures and usage figures. Libraries are increasingly finding ways to move beyond treating these products as add-ons, integrating them instead into the ways that librarians conceive their collections and services. Patrons frequently take them for granted.

An aspect of ER management that poses particular difficulties for technical services is the ethereality of resources available over the Internet. Janet Swan Hill makes this point, among others, in her article, "The Elephant in the Catalog."[6] The lack of a tangible item makes it difficult to fit these titles into existing, standard work flows—acquisitions check-in, cataloging, and provision of access. We do not know how to handle them.

The fact that ER management crosses not only departmental but divisional lines complicates the situation, as adding an ER title necessitates more back and forth communication, rather than a linear pathway through technical services to public services. A title may be selected, but its licensing agreement may turn out to be problematic. It may require additional decisions regarding coverage, number of simultaneous users, or choice of platform. It may have equipment or software requirements that do not mesh with local systems. These issues also serve to draw automated systems staff deeper into an ordering, receipt, and processing system that normally involves systems staff only peripherally.

Further, the unpredictability of ERs also prevents us from writing a simple, one-size-fits-all procedure for handling them. Licensing agreements and technical requirements continue to vary widely from title to title; pricing may include unlimited site access, single-user access, or value-added features such as current awareness or full-text options. Access may be by IP number, domain name, or password. Software that works appropriately to provide access through local systems and within local policy constraints may or may not be available for any given title. Rigid, linear processes will not deal adequately with electronic resources management.

Library organizations need models for the integration of electronic resources management into library collections and services. We cannot afford to create solutions ex nihilo in every library. What follows is a description of one possible model, that of collaborative coordination. Although we cannot plan with an assumption that the information marketplace will settle down in the future, we can pool our experiences, allowing each library to select the most useful approach for local organizational development.

THE COLLABORATIVE ELECTRONIC RESOURCES COORDINATION APPROACH

Position advertisements for electronic resource or digital resource librarians in academic libraries are increasingly common. In January 1996, Iowa State University Library joined these ranks by creating an electronic resources coordinator position within the technical services division. The underlying goal in creating this position was to ensure that issues arising from the increasing numbers of electronic titles are handled effectively and with some kind of efficiency. Because of cost constraints, this position was created by shuffling existing responsibilities among existing staff, de-emphasizing some responsibilities, while adding the tasks necessary to coordinate acquisition and access for electronic resources. It was expected that the position would grow and change over time as needs were assessed and responsibilities assigned.

At the point when this position was created, there was no single person in technical services overseeing the acquisition or cataloging of ERs. Titles were handled largely on a case-by-case basis, with the bulk of the work done by the head of the Acquisitions Department. When cataloging was needed, networked resources (mainly CDs on individual workstations or the Reference Department LAN) were referred to the appropriate staff in the Serials and Monographs Original Cataloging Department. Separate procedures for CD-ROMs had been created by the cataloger responsible for the nonbook cataloging work flow, but no provision had been made for cataloging titles available through Internet access.

We were not an unusual academic library. The new environment required adaptation and adjustment. Our initial response was split between assigning responsibilities to those with related existing responsibilities, and establishing task forces to work through policy issues.

In other areas of the library, an ER collection development policy was being drafted. A library-wide task force had made some recommendations about which ERs to catalog; another task force had been working intermittently on the issues of electronic resource management—budget, selection, and so on. The assistant director for collections was responsible for significant license negotiations. The Reference and Informational Services Department was regularly reviewing the electronic reference sources we offer patrons, adjusting the access and products based on budget and usage. Systems staff kept the library's home page up to date, made connections with subject guides to the Internet created by collection development and reference librarians, and kept the reference resources running. In short, there was a lot to coordinate.

The creation of an electronic resources coordinator position in technical services paralleled the establishment of a series of committees focused on various aspects of electronic resources, with composition based on expertise. The groups included three task forces dealing with various aspects of the library's Web site, a committee on Computer Networking and Architecture, and an Electronic Resources Management Discussion Group, whose charge was to bring issues needing library-wide discussion to the staff and facilitate discussion. Ultimately, virtually every librarian at Iowa State contributed to one or more aspects of the handling of electronic serials.

Advantages of the Coordinator Approach

Creating a position in technical services to coordinate work with electronic resources has certain advantages. Having one person coordinating the activities related to acquisitions and cataloging means that a critical bulk of information can be unified and maintained by that person. By no means does this diminish the need for others to maintain their own expertise; rather, it provides a mechanism to ensure that there is consistency in library policy and procedures, and in their application. The coordinator serves as a funnel and gathering point for relevant information from all sources.

A second advantage is that the coordinator puts a human face on technical services for staff in other parts of the library. Many of the issues involved in managing electronic journals cross departmental lines. Technical services is often the inner temple of the library, where mysterious internal processes eventually yield up the desired materials in organized form. It is important for staff in other areas to have a contact person to whom they can bring often complex questions, issues, and concerns regarding electronic resources. Trying to discern who on an organizational chart or contact list might be responsible for a given aspect of the electronic resource with which a resource librarian is dealing is not likely to have a successful outcome. We are in a new world, where we cannot afford linear, isolated processes. We need flexibility and responsiveness.

Third, having a coordinator to keep on top of ERs provides for a series of one-on-one discussions and shared insights. The coordinator is responsible for maintaining a flow of information about electronic resources across and within functions, departments, and divisions. This does not mean being the provider of information so much as trying to facilitate conversations, to listen, and to bring together staff with related information and/or information needs. It also requires periodic checking with library administrators, to ensure that the course being steered is in a desired direction.

Potential Pitfalls of the Coordinator Approach

The coordinator approach has two potential pitfalls. First, there is no single person to provide backup when the workload is heavy or the coordinator is absent. This can be overcome in a number of ways. It is important to continue to build and support expertise throughout the library, so that various aspects of this work can be covered under varying circumstances. Also, over time, various aspects of the position as initially described will become routinized or established to the point that they can be handed off to other staff members. Much of the first year of the coordinator position at Iowa State was divided between the learning curve and working out procedures for ER cataloging. Since then, maintenance of the divisional Web pages, maintenance of access to cataloged Internet resources, and coordination of cataloging of electronic titles have been moved to others. This has allowed the ER coordinator position to evolve and meet new challenges and needs. The second pitfall is that a coordinating position requires an extraordinary amount of communication—near-constant communication among a wide variety of individuals and groups. It is all too easy to overlook, unwittingly, an interested party or a piece of needed information. Vigilance, and the goodwill of one's colleagues, provide the only saving graces.

CONCLUSION

The growth of ERs, in volume and in prominence, requires that library organizations develop a proactive approach to handling these titles. A combination of coordination and collaboration provides one practical model for the management of electronic resources in academic libraries.

In the end, one hopes that this integrated approach to electronic resources management can contribute to a less fragmented vision of what library collections and services might become.

NOTES

1. Kristin H. Gerhard, "Cataloging Internet Resources: Practical Issues and Concerns," *The Serials Librarian* 32(1/2) (1997): 123-137.

2. Mary Jo Lynch, *Electronic Services in Academic Libraries: ALA Survey Report* (Chicago and London: American Library Association, 1996): 6.

3. Ibid., 7.

4. See Introduction, *ARL Supplementary Statistics 1999-2000,* compiled and edited by Martha Kyrillidou and Mark Young (Washington, DC: ARL, 2000): 7. Also available at <http://www.arl.org/stats/sup/sup00.pdf>.

5. Walt Crawford and Michael Gorman, *Future Libraries: Dreams, Madness,& Reality* (Chicago and London: American Library Association, 1995).

6. Janet Swan Hill, "The Elephant in the Catalog," *Cataloging and Classification Quarterly* 23(1) (1996): 5-25.

CATALOGING AND METADATA

Chapter 8

A Square Peg in a Round Hole: Applying AACR2 to Electronic Journals

Steven C. Shadle

INTRODUCTION

It has been said the *Anglo-American Cataloguing Rules* (AACR) and the International Standard Bibliographic Description (ISBD) were written largely for a print, monograph world and that the descriptive bibliographic standards for serials and for other physical formats are variations on those basic standards. If that is too strong a statement, one can at least say that there are certain principles, such as:

- transcription from an item can serve as the basis for bibliographic identification;
- sources of bibliographic information can be consistently identified on an item; and
- an item's physical format is the basis for bibliographic description.

These principles work relatively well for static, monographic items and have been applied to the cataloging of materials in all formats.

With the use of the Internet as a supplement to, or replacement for, the traditional publishing process, the flaws of a cataloging code developed for a different information environment are becoming more apparent. This chapter examines some specific problematic areas in the current American cataloging code (*Anglo-American Cataloguing Rules*, Second Edition, 1988 revision [AACR2]) that affect the bibliographic description of electronic journals and discusses the current policies and practices that the serials cataloging community has developed as interim solutions to address those problems.

BACKGROUND

Anderson and Hawkins provide an overview of the developments in cataloging standards for computer files. These include the development of AACR2 Chapter 9, developments in USMARC to accommodate Internet resources (specifically the 008, 256, 516, and 856 fields), and developments in CONSER policies that were the results of early efforts to catalog electronic serials.[1] The resulting CONSER policies have been formally developed as Module 31 of the *CONSER Cataloging Manual: Remote Access Computer File Serials*.[2] Many of the examples and the discussion presented in this chapter are taken from that source.

Definition of a Serial, or "What Exactly Is a Journal, Anyway?"

A serial, as defined in AACR2, is

> [a] publication in any medium issued in successive parts bearing numeric or chronological designations and intended to be continued indefinitely. Serials include periodicals; newspapers; annuals (reports, yearbooks, etc.); the journals, memoirs, proceedings, transactions, etc., of societies; and numbered monographic series.[3]

Three conditions must be met under this definition for a publication to be considered a serial:

- It must be issued in successive parts.
- The successive parts must have some type of unique identification.
- There must be an intention to continue publication indefinitely.

In her discussion of cataloging electronic journals, Geller provides four examples of self-identified electronic journals, two of which fail to fit the AACR2 definition of a serial because they are not issued in uniquely identifiable successive parts.[4] The *Journal of Electronic Publishing* (JEP) provides what appears to be volume and issue numbering. When users access the home page at <http://www.press. umich.edu/jep/> they are presented with a list of article links for the current issue, a list of issue links for Volumes 3 to the current issue, *and* a link to Volumes 1 and 2 of JEP's backlist. Clicking on the Volume 1 backlist link sends the user to a page headed "Volume 1, issues 1 and 2, January and February 1995." The user is presented with three links for searching the Volume 1 archives by subject, author, or title. The corresponding indexes provide information about which issue the article was originally published in by listing the date after the article title (e.g., 1/95). The first issue *could* be re-created (to a certain degree) by identifying the articles appearing in that first issue and rebundling them in some way. This "unbundling" of articles from their original issue seems to be a common characteristic of many electronic journals. JEP follows an organization common to many electronic journals of identifying a "current" issue (often using some kind of standard issue numbering) and then providing an archival database of articles from earlier issues.

The other issue-less journal that Geller describes was a publication of the University of Arizona (UA) School of Library Science titled *The Olive Tree*. It described itself as "a cumulative publication to which new articles are periodically added."[5] This description sounds like a Web page with no identifiable issues, only links directly to articles. The use of the past tense in describing this publication is quite appropriate, as any trace of *The Olive Tree* has disappeared from the UA School of Library Science Web space. Nonetheless, many examples can still be provided which fit this model of electronic journal as Web page. The ones that have the most potential for confusion are those that call themselves the electronic version of a print journal. Examples of these include:

- *The PM Zone:* an electronic version of *Popular Mechanics* that provides the contents of the current issue, archives of selected previous editorial content (organized topically) and much original material tailored specifically for the World Wide Web (http://popularmechanics.com).
- *Frontiers in Bioscience:* (like JEP) provides a current issue and archives of earlier articles organized by volume. There is also additional material consistently available in the current issue that is not in the print version (http://www.bioscience.org/).
- *Red Tape: The Official Newsletter of the Government Documents Round Table of Michigan:* Each issue of the print version consists of a series of titled columns. The online version is organized by column title, not by issue, so that the columns of individual issues are accessible, but there is no online issue corresponding to the entire print issue (http://www.lib.msu.edu/harris23/red%5Ftape/red%5Ftape.htm).

According to AACR2, all of these examples could be considered monographs, as they are nonserial items.

Even though "publishers do not consciously set out to create serials as defined by AACR2,"[6] the journal publication pattern of successive issues has been closely enough identified with the genre of the journal ("users recognize journals because of their intrinsic characteristics, i.e., an assemblage of articles on various topics, usually with some unifying purpose, subject, slant, or field of enquiry"[7]) that the use of the AACR2 successive issuance serial definition to identify journals has worked relatively well in catalogs to date. However, following the letter of AACR2 in the cataloging of these items introduces two inconsistencies into the catalog:

- Some electronic journals will be cataloged as serials and some as monographs depending on whether they fit the AACR2 definition of a serial.
- Print journals which are cataloged as serials may have their electronic versions cataloged as monographs.

Philosophically, these discrepancies may or may not cause problems. Jones, and Graham and Ringler, both make the case that electronic journals which are not serials should not be treated as such since there is functionality built into the serial record (serials control, successive records, ISSN) which is not necessary for the electronic journal not distributed in successive issues.[8,9] However, Jones also points out that treating electronic journals as monographs can create problems for systems which

> segregate their catalog records by type of material and biblio-graphic level, so that some resources calling themselves "jour-nals" will not be found in the serials file of such systems. And this is not desirable from the point of view of addressing user expectations in such a system.[10]

Even if systems do not store serials records in separate files, many systems still use the information from serial specific fields (such as Leader byte 06/07, 006 byte 00) to identify serials. In addition, users have been known to use other areas of the serial record such as frequency or subject headings to identify serials. In cataloging issue-less electronic journals as monographs, these markers to provide identification for this genre of material will be lost.

Catalogers have developed a variety of strategies to help identify the journal nature of these items regardless of whether they fit the AACR2 definition of a serial.[11] Catalogers at the University of Michigan are locally using the nonstandard general material designator (GMD) "[electronic serial]" to help users identify the nature of the resource from brief catalog displays. The *CONSER Cataloging Manual* suggests the use of the Type of Computer File or Data Note (USMARC 516) to help identify these resources:

> 516   Electronic journal available in ASCII, Acrobat, and Post-Script file formats.

In addition, the newly approved International Standard Bibliographic Description for Electronic Resources (ISBD(ER)) uses a wider variety of specific material designators (SMDs), including the terms "computer journal" and "computer newsletter." The intent is that these SMDs may eventually be used in the Computer File Characteristics field (USMARC 256). Other libraries are providing additional identification of these resources through the local use of genre/form headings or subdivisions (USMARC 655, 650$v) such as "Computer network resources" or "Electronic journals," and at least one major subject heading system (Medical Subject Headings) has established the use of "electronic journal" as a form subject subdivision. In addition, many libraries are cataloging these resources as serials even though they do not fit the AACR2 definition of a serial.

PROBLEMS OF BIBLIOGRAPHIC DESCRIPTION

The developing environment of the Internet has produced information resources that differ from print publications in significant ways:

- They are organized differently, often in distributed files or databases.
- They are mutable.
- They often have additional functionality.
- They do not follow the same standards for display of bibliographic information..

The next section discusses some specific problems of bibliographic description that are commonly encountered in the process of cataloging electronic journals.

Identification of a First Issue, or "Where Have You Gone, Joe DiMaggio?"

Both AACR2 12.0B1 and the *CONSER Cataloging Manual* Module 3.1 instruct the cataloger to use the chief source of the first or earliest available issue as the primary source of transcription of the title and statement of responsibility. One of the advantages to using the first issue as the basis for bibliographic description is that the description will remain unchanged over the life of a serial title. Changes that will not result in the creation of a new bibliographic record (e.g., changes in imprint) are recorded in notes. This works well in the print environment where the issue is what a subscriber receives in the mail every month. It even works relatively well for serially issued direct-access computer files, as the physical piece (either diskette, CD-ROM, or magnetic tape) is understood to be the issue. However, with the Internet, the delivery of information is no longer tied to the delivery of a physical object. The result is that electronic journals no longer need to be organized in issues in order to provide articles to their readers. So how does the librarian identify a first issue when no issue exists? In some cases, individual articles will have some type of numbering or date that can be used to identify it, thereby turning the article into the "successive part" that was formerly the issue. Another common pattern is to see evidence of original issue numbering which is no longer used to organize articles on the Web site, as the issues themselves have been unbundled. This appears to be the case in JEP where there is evidence from the archive page that there was originally a Volume 1, Issue 1 dated January 1995. Many catalogers are using this as a first issue and attempt to create a bibliographic description by transcribing information from the individual articles if possible.

The publications of Project Muse (http://muse.jhu.edu) present another case in point. The home page for a specific journal provides links to the tables of contents of specific issues. The tables of contents then provide links to the individual articles. In one respect, the issue consists of the table of contents of a specific issue and the individual articles that are linked to that table of contents. In many catalogers' judgment these pages would serve as the first issue and potentially the chief source for transcription. Generally in a print journal, an issue will have additional sources such as cover, masthead, colophon, editorial or publisher statements, etc., that are formal presentations of bibliographic information by the publisher. In print journals, the more formal presentations of title page, cover, or masthead generally provide the basis for transcription. These additional sources are necessary in the print journal as the individual issues serve as a delivery mechanism and therefore must be identifiable. However, in electronic journals, this same information is provided in abbreviated form or not at all at the issue level, but instead is provided at a higher level, such as a journal home page. Many catalogers consider the presentation of bibliographic information at the home page to be the equivalent of the title page or cover of a journal (even though it is not specific to an individual issue) and will cite this page as the chief source, instead of an issue-specific source.

One interesting development is that some resources that had previously been described as not providing distinct issues online (such as the *CONSER Cataloging Manual*'s reference to *Mother Jones*), are now providing access to articles through the use of distinctive issues. One can only hope that publishers have begun to recognize that the unique identification of successive parts (whether articles or issues) will help with article identification and citation.

Identifying the Chief Source,
or "A Title Screen by Any Other Name"

There is another interesting example of applying a print analogy to a nonprint medium. The chief source for print serials is the title page or title page substitute. The AACR2 definition of a title page is:

> A page at the beginning of an item bearing the title proper and usually, though not necessarily, the statement of responsibility and the data relating to publication.[12]

In addition, the *CONSER Cataloging Manual* gives further guidance on what does *not* constitute a title page:

> A title page is not: a page that contains text, tables of contents, or extensive editorial information, i.e., a page that has been designed to fulfill a different function.[13]

The title page provides the formal presentation of the title and also, possibly, a statement of responsibility and publication information. This is an important point in cataloging print journals because few journal publishers dedicate an entire page of a journal to providing a formal presentation of title, instead incorporating the presentation of the title into other sources (e.g., cover, masthead, table of contents, text). AACR2 provides an ordered list of title page substitutes (analytic title page, cover, caption, masthead, editorial pages, colophon, other pages) to use in case there is no title page.

Now, for computer files, the relevant rule from Chapter 9 (9.0B) states that the chief source of information for computer files is the title screen. The AACR2 definition of a title screen is:

> A display of data that includes the title proper and usually, though not necessarily, the statement of responsibility and the data relating to publication."[14]

Catalogers of direct-access computer files know exactly what a title screen is. On starting up a program, the title screen is usually the first or second screen that appears; it briefly and formally displays the title and oftentimes a statement of responsibility or publication information. What truly identifies the title screen is that it appears for such a brief period of time that the cataloger is required to reload the program several times in order to transcribe the appropriate information! As in the print model, the title screen is identified by its function of formally presenting the title. If this were not the case, then according to the strict definition of the term, any display of data that includes the title proper could be considered the title screen, resulting in a large number of sources, all of which could legitimately be called a title screen.

Unfortunately, electronic journals available over the Web generally follow the same practice as their print counterparts of not providing a display of data whose function is *solely* to provide a formal presentation of the title. Instead, there are a large number of possible sources for title transcription, including the following:

- The issues (if one exists)
- The home page or Web site of the journal
- Source document metadata
- "About" or "readme" files
- Links from other pages

Unlike AACR2 Chapter 12, Chapter 9 provides no additional guidance in choosing the title screen substitute other than this:

> In case of variation in fullness of information found in these sources, prefer the source with the most complete information.[15]

No ordered list of sources exists, so it is left to the cataloger's judgment to determine which source has the most complete information. An example of the kind of judgment required of a cataloger is illustrated in the cataloging of the newsletter of the Oregon Flora Project at <http://www.orst.edu/Dept/botany/herbarium/projects/ofn/index.html>.

Figure 8.1 is the home page for the project's newsletter. On this one screen there are several variant forms of title. "Oregon Flora Newsletter" is presented within the graphic at the head of the display. "Oregon Flora On-Line Newsletter" is presented formally as the title and is also tagged as the title in the source code. This is evident by the fact that it appears in the window header. A look at the source code in

FIGURE 8.1. Home Page of the *Oregon Flora Newsletter*

Figure 8.2 will confirm that it has been marked up as the title. "Oregon Flora Newsletter On-Line" is presented in the equivalent of a print journal masthead. In addition, the box, which serves as a link to the top of the page, has the title "Flora Newsletter." (Note that all of the screen shots are from the newsletter as of 1998; the site has since been redesigned and relocated to <http://www.oregonflora.org/>.)

Using a non–graphic-based Web browser (such as Lynx) will produce the display seen in Figure 8.3. Note that the graphic, which contained the title "Oregon Flora Newsletter," was replaced with the text "Welcome to the" which is grammatically connected to the formal title presentation "Oregon Flora On-Line Newsletter." A cataloger using this browser will not be aware of the other title presentation and would probably be less confused about the choice of title proper.

The continuation of the original home page seen in Figure 8.4 provides the links to the individual articles. Note that the articles are organized into issues, but there is no page or source that serves as an actual issue. "OFN" is what appears as the title most closely associated

```
<html>

<body bgcolor=#FFFFFF>

<p align=center>

<IMG border=2 SRC="../../images/OFN_title.GIF" ALT="Welcome to the">

</P>
```

`<TITLE>Oregon Flora On-Line Newsletter</TITLE>`

```
<H2 align=center>Oregon Flora On-Line Newsletter</H2>
```

The `<cite>`Oregon Flora Newsletter On-line`</cite>` is published three times

a year

and is a publication of the`<A HREF="../OFP/ofp.html">`Oregon Flora

Project`</A>` news. It

is edited by Rhoda Love and put on-line by Douglas Linn.`<P>`

FIGURE 8.2. Source Code of *Oregon Flora Newsletter* Home Page

with the issue itself at this point. In lieu of having an actual issue, should this link be chosen as the chief source?

Clicking on the first article of the first issue produces the display seen in Figure 8.5. On what appears to be the first page of the first issue, there are only two title presentations. Although this presentation is similar to the home page presentation, the masthead title "The Oregon Flora Newsletter On-line" does not appear. It does appear that this banner is meant solely for the purpose of formally presenting the title. The AACR2 definition of title screen talks about a "display of data," not about a "screen of data." Can this formal presentation be considered a separate display so that the use of the phrase "title screen" is appropriate to describe it? Or is this analogous to the case of a print newsletter, where the banner title is considered a caption ti-

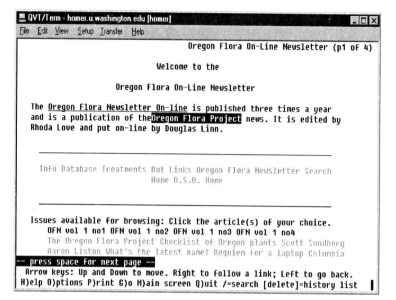

FIGURE 8.3. Home Page of *Oregon Flora Newsletter* Using a Nongraphics Browser

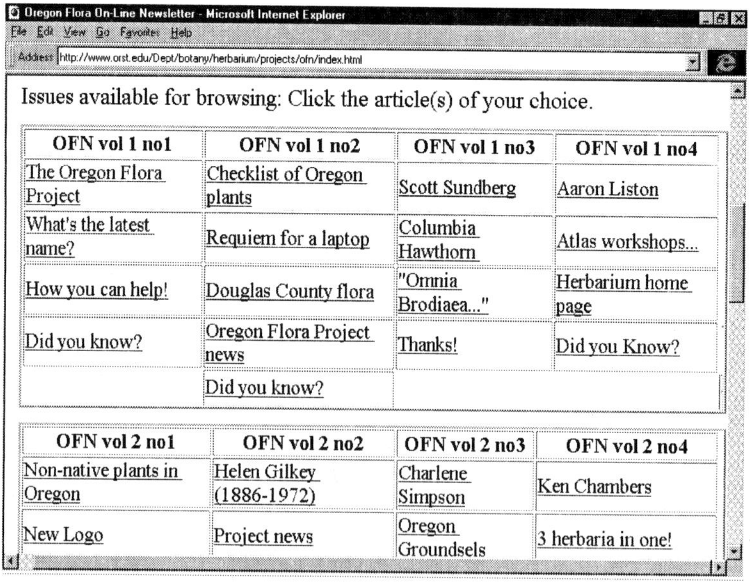

FIGURE 8.4. Continuation of Home Page of *Oregon Flora Newsletter*

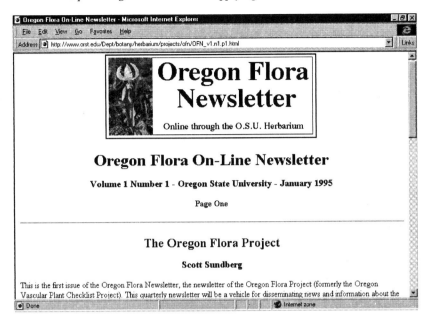

FIGURE 8.5. First Article of First Issue of *Oregon Flora Newsletter*

tle because it is given at the beginning of the first page of text? *Library of Congress Rule Interpretation* 12.0 states:

> If a serial lacking a title page has a title (the same title or different titles) on more than one source in the item, choose as the title page substitute the source that appears first in the preferred order of sources listed in the rule. *Use the entire page from which the title was taken as the title page substitute, not just the caption area, masthead area, etc.*[16] [author's emphasis]

By analogy, does this same concept apply to Web pages so that the entire Web document is considered a single source and the function of the entire document is considered to determine whether a source is a "title screen" or a "home page"? And is it still appropriate to examine an issue to identify the chief source, or is it more appropriate to examine formal presentations of the title which are not associated with a specific issue (e.g., home page) to identify the publication?

The problems with the cataloging code that these questions have raised are:

- First issue may not be an appropriate chief source for identification and description of electronic journals.
- Just as with print journals, an ordered list of potential sources may help with inter-cataloger consistency.
- Chapter 9 needs to be updated to reflect the nature of the Web. This includes the introduction of Web terminology and changing concepts such as "title screen" which still work relatively well for direct-access computer files, but are not applicable in the Web environment.

Some of the work necessary to address these problems has begun in the American cataloging community. A committee of the Online Audiovisual Catalogers (OLAC) has provided recommendations for the terms to be used in describing online sources for cataloging information.[17] Additionally, Hirons and Graham recommend that the concept of chief source needs to be examined and possibly replaced with the concept of "source of title" which would allow for "greater flexibility in the selection of title within the parameters of the prescribed sources."[18]

General strategies for coping with the proliferation of titles and lack of specificity in the catalog code include the following:

- Always citing the source of title proper (this is required per AACR2 9.7B3) and citing a specific source rather than "Title screen" unless the source primarily serves the specific function of a title screen. Users of text-based browser software may understand why the title that is cited in a bibliographic record is not displayed if they know the title was taken from a graphic element.
- Generously using title added entries, so that other catalogers and users will be able to retrieve the catalog record no matter which title is considered *the* title.

Mutability of Materials, or "All Is Flux, Nothing Stays Still"

In the world of AACR2 title changes (specifically rule 21.2), works are either successively serial, single-part monographs that change from one edition to the next, or multi-part monographs that change from one physical part to the next. There is no allowance in the cataloging code for the mutable, single-part work. Hirons and Graham cite this as a problem in the current cataloging code that affects all ongoing publications which do not fit the AACR2 serial definition whether they are loose-leaf publications, databases, Web sites, or unnumbered series.[19] In their examination of serials cataloging principles, they cite several which do not lend themselves well to mutable, single-part works. Two that specifically have to do with the changing nature of these materials are as follows:

- *Description based on earliest issue.* Bibliographic description based on the first issue is not practical for mutable, single-part works in which the earlier version of the chief source has completely disappeared. They recommend the retention of description based on earliest issue for publications issued successively, and description based on latest iteration for updated, single-part works. In the meantime, serials catalogers are still attempting to identify a date or numbering that can be used in a formatted MARC 362 field or a "description based on" note for electronic journals without issues.
- *Successive entry.* When all traces of an earlier title disappear, what is the purpose of creating or maintaining a bibliographic record for a nonexistent earlier title? Hirons and Graham recommend following a successive entry approach for successively issued publications and a latest entry approach for updated, single-part works. Some catalogers have experimented with this approach both locally and nationally by using "Title history" or "Previous title" title added entries, thus providing access for users who may find citations for a Web site or electronic journal under its previous title. However, CONSER policy as represented in the *CONSER Cataloging Manual* is to create a new record when a change in title or main entry occurs.[20]

Multiple Versions, or "They Walk Alike, They Talk Alike . . ."

In this brave new world of digital reproductions, AACR and the mainstream cataloging community have not yet developed a set of cataloging standards or a record structure which addresses the question of multiple versions. Current cataloging practice involves the creation of a separate (and nearly identical) record for each version that is published. Jones provides a good summary of the developments that have led to current cataloging practices for reproductions,[21] and discusses the *Functional Requirements of Bibliographic Records* (FRBR) specifically in the context of electronic documents.[22] Given the process and the environment within which cataloging standards exist, FRBR can be considered a long-term goal to aspire to rather than an immediate solution (considering the changes to systems that would be required by the relational record structures that are inherent within the FRBR entry-relationship model). In the meantime, the Library of Congress and CONSER have expanded existing cataloging practices in order to streamline the cataloging of electronic versions.

The Library of Congress approach to electronic reproductions has been to expand the *Library of Congress Rule Interpretation* (LCRI) 1.11A to include nonmicroform reproductions. Microform reproduction cataloging is one of the areas in which Library of Congress practice diverges from AACR2. The general principle in AACR2 is to catalog the reproduction as an original publication and to note details of the original publication. The Library of Congress practice (based on Chapter 9 of the 1967 *Anglo-American Cataloguing Rules* (AACR1) is basically the reverse: the microform reproduction record describes the original publication (if possible) and notes the details of the reproduction.[23] In May 2000, a revised version of the Library of Congress rule interpretation was issued which expanded its use to *non*microform reproductions. This practice follows the same principle of having the reproduction record be the same as the original publication record with these exceptions:

- The general material designation is that of the reproduction.
- The final note provides the details relating to the reproduction.
- An 007 is added for the reproduction physical characteristics.
- If the resource is a remote-access resource, a MARC field 856 is provided for the online address.

The revision includes a more precise definition of a reproduction (which is a difficult concept in an era when the cataloger may not definitively know what the "original" manifestation was), and examples of sound recordings, photocopies, and digitized documents.

CONSER has made an interim decision not to use this rule interpretation in cataloging online versions of print serials. Instead, CONSER participants will catalog all online serials as digital versions rather than digital reproductions.[24] There are several problems in applying the Library of Congress rule interpretation to serials:

- It requires the cataloger to make a distinction between reproduction and original version which is not always possible and not always relevant to users.
- It would result in mixed approaches to the same electronic journal if one is mechanically reproduced (digitized) and the other is an online version (with additional content or other changes).

With current cataloging standards in flux and with several groups working on issues related to the cataloging of electronic versions and multiple manifestations, CONSER felt that it was best at this point in time to continue their current practices, which are documented in the *CONSER Cataloging Manual*, Module 31.

For now, both the Library of Congress[25] and CONSER[26, 27] have adopted the interim practice of representing both a print resource and its online version with a single bibliographic record. This policy allows for the noting of the existence and electronic location of the online version in the record for the printed serial by:

- noting the availability of the online version in field 530, and
- identifying its electronic location in field 856.

Figure 8.6 shows that the only additions made to the print record are the additions of the 530 and 856 fields. This is very clearly *not* a multiple versions record as there is information specific to the online version (such as computer file characteristics) that is not noted in this record. AACR2 requires that separate records be created for versions in different physical formats. However, catalogers may follow the one-record approach for versions for which they feel a separate re-

Type:	a	ELvl:	Srce: d	GPub:	Ctrl:	Lang: eng
BLvl:	s	Form:	Conf: 0	Freq: m	MRec:	Ctry: be
S/L:	0	Orig:	EntS:	Regl: r	ISSN:	Alph:
Desc:	a	SrTp: p	Cont:	DtSt: c	Dates: 1996, 1999	

```
1    010        sn97-46009
2    040        MIA $c MIA $d PIT $d WAU
3    012        $i 9702
4    0037       $B EUR-OP (Information Society News) 2, rue Mercier (MER
193-195), L-2985, Luxembourg
5    042        lcd
6    043        e-------
7    090        HE8081 $b .E875
8    090        $b
9    049        WAUW
10   110  2     European Commission. $b Information Society Project Of-
fice.
11   245  10    Information Society news / $c ISPO.
12   246  10    IS news
13   246  13    ISPO Information society news
14   260        Brussels : $b ISPO, $c 1996-
15   300        v.. : $b ill. ; $c 30 cm.
16   310        Monthly
17   362  0     No. 1 (Apr. 1996)-
18   530        Also available on the World Wide Web.
19   650  0     Telecommunication $z European Union countries $v Periodi-
cals.
20   650  0     Telecommunication policy $z European Union countries $v
Periodicals.
21   650  0     Information technology $z European Union countries $v Peri-
odicals.
22   610  20    European Commission. $b Information Society Project Office
$v Periodicals.
23   856  41    $u http://www.ispo.cec.be/ispo/newsletter/
24   850        PPiU $a WaU
25   936        No. 9 (Jan. 1997) LIC
```

FIGURE 8.6. CONSER Record for Print Version Used to Catalog the Electronic Version

cord is not necessary. A CONSER working group reported on various situations where it would be best to apply the single-record approach:

- The online version contains sufficient full text to be a satisfactory substitute for the print and has no significant additional content (meaning they basically have equivalent content).
- The online version does not contain sufficient full text to be considered an adequate substitute for the original. The online site

may not be considered worth cataloging separately in many such cases, so its existence and electronic location are noted on the record for the original, with appropriate indication of its relationship to the original version (including online versions whose continued publication may be questionable or online versions that may be difficult to catalog separately for whatever reason).

- The online version is actually a related site (e.g., finding aid, publisher site) and also may not be considered worth cataloging separately.[28]

The option of using the single-record approach has been generally accepted by the cataloging community[29] as it allows for the creation of separate records by those institutions who, for local reasons—such as subscription control or catalog access—are required to create separate records, yet it provides enough information on the print record so that users can access the electronic version of the resource. It can be a useful approach for many of the electronic journals cited in this chapter, for which the application of current cataloging practices can be problematic.

SUMMARY

Many libraries have, with varying degrees of success, integrated electronic journals into their catalogs, and Web catalogs are providing direct access to these journals. This chapter has investigated aspects of the current cataloging code that are not easily applicable to the environment of the electronic journal published and distributed on the Internet. Changes in the cataloging code will be required in order for the cataloging community to better integrate electronic journals into library catalogs and collections. A much more detailed and principled discussion of many of these same issues is available in "Issues Related to Seriality," a paper presented by Jean Hirons and Crystal Graham at the International Conference on the Principles and Future Development of AACR.[30] Since this paper was presented at the conference, many groups within the cataloging community have worked on AACR revisions to better accommodate electronic resources. The current status of proposals reviewed by the Joint Steering Committee is available from their Web site at <http://www.nlc.bnc.ca/jsc/current.html>.

NOTES

1. Bill Anderson and Les Hawkins, "Development of CONSER Cataloging Policies for Remote Access Computer File Serials," *The Public-Access Computer Systems Review* 7(1) (1996), <http://info.lib.uh.edu/pr/v7/n1/ande7n1.html> (viewed May 26, 2001).

2. Melissa Beck, "Remote Access Computer File Serials," in *CONSER Cataloging Manual*, ed. Jean Hirons (Washington, DC: Library of Congress, 1996), Module 31. Fall 2000 revision available: <http://lcweb.loc.gov/acq/conser/module31.html>.

3. *Anglo-American Cataloguing Rules,* Second Edition, 1988 Revision, eds. Michael Gorman and Paul W. Winkler (Ottawa: Canadian Library Association; Chicago: American Library Association, 1988), p. 622.

4. Marilyn Geller, "A Better Mousetrap Is Still a Mousetrap," *Serials Review* 22(1) (spring 1996): 72.

5. Ibid.

6. Ed Jones, "Serials in the Realm of the Remotely-Accessible: An Exploration," *Serials Review* 22(1) (spring 1996): 77.

7. Jean Hirons and Crystal Graham, "Issues Related to Seriality" in *The Principles and Future of* AACR: *Proceedings of the International Conference on the Principles and Future Development of AACR*, ed. Jean Weihs (Ottawa: Canadian Library Association; London: Library Association Publishing; Chicago: American Library Association, 1998), p. 191.

8. Jones, "Serials in the Realm," p. 78.

9. Crystal Graham and Rebecca Ringler, "Hermaphrodites & Herrings," *Serials Review* 22(1) (spring 1996): 76.

10. Jones, "Serials in the Realm," p. 78.

11. Steve Shadle, "Identification of Electronic Journals in the Online Catalog," *Serials Review* 24(2) (summer 1998): 105-106.

12. *Anglo-American Cataloguing Rules,* p. 624.

13. *CONSER Cataloging Manual*, Module 3, p. 10.

14. *Anglo-American Cataloguing Rules,* p. 624.

15. Ibid., p. 222.

16. *Library of Congress Rule Interpretations*, Second Edition, ed. Robert M. Hiatt (Washington, DC: Cataloging Distribution Service, Library of Congress, 1989), 12.0B1, p. 1.

17. Online Audiovisual Catalogers, Cataloging Policy Committee. *Source of Title Note for Internet Resources,* <http://ublib.buffalo.edu/libraries/units/cts/olac/capc/stnir.html> (viewed May 21, 2001).

18. Hirons and Graham, "Issues Related to Seriality," pp. 201-202.

19. Ibid., pp. 185-187.

20. Melissa Beck, "Remote Access Computer File Serials," Module 31.19.

21. Edgar A. Jones, "Multiple Versions Revisited," *Serials Librarian* 32(1/2) (1997): 177-198.

22. *Functional Requirements of Bibliographic Records* (Munchen: K.G. Saur, 1998). Available: <http://www.ifla.org/VII/s13/frbr/frbr.htm> (viewed May 24, 2001).

23. Jim Cole, "The Cataloging of Digitized Texts," *Cataloging & Classification Quarterly*, 28(3) (1999): 47-48.

24. Jean Hirons, "Decision on E-serial Issues," *CONSER Cataloging Discussion List*, posted October 25, 2000.

25. Library of Congress, Cataloging Policy and Support Office, *Draft Interim Guidelines for Cataloging Electronic Resources*, <http://lcweb.loc.gov/catdir/cpso/dcmb19_4.html> (viewed June 26, 2001).

26. CONSER Working Group. *Single or Separate Records? What's Appropriate and When*, March 1999, <http://wwwtest.library.ucla.edu/libraries/cataloging/sercat/conserwg/> (viewed May 25, 2001).

27. *CONSER Cataloging Manual*, Module 31.3.5.

28. CONSER Working Group. *Single or Separate Records? What's Appropriate and When*, March 1999, <http://wwwtest.library.ucla.edu/libraries/cataloging/sercat/conserwg/> (viewed May 25, 2001).

29. Steve Shadle. "Survey Results" in CONSER Working Group. *Single or Separate Records? What's Appropriate and When*, March 1999, <http://wwwtest.library.ucla.edu/libraries/cataloging/sercat/conserwg/index2.html> (viewed May 29, 2001).

30. Hirons and Graham, "Issues Related to Seriality," pp. 180-213.

Chapter 9

Electronic Serials: Searching for a Chief Source of Information

Jim Cole

The electronic era has introduced an array of new carriers of information, from the early magnetic tapes to floppy disks, CD-ROMs, and the Internet, where information can be distributed in various ways, ranging from e-mail to the now-ubiquitous World Wide Web. Cataloging practices have been greatly impacted by the development of these new electronic media. Witness, for instance, the continuing evolution in the International Standard Bibliographic Description program. In 1977, *ISBD(NBM): International Standard Bibliographic Description for Non-Book Materials* originally provided instructions for the description of machine-readable data files. A specialized ISBD—*ISBD(CF): International Standard Bibliographic Description for Computer Files*—was later written, with a final draft appearing in 1988. This now has grown into *ISBD(ER): International Standard Bibliographic Description for Electronic Resources.*[1]

As new forms of communication have developed and international standards have evolved to provide for their bibliographic description, the *Anglo-American Cataloguing Rules* have likewise adapted. Chapter 9 of the second edition of the code (AACR2), dealing with computer files, is being revised to bring it into alignment with ISBD(ER) and to expand its scope to include new types of electronic resources, including interactive multimedia. The Joint Steering Committee has kept the library community apprised of its progress in the work, posting reports on the Web.[2] At the same time—and again prompted by the emergence of electronic resources—Chapter 12, which has until now dealt with serials, is being revised to cover the entire gamut of "continuing resources."

This chapter focuses on the selection of the chief source of information for electronic serials. It looks not only at the proposed revisions found in Chapters 9 and 12 of AACR2, but at CONSER's application of the present rules, and proposes an alternate approach that, it might be hoped, could be more uniformly and easily applied.

AACR2 REVISIONS

In its posted reports, the Joint Steering Committee states that the revision of rule 9.0B1 would specify the entire resource as the chief source of information for electronic media. The proposed revisions to Chapter 12, however, provide added direction to the cataloger. Proposed rule 12.0B1 instructs the cataloger to

> [b]ase the description of a serial on the first issue or, lacking this, on the earliest available issue. If a remote access serial is not organized in issues or issues do not contain relevant bibliographic information, base the description on the entire resource, according to 9.0B1.[3]

A newly constructed rule 12.0B2 then states that for resources which currently have both a print and an electronic version, the chief source of information is the title page or title page substitute. The rule directs the cataloger when dealing with a wholly electronic resource to consider the entire resource as the chief source according to 9.0B1. It then states, however:

> For **remote access electronic serials,** prefer a source associated with the first issue (rather than a home page for example) when the title given on that source is formally presented and is not in abbreviated form.[4]

Thus, for both printed and remote access electronic serials, the chief source of information has a relationship with the first issue. The relationship is clear for printed serials—the chief source is to be *from* that issue. For remote access serials, the relationship is perhaps a bit more ambiguous—the chief source is, preferably, a source merely *associated* with the first issue.

A LOOK AT CONSER DOCUMENTATION

To help clarify this ambiguity, a look at current CONSER documentation might be useful. Although this is, admittedly, an attempt to predict what lies ahead from what has gone before, a view of the road that we have traveled thus far may help us plan how best to deal with the trouble spots on the long stretch still facing us.

In module 31 of the *CONSER Cataloging Manual,* Melissa Beck has for the past several years provided catalogers guidance in the description of remote access electronic serials. Beck has endeavored to strike a balance between the provisions of Chapters 9 and 12 of the code, saying most recently in section 31.4.1 that

> [c]atalogers continue to look to the first issue for bibliographic information in online serials and AACR2 9.0B1 establishes the "title screen" as the chief source for computer files (see also 31.4.2). When cataloging online serials, catalogers should also consider common sources for bibliographic information: journal home pages, welcome screens, other types of opening screens, publisher information pages, table of contents screens, the browser title bar, etc. Although the first issue is the preferred basis for description, online serials sometimes do not give necessary information in the first issue or may not have a first issue easily recognizable as such, so that the description then must be based on the whole resource available at the time of cataloging.[5]

It can be difficult to determine if a publication has the required "title screen," a problem that Beck addresses in section 31.4.2:

> While many remote access serials such as commercially-published electronic journals have title presentations with clear layout and design similar to their printed counterparts, this is not always the case. If there does not appear to be a clear title screen, base the description on any formal statements found in the publication that indicate the title, publisher, and/or designation of the remote access serial.[6]

She goes on to state:

> When different information is presented in different sources, the question arises as to *which* "title screen" is the chief source. Review the earliest issue and other files that contain formal presentations of bibliographic information. Review as much as is reasonable and select as the chief source a formal presentation of the title proper and related bibliographic information which is likely to be stable over time, and note any variant bibliographic information and the source(s) from which it is taken.
>
> The description of remote access computer file serials begs for both flexibility and the exercise of cataloger judgment in determining the appropriate sources of information. When in doubt, record what seems reasonable, remembering that the first step is to accurately identify and provide access to the publication. The more non-traditional the description, the more necessary it becomes to make explicit notes that explain the sources of information used.[7]

Finally, in section 31.4.3, she advises catalogers, when selecting the source of the title proper, to

> [u]se the first designated part or issue of the serial if it has a source with a formal title presentation that can be considered the chief source of information. To cite the source of title, use a term that is as specific as possible to describe the source, e.g. "title from table of contents screen," "title from title bar" etc. in preference to a more general term such as the phrase "title from title screen."[8]

In the same section, however, she includes a sample note "Title from printout of title screen"; example 31.20.2 also cites the title screen as the source of the title proper.[9]

CONSER participants—and indeed other libraries as well—have striven to apply these guidelines in their cataloging of online serials. In doing so, they face a number of challenges.

The first is the fact that if the form of the title varies within the serial, the choice of the chief source of information can affect the stability of the resultant bibliographic description. The ideal record is one that not only identifies and describes the serial, but one that will stand the test of time as well as possible. A serial is, by its very nature, subject to change; the addition of the Web introduces still another degree of instability to an already unstable publication. This fact will affect the cataloger's decisions, including whether to select a title source from the first issue of the serial or one from the overall Web site.

The next challenge is determining whether or not the online serial has, to use Beck's terminology, a "clear title screen." Beck, perhaps deliberately, does not elaborate to a great extent upon her ideas as to what does—or, more important, does not—constitute such a screen. To gain a better understanding of this, one must refer, therefore, to the AACR2 definition of "title screen":

> **Title screen (Computer files).** In the case of a computer file, a display of data that includes the title proper and usually, though not necessarily, the statement of responsibility and the data relating to publication.[10]

Beck aptly compares online and print serials, writing that an online serial may have a title presentation with a "clear layout and design similar" to a print serial—in other words, similar to a title page. After all, the definition of a title screen closely resembles that of a title page ("A page at the beginning of an item bearing the title proper and usually, though not necessarily, the statement of responsibility and the data relating to publication . . ."[11]). Given this, one may logically surmise that the criteria used to assess whether a printed source is actually a title page are equally applicable here. Turning, therefore, to section 3.2.1 of the *CONSER Cataloging Manual,* one finds that a title page is not to contain text, tables of contents, or extensive editorial information; in other words, it is not "a page that has been designed to fulfill a different function."[12] A rigid interpretation such as this could, however, mean that very few if any online serials would have actual title screens—or, more properly, title pages, since a Web site is a collection of interlinked Web pages rather than screens[13]—because the initial pages of many online serials' Web sites serve a multiplicity of functions.

Last of all, if an online serial lacks a title screen or page, the cataloger is faced with selecting an appropriate alternative source to use as a substitute. Here, as Beck points out, the cataloger is to remember that as the description becomes more nontraditional, explicit notes must be added to clarify what the source actually was.

Thus, from CONSER documentation, one sees that the principal consideration is the creation of a stable record that both identifies and describes the online serial. The chief source of information may be a "clear title screen" or an alternative. The source may, or may not, have a direct relationship with the first or earliest issue of the serial, but it should be identifiable from the cataloging.

How are the present CONSER guidelines put into practice by CONSER participants and other libraries? This can best be determined by looking at a selection of records. First, although one can argue for a strict interpretation of the term "title screen," the term has, at least until now, been frequently used in the catalog record. For instance, the record for *The Electronic Journal of Combinatorics* (sn94-5314) contains the note "Title from title screen." The page in question, which does contain a formal presentation of the serial title, consists of two frames—a left frame containing editorial information, and a right frame with more than a dozen different hypertext links, divided into the categories "View the Journal," "About the Journal," and "The World Combinatorics Exchange." In general parlance, this would be a home page—"a starting page with links to other related pages," to use Crumlish's definition[14]—and may have been considered as such by some catalogers. The *CONSER Cataloging Manual,* however, defines a home page as a "hypertext document that serves as the 'preface' for a service or publication mounted on the World Wide Web. It is normally an introductory screen that provides general information about the institution maintaining the site, or a publication or group of publications available. Hypertext links are included to access specific documents or files archived at the site."[15] Perhaps the *Manual*'s definition is sufficiently restrictive that the source in question can no longer be termed a home page. Whatever the case, a serial's home page is itself a somewhat frequently cited source of the title, as evidenced by the record for *School Library Media Research* (sn99-3244).

The title may be taken from a source within a given issue of an online serial. For example, the record for *Learned Publishing* (00-253290) contains the note "Description based on: Vol. 10, no. 1 (Jan 1997); title from contents page caption (viewed Aug. 28, 2000)." One frequently encounters, however, notes such as "Description based on:

Vol. 46, no. 2 (spring 1999); title from title screen (viewed Oct. 13, 1999)," found on the record for *Africa Today* (sn99-4666). Volume 46, no. 2 has a contents page, but no title screen or page of its own. The URL in the record's 856 field links to the journal's opening page, referred to elsewhere on the site as "This Journal"—but that page does not constitute a part of the issue. If the title is from the contents page of volume 46, number 2, it should be identified as such; if it is from the opening "This Journal" page, it is not logical to say the description was based on an issue when the title was in actuality transcribed from the opening page. The question again arises, too, as to whether the *Africa Today* opening page—if that is the source of the title—would be better described as a home page. *Africa Today* is a Project MUSE title, as is *Differences*; both have opening pages with identical layouts. The latter's bibliographic record (sn99-4667), however, says "Description based on: Vol. 10, no. 3 (fall 1998); title from journal home page (viewed Oct. 13, 1999)."

A frequent source of information is what is termed the "journal information screen." For instance, the record for The FASEB Journal (sn99-34658) informs the user, "Description based on: Vol. 12, no. 1 (Jan. 1998), viewed Sept. 24, 1999; title from journal information screen." Identifying the page in question is a bit of a difficulty, since nothing termed a "Journal Information" screen or page can be found. The journal's home page (http://www.fasebj.org) has a "General Info." link to the URL <http://www.fasebj.org/subscriptions/trial.shtml>. The primary function of this page, which contains an announcement of the online availability of the journal as well as information about the Web site, clearly is not the presentation of the title, the statement of responsibility, and the data relating to publication. The "General Info." page, in turn, has a link to "Subscription Information"—still another page with "information." The user is thus faced with a certain ambiguity that the bibliographic record makes no attempt to resolve decisively.

Finally, the title may be taken from a source that eventually disappears completely from the site. For example, the record for the *Electronic Journal of Differential Equations* (95-647857) says "Title from 'Scope and dissemination' file"—a file that can no longer be accessed through any of the four Internet addresses (two Web, one ftp, one gopher) on the record.

However well or poorly the CONSER guidelines are being put into practice, they do reflect a desire for a descriptive, identifying, yet stable record, something that has always been a hallmark of serials cataloging. One cannot easily envision the abandonment of that objective solely to base the description of an online serial whenever possible upon a source "associated with the first issue." The practices of today—tested now for several years—will undoubtedly continue into the future unless a workable alternative can be found.

SEARCHING FOR AN ALTERNATIVE

Before one begins to consider other possibilities for a chief source of information, it might be well to look at the structure of an electronic serial. Each one, admittedly, is different. Generally, serials from the same publisher will have a similar structure, but even that is not always the case. Some characteristics, appear to be common to most, especially those that are commercially published. First, although there are exceptions, most serials have a starting or opening page (some publications of societies, institutions, and the like must be accessed through the organization's main page). The serial's opening page—whether it is the home page, the "title screen," or something else in cataloging terms—usually has one or more links to the online issues. Sometimes the page contains a list of volumes or even a list of volumes and issues, as CatchWord provides for the Taylor and Francis journals. At other times, one finds a link to the current issue and another to an archive of all the issues (which itself may be one or more "clicks" removed). If the serial one is accessing is a periodical, when one is ultimately able to click on an issue number, what generally appears is not a digitized cover or a title page, but a contents page. From there, one can generally view the abstract or the full text, sometimes in a variety of formats such as RealPage, PDF, PostScript, and HTML.

Thus, for an online periodical at least, issues usually consist of a contents page and individual articles, which in turn may have a separate abstract page in addition to full text. Generally there is no easily readable digitization of the cover. Most of the additional material traditionally appearing in a printed issue of a journal—the list of editorial board members, the statement of the scope and purpose of the journal, instructions for authors, subscription information, masthead data, and the like—is at what may be considered the journal level; it appears only once and applies to the entire publication.

Even the contents page now can present a problem for the bibliographic description, since, as is the case with the above-mentioned Taylor and Francis journals, it may be available in both HTML and "original" (RealPage or PDF) formats. If the contents page is cited as the title source, the format of the page should probably be included to avoid ambiguity.

What could one, then, suggest as an alternative title source for an electronic serial—an alternative chief source of information? A look at our cataloging roots may provide an answer. All serials catalogers know that when a printed serial lacks a title page, AACR2 directs the cataloger to select a chief source from among a list of substitutes, with the cover most often given preference. This was the case with the first edition of the code as well (AACR1). However, rule 161A— the very rule that contained the prioritized list of title page substitutes—also stated that "[t]he title and imprint are taken from a single source as far as possible."[16] Moreover, the introductory notes to Chapter 7 of AACR1, which dealt with the description of serials, said that "wherever suitable, the rules for the cataloging of monographs are to be applied to serials," and rule 132B1, pertaining to monographs, said that "[t]he part of the work supplying the most complete information is used as the [title page] substitute."[17] One wondered, therefore, why preference was given to the cover as a title page substitute, when the contents page (which often contained the masthead) was the more "complete" source. The traditional answer, of course, was that the cover was what the patron saw first.

Most online serials have a starting or opening page. That page is analogous to a cover of a printed serial—it is what, again, the user sees first. It functions as a "cover" for the entire online publication, and not just an issue. If one considers the opening page to be the "cover," then perhaps it is the most logical chief source of information when it contains a formal presentation of the title.

ADVANTAGES OF ADOPTING THE OPENING PAGE AS THE CHIEF SOURCE

Several advantages would accrue from adopting the opening page as the chief source of information for an online serial. First and foremost, although the information on that page may change, the page itself, if it exists, is unlikely to disappear from the site. On the other hand, a "Scope and dissemination" page or file such as the *Electronic Journal of Differential Equations* once had can easily disappear without ill effect to the overall site (as well could the "General Info." page [http://www.fasebj.org/subscriptions/trial.shtml] of *The FASEB Journal*). Even if the title is taken from the contents page of the earliest issue, that may not be a permanently available source—all too often, one finds that older issues are removed from a site as newer issues are added. Without a permanently available source for the title, one has no valid basis of comparison to see if the title has changed. If the opening screen is the source of the title, however, one can observe any changes and make whatever corrections are necessary, much as one would in the description of a loose-leaf publication (an "integrating resource," to use the terminology of the proposed revisions of Chapter 12 of AACR2[18]).

Next, a simple note, "Title from opening page (viewed [date])," could be used to record the title source. This would have two advantages. First, the cataloger would not have to wrestle with the definitions of a "title screen" and a home page, trying, sometimes futilely, to distinguish between the two, as evidenced from the earlier discussion of the cataloging of *Africa Today* and *Differences*. Second, the cataloger would no longer need to struggle to construct explicit terminology to describe the page. It would be easily identifiable to both the cataloger and the user alike. If the bibliographic record contained more than one 856 field, the first would link to the opening page upon which the description was based.

Also, since for most serials the opening page would not be considered part of an issue, a needless repetition of data in the bibliographic record for an online version of a print publication could be avoided: the issue number would no longer be recorded in both an unformatted 362 field and in an illogical, contradictory statement regarding the item described. For instance, the record for *Differences* contains the following:

362 1   Coverage as of October 13, 1999: Vol. 10, no. 3 (fall 1998)-

500   Description based on: Vol. 10, no. 3 (fall 1998); title from journal home page (viewed Oct. 13, 1999).

If the opening page were used as the chief source, this would be simplified to read:

362 1   Coverage as of October 13, 1999: Vol. 10, no. 3 (fall 1998)-

500   Title from opening page (viewed Oct. 13, 1999).

One of the advantages of the "Description based on" or, to use the proposed new terminology, the "Earliest issue consulted"[19] note is that it "dates" the description. Since the date of viewing is incorporated into the "Title from opening screen note," this advantage is preserved.

Electronic serials are just as prone to change their titles as printed serials are. The adoption of the opening page as chief source of information would at times simplify matters here as well. The presentation of the title on that page would serve as the basis for the decision whether or not to create a new record. When there is just a single URL for the overall serial (instead of two, one for the earlier title, and one for the later), only a single record would be created, using the title from the opening page, with notes and access points for the variant titles. The proposed revision of Rule 21.2C1a, on the other hand, admits of two possibilities—separate records for the earlier and later titles if individual issues reflect both, but a single record if the earlier title is no longer formally presented on the issues.[20] Curiously, both possibilities, but in reverse, have over the course of time been the case with the *International Update* issued by the College of Agriculture of Iowa State University. The serial had a single URL, and the opening page had the title *International Update*. The individual issues published through 1998 also had that title, while all the later issues consistently had the title *International Agriculture*. On September 26, 2000, the Iowa State University Library therefore created two records for the serial, one with the title field

245 10 International update $h [computer file] : $b newsletter.

and the other with the title field and note

245 10 International agriculture $h [computer file] : $b a newsletter from International Agriculture Programs, College of Agriculture, Iowa State University.

246 1 $i Title on opening screen: $a International update

Sometime between September 26, 2000, when the two records were created, and January 15, 2001, the College of Agriculture changed the title of the individual issues to reflect once again the serial's opening page. Since there was only one URL for the serial, selecting the opening page—the "cover" of the serial—as the chief source of information would have allowed the creation of a single record and would have eliminated the eventual need to recatalog the serial, collapsing the two records into one.

CONCLUSION

The choice of the opening page as the preferred chief source of information for an online serial has a number of advantages, as demonstrated. These include the continued existence of the title source, the simplification (and standardization) of the process of selecting the title source and then identifying it in the catalog record, the elimination of repetitious data from the record, and the simplification of the handling of title changes. While a "Description based on" or "Earliest issue consulted" note would not be included if the serial had an opening page, the chief advantage of that note—the "dating" of the description—would be retained, since the date of viewing would continue to be recorded.

Adopting the opening page as the chief source is not without precedent: it is in keeping with Nancy Olson's general recommendations in her *Cataloging Internet Resources,* when she says that "[i]f there is no special [title screen] display, information may be taken from the home page, web page, or file itself. . . . "[21] The advantages of doing so far outweigh the mere adherence to the principle of taking the title from the first or earliest issue, or in the case of an online serial, from a source "associated" with that issue.

NOTES

1. ISBD(CF) Review Group, *ISBD(ER): International Standard Bibliographic Description for Electronic Resources.* July 2, 1999. <http://ifla.org/VII/s13/pubs/ isbd.htm> (December 21, 2000).

2. Joint Steering Committee for Revision of AACR, "Outcomes of the Meeting of the Joint Steering Committee Held in Brisbane, Australia, 18-20 October 1999."

November 20, 1999. <http://www.nlc-bnc.ca/jsc/9910out.html> (June 20, 2001); Joint Steering Committee for Revision of AACR, "Outcomes of the Meeting of the Joint Steering Committee Held in San Diego, California, USA, 22-24 March 2000." May 30, 2000. <http://www.nlc-bnc.ca/jsc/0003out.html> (December 21, 2000).

3. Jean Hirons and members of the CONSER AACR Review Task Force, "Revising AACR2 to Accommodate Seriality: Rule Revision Proposals," p. 7. February 28, 2000. <http://www.nlc-bnc.ca/jsc/ch12.pdf> (June 20, 2001).

4. Hirons, "Revising AACR2," p. 8.

5. Melissa Beck, "Remote Access Computer File Serials." *CONSER Cataloging Manual*, Module 31. January 2, 2001. <http://lcweb.loc.gov/acq/conser/module31.html> (April 9, 2001).

6. Ibid.

7. Ibid.

8. Ibid.

9. Ibid.

10. *Anglo-American Cataloguing Rules*, Second Edition, 1998 Revision (Ottawa: Canadian Library Association, 1998), p. 624.

11. Ibid., p. 623.

12. *CONSER Cataloging Manual* (Washington, DC: Library of Congress, Cataloging Distribution Service), Module: 3 (fall 1995): 10.

13. Edward T. O'Neill and Brian F. Lavoie, "Bibliographic Control for the Web," *The Serials Librarian* 37(3) (2000): 59.

14. Christian Crumlish, *The Internet Dictionary* (San Francisco: Sybex, 1995): 89.

15. Beck, "Remote Access Computer File Serials."

16. *Anglo-American Cataloging Rules*, North American text (Chicago: American Library Association, 1967): 232.

17. Ibid., p. 231, 193.

18. Hirons, "Revising AACR2," p. 6.

19. Ibid., p. 38.

20. Ibid., p. 45.

21. Nancy B. Olson, ed., *Cataloging Internet Resources,* Second Edition. 1997. <http://www.purl.org/oclc/cataloging-internet> (January 16, 2001).

Chapter 10

A Meditation on Metadata

Gregory Wool

INTRODUCTION

In the last few years the term "metadata" has become a buzzword in the realm of online information access. The word figures prominently in discussions of how to improve electronic data retrieval. The Institute of Electrical and Electronics Engineers (IEEE) has begun organizing conferences devoted entirely to metadata. At the same time Clifford Lynch has advised at least one audience of library catalogers that if they tell their directors they create metadata, they could improve their chances for a higher salary.[1]

This chapter was written to help show how metadata can be applied to online serials. Its specific task, however, is to establish (with apologies to the late short-story writer Raymond Carver) what we talk about when we talk about metadata.

Two overlapping but somewhat contradictory definitions of metadata are worth considering. The first is from Priscilla Caplan, Assistant Director for Digital Library Services at the Florida Center for Library Automation and a participant in the discussions that produced the Dublin Core metadata standard:

> Metadata really is nothing more than data about data; a catalog record is metadata; so is a TEI header, or any other form of description.[2]

The author wishes to acknowledge the suggestions and comments of Crystal Graham, Gerry McKiernan, and Kris Gerhard, from which the original version of this chapter, and by extension the present version, have benefitted.

The second is from the International Federation of Library Associations and Institutions (IFLA) "Metadata Resources" home page:

> Metadata is data about data. The term refers to any data used to aid the identification, description and location of networked electronic resources.[3]

Caplan's definition is preferable because it encompasses the print as well as the online environment. It also reassures us that metadata are not something new and strange, but have been created and used for centuries, by publishers as well as librarians. At the same time, the more restrictive IFLA definition contributes to our understanding of the topic by reminding us of the term's origins in the world of digital information. It implies that metadata can take many forms, exist on many levels, and be manipulated in many ways in order to fulfill their stated purpose. It also implies that new approaches to metadata are not only possible but necessary.

Just as online serials represent a familiar document type with new characteristics and possibilities, metadata are essentially the cataloging and other identifying data that librarians (and other information workers) have always recorded and used—but with new forms and capabilities in the online environment. In addition—to the extent technology has allowed—such data have always been borrowed, adapted, and further distributed in the interests of promoting the efficient use of information. As such, metadata are the special province of librarians, who have a vital interest in ensuring that the right metadata are created, preserved, and put to optimal use. To alter slightly the old folk rhyme prescribing what a bride should wear on her wedding day for good luck, metadata are something old, something new, something borrowed, something we (i.e., librarians) "do."

METADATA AS SOMETHING OLD

The catalog record, usually containing such identifying information as title, author, publisher, subject categories, and physical description, is (to librarians at least) the most obvious metadata application in the print environment. Such "document surrogates" have existed probably as long as there have been libraries (and certainly since the Middle Ages) as components of a catalog—the authoritative record of a library's holdings—which functions as both a management tool and a finding aid for the library's users. For the past several decades, bibliographic records from various libraries have been collected and published in "union catalogs" as well. Publishing firms also issue catalogs, listing for potential customers the titles they offer, usually with brief identifying data and perhaps tables or summaries of contents. Subject bibliographies have a long history, and their contents, too, are metadata.

Printed documents usually contain their own metadata, in the form of title pages, cover information, colophons, tables of contents, and indexes. Such information, besides being transcribed in catalogs and bibliographies, is compiled and organized for access in periodical indexes and other reference databases. Metadata have long been used not only to locate books and journals, but also individual articles, chapters of books, and concepts within documents. Indexes and concordances employ words from the text itself as metadata.

Finally, metadata include the various sorts of information libraries keep about their serials for internal management purposes. Such items of interest as subscription cost, vendor used, issues checked in, binding status of volumes, and retention policies, while not bibliographic in nature, are just as surely "data about data" and warrant appropriate consideration in any metadata strategy.

Many of the metadata applications we see in the online information environment are extensions of techniques long used in the print domain, enhanced with uniquely online capabilities. Perhaps the most obvious is OCLC's Intercat project, which provides a hypertext link within a catalog record for an Internet resource for direct access to that resource.[4] This functionality can also be found in many of the new metadata schemes consciously or unconsciously modeled on library cataloging standards. Hotlinked subject "Webliographies" and search engines matching natural language queries to words or phrases in file headers serve as less obvious examples.

METADATA AS SOMETHING NEW

Though in many ways the forms and functions of metadata remain substantially the same in the online environment and for online information objects, as with their print counterparts, the technology has brought structural innovations. These can be classified as new elements, new functionalities, and new paradigms.

New Elements

The new elements actually result from the new technologies of data objects rather than those of information management systems. A good information manager will make available all the types of metadata necessary to answer common questions about a resource. Not surprisingly, electronic resources have a number of characteristics not found in printed materials. Moreover, there are multiple electronic resource formats (e.g., numeric data files, Web sites, CD-ROMs), each with its peculiar set of characteristics, and a new format seems to come along every few months. (Thus we have serials catalogers learning to record Uniform Resource Locators (URLs) for Web-based journals and required machine specifications for CD-ROMs.) Library standards such as AACR2 and MARC have been scrambling to keep up, but with their need for general applicability, they cannot provide the level of detail for specialized formats their user groups demand. Hence, there is a proliferation of metadata schemes for such resource types as geographic information system (GIS) coverages and humanities text files.

New Functionalities

Some of the new functionalities have been referred to already. The hotlinking of metadata elements in a catalog record, a title list, or elsewhere, accomplished through the use of Hypertext Markup Language (HTML), creates a direct link for the searcher from externally produced metadata to the item itself.[5] Through algorithms using such techniques as relevance ranking and concept mapping, search engines generate metadata on the fly while mimicking the performance of human indexers. Perhaps more significantly, the growing use of HTML and other applications of SGML (Standard Generalized Markup Language) creates a class of metadata that govern or facilitate retrieval and display while remaining hidden from the user.[6] Catalog and database search software can be configured to conceal metadata as well, whether for brief record displays or for natural language search assistance.

New Paradigms

The development of computer storage and networked retrieval of information has resulted in at least two new paradigms for metadata which make it seem like a new phenomenon rather than the ancient art of cataloging in a new environment. One might be called the Database Paradigm. In it, metadata associated with a data object are recorded as attributes with values; the attributes are registered with definitions in a data dictionary. (This contrasts with the tagless, citations-with-annotations approach typical of catalog cards.) The metadata are stored in a record, which could display in full or in any possible subset (e.g., brief entries in a catalog or list of search results) depending on what choices are programmed. Metadata shared by several data objects may reside in a separate record linked to the objects' metadata records, especially if the metadata have cross-references (for example, an author's name known in several forms).[7] Each metadata item is autonomous, depending only on its definition in the data dictionary and the identifier of the data object for its meaning, not on the other metadata; thus it can be displayed in a variety of sequences and tagging schemes without loss of meaning.

Online library catalogs using the MARC formats mimic the Database Paradigm, but critically lack an effective data dictionary, as records are still created using rules set up for a structured prose-like citation-with-annotations scheme (the International Standard Bibliographic Description, or ISBD), and then "translated" by the catalog software into a list of attributes and values. The redundancy, inflexibility, potential for confusion, and two-dimensionality that result are well documented elsewhere.[8]

The Markup Paradigm involves the embedding of metadata in the data object, usually by tagging the data using an SGML document type definition. Typically, SGML tagging is used to control the display of data rather than describe the data object, but by marking data elements crucial to identification, it can index a data object and facilitate its direct retrieval. In addition, such tagging can be used to automatically generate catalog records. By contrast, printed books and serials contain metadata (on a title page, cover, or elsewhere) with either unstandardized or no tagging, making their interpretation by a trained cataloger necessary for future identification and retrieval. Perhaps the greatest potential for the Markup Paradigm involves the encoding of relationships within a body of data for use in data mining applications and precision retrieval systems based on artificial intelligence.[9]

METADATA AS SOMETHING BORROWED

At least since the invention of title pages, metadata have been attached to information objects by their creators or publishers and later adapted for catalog records and other third-party reference or management applications. The extent to which such information has been altered or used unchanged varies with the type of metadata as well as the metadata scheme being used. It has also varied over time; a look at North American cataloging standards over the past century reveals a trend, not so much away from interpretation and toward faithful transcription, as toward the recording of parallel versions of the same metadata: one transcribed verbatim from the item being described, a second altered as necessary to enable collocation with other records bearing the same characteristic (e.g., association with a particular person or corporate body), perhaps a third in encoded form. An element of interpretation is always present in the reuse of author/publisher-supplied metadata, even when selecting the data to transcribe.[10]

With the growth in the number (and variety) of information objects outstripping that of the resources available for their management, interest in expanding the role of authors and publishers in creating metadata is greater than ever (as is, of course, interest in sharing metadata among libraries). Over a decade ago Maurice Line, a library consultant who had previously been an administrator of the British Library, proposed the creation of an "all-through system" whereby library catalog records would be produced by book publishers and sent to libraries along with the books.[11] Although that has not yet materialized, many book jobbers and subscription vendors now offer catalog-ready records, whether created in-house or derived from a bibliographic utility, for the materials they supply. Increasingly, access to "virtual collections" on the Internet such as the Government Information Locator Service (GILS) and the National Engineering Education Delivery System (NEEDS) is built upon the use of metadata templates, with the producers of data objects filling in the values for a predefined list of attributes.[12] The Text Encoding Initiative (TEI) header standard is a more elaborate version of such a template (as well as one created and used more from a librarian's perspective), but its use of SGML also allows the same set of metadata to function as both a title page and a catalog record.[13]

Inevitably, increasing reliance on what might be called "source" metadata in the library environment (including Internet-based "digital libraries") raises the question of how such unstandardized metadata can be managed to improve retrieval effectiveness. Many players appear to be betting the farm on future breakthroughs in artificial intelligence, although human language (the very stuff of metadata) is notoriously resistant to machine comprehension. In the meantime, solutions mean finding the most effective ways to leverage the intervention of human organizers.

METADATA AS SOMETHING WE DO

If, then, people are to provide and manage the metadata needed to administer and maintain access to collections of recorded information, how does one get started? One ready answer might be, "Plug into an existing system." But which one? There are dozens. Next ready answer: "The one that best meets your needs." Ah, but what are those needs?

Several years ago, when the World Wide Web was still in its infancy, I had the opportunity to build a prototype online catalog for remotely held (but not networked!) files of machine-readable databases and numeric data files. I found the following four-part question helpful in not only planning my work, but also explaining it to the agencies funding my project: What kinds of information do you want to (1) collect, (2) display, (3) label, or (4) index?[14] Seen as a decision model, this question has two underlying assumptions: first, each part represents a separate decision; second, the answer to each part determines the pool of choices for the next part. As may be surmised, this second assumption will not be entirely applicable to all metadata situations (e.g., one may want to index information but not display it in a record). Nonetheless, the model can provide a useful framework for thinking about metadata because the question addresses not only the basic information need, but also the structure and use of the information.

Collect

Collecting is the first cut. What sorts of information about your data objects will you want to make available, whether to an external audience or for internal management needs? Each type of information should be recorded for every data object as applicable. What will be done with the information is not at issue here. If it is not collected, it cannot be used.

Display

"Display" refers to record displays for external users. Some things you may want to collect for internal use only. If there are multiple display formats (search results list entry, brief record, full record, in-between record, etc.) the decisions to be made are correspondingly multiplied.

Label

What separates the label from the display decision is that this puts the metadata into categories, at least for public display. (In relational database terms, it defines the attributes for which the metadata are values.) For example, you may choose to collect names of personal authors and of corporate authors, and to display them, but decide to use a single label for the two types of authors, thus creating a single category. For that matter, are editors "authors"? Here is where you would decide.

Index

Under "index" you would decide what types of metadata users could search. In most online catalog systems, of course, several indexes are configured (typically for titles, authors/names, and subjects) and someone has to decide what types of data go into each one.

Some Added Wrinkles in the Decision-Making Process

With online catalog systems, many of the decisions described above have been made during system configuration. On the other hand, in a client-server environment, the advent of clients that can search multiple database systems using the Z39.50 standard raises the possibility that searchers from remote sites will be able, through the configuration of their Z39.50 client, to make their own decisions regarding display, labeling, and indexing of your metadata.[15] This means that as far as possible, metadata should be recorded (and categorized) in a way that minimizes dependence on context for its meaning.[16]

CONCLUSION

The intent of this chapter has been to demystify metadata for librarians by showing that cataloging and metadata collection are essentially the same task. It sets out to do so by emphasizing the broader definitions of both "cataloging" and "metadata," so that cataloging is seen as more than just the creation of bibliographic records in libraries, and metadata as more than just the documentation of electronic datasets. In the process, two things should have become apparent. One, cataloging is changing and will change further under the influence of online information technology. Two, the creation and maintenance of metadata for online serials are at most an extension of the processes used in online cataloging and catalog maintenance for their printed counterparts.

NOTES

1. Clifford Lynch, *Descriptive Cataloging Hits the Net: Metadata, Uniform Resource Identifier Systems and New Descriptive Requirements* (Paper presented at AACR2000: Toward the Future of the Descriptive Cataloging Rules, preconference institute sponsored by the Association for Library Collections and Technical Services, Chicago, IL, June 22, 1995).

2. Priscilla Caplan, "You Call It Corn, We Call It Syntax-Independent Metadata for Document-Like Objects," *The Public-Access Computer Systems Review* 6(4) (1995). Available: <http://info.lib.uh.edu/pr/v6/n4/capl6n4.html>.

3. International Federation of Library Associations, *Digital Libraries: Metadata Resources*. Available: <http://www.ifla.org/II/metadata.htm>.

4. Cf. *Intercat: A Catalog of Internet Resources.* Available: <http://purl.oclc. org/NET/INTERCAT>.

5. Cf. W3C, *Hypertext Markup Language (HTML): Home Page.* Available: <http://www.w3.org/pub/WWW/MarkUp/MarkUp.html>.

6. Cf. David Seaman, "About Standard Generalized Markup Language (SGML)." Available: <http://etext.lib.virginia.edu/sgml.htm>.

7. Proposals for this type of functionality in online catalogs can be found in Michael Carpenter, "Does Cataloging Theory Rest on a Mistake?" in *Origins, Content, and Future of AACR2 Revised,* ed. Richard P. Smiraglia (Chicago: American Library Association, 1992), 98-100; Michael Gorman, "After *AACR2R*: The Future of the Anglo-American Cataloging Rules," in *Origins,* 91-93; and Barbara B. Tillett, "Bibliographic Structures: The Evolution of Catalog Entries, References, and Tracings," in *The Conceptual Foundations of Descriptive Cataloging,* ed. Elaine Svenonius (San Diego, CA: Academic, 1989), 161-162.

8. Cf. Gregory H. Leazer, "An Examination of Data Elements for Bibliographic Description: Toward a Conceptual Schema for the USMARC Formats," *Library Resources and Technical Services* 36 (April 1992): 189-208; Michael Heaney, "Object-Oriented Cataloging," *Information Technology and Libraries* 14 (September 1995): 135-153; Gregory J. Wool, Bart Austhof, Anita Breckbill, and B. Larry Mozzer, "Cataloging Standards and Machine Translation: A Study of Reformatted ISBD Records in an Online Catalog," *Information Technology and Libraries* 12 (Dec. 1993): 383-403.

9. "Data mining (also known as Knowledge Discovery in Databases—KDD) has been defined as 'the nontrivial extraction of implicit, previously unknown, and potentially useful information from data.' It uses machine learning, statistical and visualization techniques to discovery [sic] and present knowledge in a form which is easily comprehensible to humans." (Andy Pryke, "Introduction to Data Mining." Available: <http://www.cs.bham.ac.uk/~anp/dm_docs/dm_intro.html>. Cf. *Kdnuggets: Data Mining, Web Mining, Knowledge Discovery, and CRM Guide.* Available: <http://www.kdnuggets.com/>; Andy Pryke, *The Data Mine.* Available: <http://www.cs.bham.ac.uk/~anp/TheDataMine.htm>; Knowledge Discovery and Data Mining Foundation, *Knowledge Discovery and Data Mining.* Available: <http://www.kdd.org/>.

10. Cf. Ben R. Tucker, "The Limits of a Title Proper; or, One Case Showing Why Human Beings, Not Machines, Must Do the Cataloging," *Library Resources and Technical Services* 34 (April 1990): 240-245.

11. Maurice B. Line, "Satisfying Bibliographic Needs in the Future—From Publisher to User," *Catalogue and Index* (90-91) (autumn-winter 1988): 10-14. A revised version of this paper appears in *Aslib Proceedings* 42 (February 1990): 41-49 under the title "Bibliographic Records for Users: From Disordered Superabundance to Cost-Effective Satisfaction."

12. Cf. *Global Information Locator Service (GILS).* Available: <http://www. usgs.gov/public/gils/>; National Archives and Records Administration, *Guidelines for the Preparation of GILS Core Entries.* Available: <http://www.dtic.mil/gils/ documents/naradoc/>; *NEEDS: A Digital Library for Engineering Education.* Available: <http://www.needs.org/>.

13. Cf. David Seaman, "Guidelines for SGML Text Mark-up at the Electronic Text Center." Available: <http://etext.lib.virginia.edu/tei/uvatei4.html>.

14. Iowa Policy and Planning Data Project, "Report, January 1, 1993 to March 31, 1993" (Ames, Iowa, 1993, photocopy), 2-7.

15. "What is Z39.50?" in *The ANSI/NISO Z39.50 Protocol: Information Retrieval in the Information Infrastructure.* Available: <http://www.cni.org/pub/NISO/docs/Z39.50-brochure/50.brochure.part01.html>.

16. Gregory J. Wool, "Bibliographical Metadata; or, We Need a Client-Server Cataloging Code!" in *Finding Common Ground: Creating the Library of the Future Without Diminishing the Library of the Past* (pp. 198-201), eds. Cheryl LaGuardia and Barbara A. Mitchell (New York: Neal-Schuman Publishers, 1998).

Chapter 11

Digital Preservation and Long-Term Access to the Content of Electronic Serials

Michael Day

INTRODUCTION

The long-term preservation of information in digital form has been a subject of growing interest for the library and information professions since the late 1970s. Initially, this was a response to the growing use of digital technologies in publishing and the suggestion by Lancaster (and others) that society was steadily moving toward the use of information systems that would be largely paperless.[1] Much recent awareness of the digital preservation issue was facilitated by the publication in 1996 of the report of the Task Force on Archiving of Digital Information commissioned by the Commission on Preservation and Access (CPA) and the Research Libraries Group (RLG).[2] The report provided a good summary of relevant issues and acted as a catalyst for further research and development.

UKOLN is funded by the Joint Information Systems Committee of the U.K. higher and further education funding councils and by Resource: The Council for Museums, Archives and Libraries, as well as by project funding from several sources. The views expressed in this chapter do not necessarily reflect those of UKOLN or its funding bodies.

Naturally, digital preservation issues apply across the whole range of digitally based information resources. This chapter is concerned with just one subset of these; i.e., the digital products of scholarly and scientific communication that have been traditionally published in printed peer-reviewed serials. In order to reflect current trends, this will include both the contents of those electronic serials that have been formally published by commercial and learned society publishers and also those papers (or e-prints) that have been "self-archived." The development of sustainable preservation strategies for both of these types of resources is essential to ensure the future viability of scholarly communication.

Initially, however, it is important to define some terms. Even the concept of "digital preservation" can be difficult to define unambiguously. The term is sometimes confused with the quite separate idea of digitizing resources as part of a preservation strategy for nondigital objects. In the context of scholarly communication, back issues of serials are often digitized and made available over networks in order to improve access to the information contained in them and, on occasion, to aid the preservation of the original item.[3] Examples of this type of service are JSTOR and the Internet Library of Early Journals (ILEJ).[4] Although it is acknowledged that digitized versions of the back issues of serials will also need to be preserved, they will not form the main focus of this chapter.

The concept of digital preservation can also get muddled with ideas of digital archiving or digital archives. Indeed, the terms sometimes appear to be used interchangeably. This can be a source of confusion. For example, members of the archives and records professions have a very different understanding of the archives concept than computer scientists, who often use the word "archive" as a verb, meaning the creation of secure backup copies for a fixed period of time. The word is used in a similar way by the developers of e-print archives. Wherever possible, this chapter uses the word "preservation" in an attempt to avoid any confusion, except in relation to e-print archives. Preservation itself is primarily concerned with the survival of information in a usable form for as long as it is required.[5] Preservation, therefore, is not just concerned with the conservation or restoration of physical artifacts, but includes all of the strategic and organizational considerations that relate to the survival of information over time. Hedstrom has usefully defined digital preservation as "the planning, resource allocation, and application of preservation methods and technologies to ensure that digital information of continuing value remains accessible and usable."[6]

A distinction is sometimes made between the preservation of the information embodied in a document (the information content) and the physical conservation of an information carrier.[7] This is especially relevant for digital information—including the content of e-serials—because most users tend not to be interested in which particular type of physical object is being used to store the information. There may be a case for retaining physical objects, for example in a museum of technology, but for e-serials, the preservation of informational content is the main issue.

Another important, often emotional, issue is how long this information should be kept. It is often assumed that preservation should be permanent, often defined with reference to loaded terms such as "in perpetuity" and "indefinitely." In the context of archives, Bearman has noted the absurdity of using concepts of permanence with regard to preservation and instead has proposed a more realistic concept of "retention for period of continuing value."[8] In consequence, this chapter will assume that preservation is normally linked to continuing access and use and not with nebulous concepts of permanence.

THE ELECTRONIC SERIAL LANDSCAPE

Scholarly and scientific papers published in peer-reviewed printed serials have fulfilled a vitally important role in the scholarly communication process since the seventeenth century. Line has correctly described them as the "established medium of record and dissemination."[9] Despite this, there has been a growing feeling that the traditional printed serial has outlived its historical role and that some kind of digitally based form of scholarly communication will soon replace it.[10] At the moment, there are two main models for the digital distribution of scholarly communication through the Internet, and both have developed relatively independently.[11] First, the publishers of traditional printed serials have begun to place digital copies of each issue on Web sites (a form of parallel publishing) and have started to experiment with the production of digital-only journals. Second, some scholars and librarians have outlined "subversive proposals" that aim to ensure free access to the scholarly and scientific literature through the self-archiving of papers by their authors. Both the publishers of e-serials and the supporters of author self-archiving initiatives hope—in different ways—that developments in the digital distribution of scholarly communication might help offset the effects of the ongoing "serials crisis."[12]

THE FUNCTIONS OF SERIALS

The idea of electronic serials has been around for a number of years. Research projects in the 1980s first proved that e-serials were technically feasible.[13] Initiatives such as EIES (Electronic Information Exchange System) and BLEND (Birmingham and Loughborough Electronic Network) demonstrated that all stages of the production of a scholarly serial (i.e., article submission, peer review, editing, and distribution) could be undertaken through computer networks.[14] However, these projects did not develop into sustainable services at the time because computer networks were immature and not ubiquitously available, even within the research community.[15] Also, in some cases, the proposed user interfaces were poor and the system developers did not always have a clear idea of the many different functions fulfilled by the printed scholarly serial. McKnight has noted that there is no incentive for either authors or readers to change unless electronic serials can do "at least the same things—and preferably more—with electronic journals as they do with paper."[16] The printed peer-reviewed serial has proved to be an extremely successful part of scholarly communication since the seventeenth century because it has fulfilled a wide range of different functions. The following list is expanded from those functions that have been identified by Rowland.[17]

- *Dissemination*—Publication of a paper in a peer-reviewed serial allows an author to disseminate important research findings to the wider research community and beyond. It is important to recognize, however, that the content of many published papers may also have been discussed informally, reported on at conferences, or distributed as preprints.

- *Quality control*—Consistently applied editorial processes can help to ensure a high written standard of papers, but the main quality control process is the peer review of all submitted papers.
- *Establishing priority*—One of the most important functions of the printed serial, especially in the science, technology, and medicine (STM) disciplines, is to be able to establish priority over a particular discovery or advance.
- *The recognition of authors*—Authors value publication in refereed serials as a means of raising their profile and as a means of gaining further research contracts or promotion.
- *The creation of a public domain "archive"*—Once published, serial papers are in the public domain, and research libraries collectively act as a distributed "archive," preserving the knowledge embodied in them for future scholars.

These are the basic functions that need to be fulfilled by any new form of digitally based scholarly communication.

ELECTRONIC SERIALS

Since the late 1980s, both commercial and not-for-profit publishers (e.g., learned societies) have invested significant amounts of time and effort into the development of electronic serials. Early efforts included the CD-ROM-based experiment in document delivery undertaken by the ADONIS consortium. This was followed by initiatives such as the American Chemical Society's Chemical Journals Online (CJO) service and collaborative ventures with libraries such as the ELVYN project, which involved the Institute of Physics Publishing and a research team based at Loughborough University.[18] Another example of library-publisher cooperation was TULIP (The University Licensing Program), in which selected serials from the Elsevier Science group were delivered to participating U.S. research libraries in an attempt to investigate some of the technical, legal, and economic issues associated with e-serials and user behavior.[19]

It was, however, the emergence of the Internet as a mass medium that finally persuaded both commercial and learned society publishers that the development of electronic serials was a viable option. Publishers have started to distribute the content of their scholarly serials through the Internet. At the present time, probably for economic reasons, most publishers are using digital technologies in an essentially conservative way.[20] Most are creating Web-based services that give access to the content of already published printed serials rather than introducing new titles that implement digital-specific features such as embedded multimedia. Examples of these services include ScienceDirect from Elsevier Science, the IDEAL Online Library from Harcourt (including Academic Press), and Project MUSE from the Johns Hopkins University Press. Many publishers "bundle" collections of e-serials together and offer institutions (and their libraries) the ability to subscribe to their entire list as a single product.[21] Halliday and Oppenheim note that this helps publishers to spread production costs across the whole subscriber base and can help reduce the scope of license negotiations.[22] At the same time, the organizations that subscribe to serials are also beginning to join together in order to collectively negotiate licenses with publishers. Examples include OhioLINK (a consortium of Ohio libraries) and the U.K. National Electronic Site Licence Initiative (NESLI). NESLI, a consortium led by the University of Manchester and Swets Blackwell, negotiates deals with publishers on behalf of the whole U.K. higher education community and, where possible, incorporates a clause for ensuring long-term access.[23]

Some research libraries are beginning to support partnerships with learned society publishers in order to provide digital outlets for existing titles and help foster the publication of new electronic serials. For example, HighWire Press—a not-for-profit initiative of the Stanford University Libraries—gives access to a large number of serials published by learned societies. These include *Science, Proceedings of the National Academy of Sciences,* and *British Medical Journal (BMJ).* Another library-led initiative is SPARC (Scholarly Publishing and Academic Resources Coalition), a coalition supported by the Association of Research Libraries (ARL). This organization looks for partnerships with learned society publishers and seeks to underwrite new serials that might be able to provide competition for more established and expensive titles. The first new titles published by SPARC partners included *Organic Letters* (published by the American Chemical Society), *PhysChem Comm* (published by the Royal Society of Chemistry), and *Evolutionary Ecology Research.*[24]

It is important to realize that most commercial and learned society publishers have not yet moved to digital-only publication. Many tend to offer access to parallel digital versions of printed articles—usually in PDF (Portable Document Format)—and some bundle both printed and digital formats into the subscription price. On occasion, however, the digital version will offer more functionality than the printed version; e.g., Springer's LINK service includes some papers that contain supplementary material such as software, multimedia, or data sets that would not be available in either the printed or PDF versions. The Web sites of some serials also become a focus of more informal communication and sometimes provide space for news items, scholarly debates, information about relevant events, links to external Internet resources, etc. The Web sites of general scientific serials such as *Nature* and *Science* are good examples of this. It is important to recognize that the Web sites of serials themselves may also be good candidates for long-term preservation.

SELF-ARCHIVING INITIATIVES

At the same time as this mainly publisher-led activity has been unfolding, other actors in the scholarly communication chain have seen the potential for more wide-ranging changes in scholarly communication, often suggesting that printed serials have no long-term future.[25] Some scholars and librarians have begun to ask why the status quo in paper serials should simply duplicate itself in the Internet age.[26] People have begun to support "subversive proposals" suggesting that the authors of scholarly and scientific papers should simply make them available for free by storing (or archiving) copies on Internet sites.[27]

Proponents of the self-archiving idea argue from the premise that peer-reviewed serials form a peculiar type of publishing that has little in common with the payment- or royalty-based trade publishing sector. So, for example, Harnad and Hemus argue that the authors of scholarly and scientific papers are not primarily interested in monetary reward, but in having their work read, used, built upon, and cited.[28] In the print world, authors have to perpetuate what Harnad has called a "Faustian bargain," whereby they trade the copyright of works to publishers in exchange for having them printed and distributed. He argues that this type of bargain made sense when publishing remained an exclusive and expensive domain, but that it has little or no relevance in the Internet age when scholars and scientists can self-archive their own papers at little or no personal cost.[29] Authors, then, are being encouraged to deposit digital copies of their papers in centralized e-print services or in e-print archives based at their own institutions, thus making them freely available to fellow scholars and scientists. Furthermore, technologies have now been developed that would enable distributed e-print archives implemented in accordance with the standards developed as part of the OAI (Open Archives Initiative) to be combined into a single global virtual archive.[30] It is argued that once users prefer to access the free online copy of papers, publishers' revenues will decline and their role eventually will be reduced to the essential one of providing quality control: chiefly the implementation of peer review. This could then be paid for directly by authors' institutions out of savings on subscription costs.

The most frequently cited model of the first stages of the "subversive proposal" in action is the e-print archive first set up by Ginsparg at the Los Alamos National Laboratory in 1991.[31] This service originally gave access to digital preprints in the domain of high-energy physics, and it very quickly became the primary means of scholarly communication in this subject area. It has since expanded to cover other areas of physics, mathematics, and computer science. Physicist Steven B. Giddings was quoted in 1994 as saying that the service had completely changed the way people in his field exchanged information. He noted that the only time that he needed to look at published serials was to find articles that predated the Los Alamos physics databases.[32] The success of the Los Alamos e-print archive has led to the development of other Web-based e-print services. This has not been without controversy. For example, in 1999, the U.S. National Institutes of Health published a proposal for a service called PubMed Central that would give free online access to published material in the biomedical sciences.[33] The original proposal suggested the creation of two separate services: one that would publish papers with peer review from the editorial board of participating serials and a second one for non-peer-reviewed papers—essentially a form of e-print archive. The non-peer-reviewed section of the proposed service received considerable criticism, largely focused on the need for the strict evaluation of clinical research, because of potential adverse impacts on public health and medical practice.[34] Consequently, the PubMed Central system, when it was officially launched in January 2000, contained only the peer-reviewed part of the proposed service. Serials currently participating in PubMed Central include the *Proceedings of the National Academy of Sciences, Molecular Biology of the Cell,* and the *BMJ.*

To date, many scholars and scientists have been reluctant to commit themselves to self-archiving. Part of this is due to cultural differences between different subject areas. Valauskas, for example, notes how different the styles of communication and verification, debate and consensus can be among different academic disciplines.[35] It is rather simplistic to say that because self-archiving appears to be accepted by most physicists then it should also be adopted by biomedical researchers or historians. Another possible reason why self-archiving has failed to take off is that scholars and scientists have been reluctant to stop publishing in established high-impact serials. Some supporters of the author self-archiving approach argue that there remain "perverse incentives" for scholars to publish their papers in expensive serials.[36] For example, the market for scholarly serials can be skewed by the fact that the organizations that actually spend money on subscriptions tend not to be the ones who actually read or submit articles to serials. For these reasons, Harnad and his supporters do not suggest that authors should completely give up publishing in high-impact serials, but only that they simultaneously self-archive copies of the same papers either in a centralized e-print service or in their institution's own e-print archive. They argue that this in itself will be enough to trigger the inevitable change.

Following the launch of the PubMed Central service, some scholars and scientists stepped up their campaign for the creation of e-print archives of published papers. A number of scientists have appealed to serial publishers in the life sciences to cooperate with initiatives such as PubMed Central by making their content available to publicly accessible e-print archives some time after publication.[37] In order to help bring this about, a group known as the Public Library of Science has recently been inviting scholars to sign an open letter. Signatories pledge their intention only to publish in, undertake peer review for, and serve on the editorial boards of those serials that will make papers freely available six months after publication. This initiative moves far beyond a general support for author self-archiving initiatives. It is using authors to put pressure on the publishers of serials to "give away" content to publicly funded e-print initiatives. The Public Library of Science group argues that this will help to facilitate free access to the scientific literature and suggests that open e-print archives can continue the historical role of research libraries with regard to preservation. The open letter states that "the permanent, archival record of scientific research and ideas should neither be owned nor controlled by publishers, but should belong to the public, and should be freely available through an international online public library."[38] This is a laudable aim, but the letter does not address precisely how this digital archival record of research would be preserved and how the preservation process would be coordinated. This is a weakness with most self-archiving models, which sometimes appear to treat long-term digital preservation as a relatively simple technical problem,[39] probably because the supporters of self-archiving publishing models tend to be concerned more with the distribution of current content than with ensuring continuing access to the scholarly record.[40]

In any case, it is probably true to say that the digital distribution of scholarly and scientific papers through either e-serials or e-print archives will not fulfill all of the functions that have been fulfilled by printed serials. So, for example, while the digital distribution of papers is extremely good for fast and timely dissemination, the volatility of digital information means that it is not so good at fulfilling the functions of establishing priority and the long-term preservation of the scholarly record. Meadows has noted that establishing priority is often the "basic motivation"of scientists, and that many consider it to be much more important than being read or cited by their peers.[41] Establishing priority in a digital environment will depend upon the implementation of secure time-stamping and other authenticity mechanisms. This is just one aspect of a wider digital preservation problem that needs to be addressed by the publishers of e-serials, the organizers of centralized-print services such as PubMed Central, and by institution-based interoperable e-print archives.

DISTRIBUTION METHODS AND FORMATS IN USE

Electronic serials have been made available in a variety of different formats. The first e-serials used relatively simple formats including plain ASCII text or bit-mapped page images. ASCII was considered to be fine for articles that were composed largely of text, but was not thought adequate for the representation of the visual complexity of some scholarly literature. With this in mind, the early publisher-led ADONIS project, for example, scanned the paper copy of the serial and distributed the pages as bit-mapped images on CD-ROMs.[42]

The most difficult, and therefore expensive, types of serial to produce in any format are STM serials because they contain specialized terminology and frequently include detailed mathematical formulas, complex artwork, or tabular data.[43] For these reasons, networked STM serials often tend to use formats that retain the features of print serials. The most popular of these formats are PostScript and the proprietary PDF.[44] PDF is particularly good for use in situations where digital versions of printed serials are being made available online; the pages look the same as in the printed version. Many commercial publishers distribute parallel editions of printed serials in PDF, largely because the format is very easy to produce as a by-product of the publication process for print, but also because they can maintain complete control over the page layout of their digital publications.[45]

Widespread use of the Web as a distribution technology has meant that the other popular format currently used for the distribution of e-serials is the Hypertext Markup Language (HTML). E-serials often use HTML because they can take advantage of the hypertextual and multimedia features of Web publishing rather than just replicating the printed page. For example, the U.K. serial *Internet Archaeology* has published a paper on Roman amphorae that contains "clickable" maps and timelines.[46] Many e-serials that were originally distributed in ASCII form by electronic mailing list software are now also available in HTML on the Web. HTML is not always an ideal format for STM serials as it has limitations in encoding some special characters and relies on inline graphics or helper applications for the full display of illustrations.[47] Accordingly, HTML is often used to create an interface for the viewing of other formats. Many commercial e-serial providers give contents page information and abstracts in HTML while the full text of the articles are made available in PDF.

Naturally, there is an interest in other formats—especially those based on logical content mark-up, e.g., the Standard Generalized Markup Language (SGML) and the Extensible Markup Language (XML). Project ELVYN, for example, had first considered PostScript as a delivery format for the Institute of Physics Publishing's serial *Modelling and Simulation in Materials Science and Engineering*, but it was eventually delivered in an SGML-based format, which was then converted to HTML for viewing via a Web browser.[48] The Chemistry Online Retrieval Experiment (CORE), which gave access to American Chemical Society (ACS) serials, converted data from the native format used by the ACS to a variant of the SGML Document Type Definition (DTD) produced by the American Association of Publishers for their Electronic Manuscript Standard.[49] Articles sometimes exist in a format that can be converted into other formats for delivery to the end user. For example, a study undertaken for the NEDLIB (Networked European Deposit Library) project found that two-thirds of the publishers in a nonrandomly selected sample generated HTML "on the fly" from SGML- or XML-encoded text.[50] There is still a problem that logical content-based mark-up (unlike PostScript or PDF) is still not very good at representing mathematical or chemical information. In order to address these requirements, the World Wide Web Consortium (W3C) is developing a Mathematics Markup Language (MathML), and chemists have published an XML-based Chemical Markup Language (CML) for molecular information.[51]

Although PDF and HTML versions of articles often replicate the functionality and sometimes appearance of papers in printed serials, the form of articles that can be published in e-serials is not fixed. An electronic serial can be a dynamic document including embedded multimedia or active links to related publications or data. Electronic serials can also be regularly updated to take account of comments made by scholars in reviews or in other publications. Murray-Rust has argued that in chemistry the "static, immutable, noninteractive paper publication" is often unable to communicate the real message of an author and that a publication could also form a data resource for analysis or for input into programs or instruments.[52] Experiments with more "dynamic" types of e-serial include *Internet Archaeology* and the CLIC electronic journal project, both initially funded by the U.K. Electronic Libraries (eLib) program.[53] For example, the CLIC project attempted to develop ways in which users could acquire three-dimensional molecular data in digital form through electronic serials that could act as a starting point for their own exploration of the content.[54] These new publication models will present a severe challenge for preservation. As some of the CLIC researchers have asked, how long should any given data be expected to reside in automatically accessible form on the Internet?[55] Also, can these data be preserved in such a way that they can be retrieved in the future without also using the specialized software tools that have been developed to process them? These are the types of issues that will have to be considered by those who have responsibility for the long-term preservation of e-serials.

E-SERIALS AND DIGITAL PRESERVATION

The root of the digital preservation problem is technological, but any proposed solution also needs to take account of organizational and economic issues. The following sections introduce the main technological problems with the long-term preservation of information in digital form, delineate some possible preservation strategies, and then outline some of the nontechnological issues.

Technological Preservation Issues

Almost all kinds of digital information need to be interpreted by machines before they can become intelligible to humans. Preservation problems are associated with three distinct aspects of digital information technologies: the medium upon which digital information is recorded and its associated hardware and software.

Media Longevity

Digital information is mostly stored on either magnetic or optical media types. Both have relatively short lifetimes in comparison with more established media such as paper and microfilm. Hedstom argues that the preservation threat posed by magnetic and optical media is "qualitatively different" in that the media are easily reusable and in the fact that they deteriorate in a matter of years, not decades.[56] One immediate technological response to this problem is known as "refreshing"—the periodic recopying of the data bits onto a new medium. The focus of digital preservation has in recent years moved away from media longevity issues, not because the problems have been solved to any great extent, but because there is a greater awareness of the significant technological problems associated with hardware and software obsolescence.

Hardware Obsolescence and Software Dependence

Mallinson noted back in 1987 that one of the most serious problems with preserving electronic information was the rapid obsolescence of electronic hardware.[57] Brichford and Maher sum up this problem when they say that a "twenty-year life for the plastic backing material used for computer tapes and disks is irrelevant if the tape or disk drives on which they were recorded become obsolete and unavailable after ten years."[58] In addition, digital information is often stored in formats that are dependent upon particular software to interpret them correctly. This is known as software dependence.

Digital Preservation Strategies

It is now becoming clear that the successful long-term preservation of digital information will depend upon relevant organizations identifying and implementing suitable preservation strategies.[59] At present, there are three main technical options: technology preservation, software emulation, and data migration.

None of these options provide a perfect solution for all types of digital resources and, as Ross notes, selecting any one strategy will require trade-offs to be made.[60]

Technology preservation is the preservation of an information object together with all of the hardware and software needed to interpret it. This approach has its supporters and may have an important short-term role for the recovery of data from obsolete storage media and platforms, but it is unlikely to become a viable long-term strategy.[61] Feeney points out that collection managers who relied only upon this approach would soon end up with "a museum of ageing and incompatible computer hardware."[62] As a result, the other proposed strategies for digital preservation are not concerned with the preservation of physical artifacts (hardware, media, etc.), but concentrate instead upon the preservation of the information objects themselves in some disembodied digital form.[63] Both emulation and migration strategies are examples of this general approach.

Emulation strategies are based on the premise that the best way to preserve the functionality and "look and feel" of digital resources would be to preserve the original software and then to run this on emulators that would mimic the behavior of the obsolete hardware and operating systems.[64] Emulation-based preservation strategies require the encapsulation of a digital data object (a byte stream) together with the application software used to create or interpret it and a description of the required hardware environment that could be used as a specification for an emulator. While preservation strategies based exclusively on emulation may be promising for helping to preserve the look and feel of complex objects—e.g., interactive molecular diagrams—they are also likely to be very complicated and could be expensive to implement.[65] It is likely, however, that the targeting of key platforms for emulation might allow a large number of digital objects to be preserved in a very cost-effective manner. In practice, emulation is most likely to work as one part of a broader preservation strategy that would also include some use of migration techniques.

Migration strategies are more tried and tested, and mean the periodic transfer of digital information from one generation of computer technology to a subsequent one.[66] The point of migration is to transfer to new formats while, wherever possible, preserving the integrity of the information. The simplest migration strategies involve transfer into a standardized format that is relatively software independent, e.g., plain ASCII text. Care must be taken with this approach. For example, ASCII might be an adequate format for e-serials consisting only of textual information, but its use would result in a considerable loss of functionality for most STM-based electronic serials or those publications that have tried to incorporate more dynamic features. A related strategy would be to migrate resources to a small number of "standard" formats on their ingestion into a digital repository. For e-serials, these formats could include, for example, HTML, PDF, or documents structured in SGML or XML together with their associated DTDs. This strategy would simplify future migration processes while helping to maintain some of the important characteristics of the original.[67] However, as Ross points out, data migration inevitably leads to some losses in functionality, accuracy, integrity, and usability.[68] Successful migration strategies will, therefore, depend upon metadata being created to record the migration history of a digital object and to record contextual information so that future users can either reconstruct or, at the very least, begin to understand the technological environment in which a particular digital object was created. In general, e-serials would be good candidates for migration strategies, except when they contain significant amounts of multimedia.

One publisher of e-serials has already announced a migration-based plan for the long-term preservation of its own Web-based titles. In February 2000, HighWire Press described how content supplied from publishers would be migrated to industry-standard formats and then stored on robust disk arrays in multiple locations.[69] These would then be migrated as necessary. Together with Sun Microsystems, Stanford University Libraries are also involved in the LOCKSS (Lots of Copies Keep Stuff Safe) program.[70] This involves the development of open-source software that would enable the content of e-serials to be cached on a large number of distributed sites. The LOCKSS system then automatically and continuously monitors these distributed caches and repairs files when it finds that their content has been damaged or removed.

Preservation Metadata

Recent developments have suggested that, regardless of which particular digital preservation strategy is chosen, the successful long-term preservation of digital resources will depend upon the creation and maintenance of metadata that will be able to record some part of a digital object's functionality and context.[71] Lynch states that, within a digital repository, "metadata accompanies and makes reference to each digital object and provides associated descriptive, structural, administrative, rights management, and other kinds of information."[72]

Much of the current focus on preservation metadata has been centered on the *Reference Model for an Open Archival Information System* (OAIS) being developed by the Consultative Committee for

Space Data Systems (CCSDS) on behalf of the International Organization for Standardization (ISO).[73] The OAIS model defines a range of functions that are applicable to any archive, whether digital or not. These functions include ingest, archival storage, data management, administration, and access. Among other things, the OAIS model aims to provide a common framework that can be used to help understand archival challenges and especially those that relate to digital information. Accordingly, the OAIS model identifies and distinguishes between the various types of metadata that will need to be recorded by a digital repository. Several digital library projects have begun to use the OAIS model as a means of helping to define digital preservation systems and their associated metadata. These include NEDLIB, which has developed a model for a deposit system for electronic publications (DSEP),[74] and the U.K. Cedars (CURL Exemplars in Digital Archives) project.[75]

Nontechnological Preservation Issues

Despite their apparent intractability, technological problems are probably not the most important factor in the preservation of e-serials. Strategies can be implemented if the need for preservation is noticed early enough. The following sections introduce some of the most important nontechnological issues that also need to be addressed to ensure the long-term preservation of scholarly information published in e-serials.

Authenticity and Intellectual Preservation

Perhaps the most important preservation requirement for scholarly communication in digital form is for its integrity to be guaranteed. In comparison with printed information, online digital information is relatively easy to change and update. Indeed, this is one of its major advantages over printed information. However, with preservation in mind, this characteristic becomes a potential problem. It is very difficult to prove that digital information has not been accidentally or deliberately corrupted at some time. It is also very difficult to know exactly when a particular version of a paper was published. This has implications for the integrity of the scholarly record and for the retrospective establishment of priority over particular discoveries or advances. In the digital world there is scope to frequently update scholarly and scientific papers to take account of new data, more recent research, and the comments of other scholars. For some, this is one of the major advantages of digital publication but, as Lynch notes, this is "culturally opposed to the view of the scholarly record as comprising a series of discrete, permanently fixed contributions of readily attributable authorship."[76]

In short, the users of e-serials will want to be sure that the version of the paper that they are referring to is the one that they intend to consult and that it has not been deliberately or accidentally corrupted since its original publication date. With relation to electronic serials, authenticity could be promoted by the adoption of techniques based on cryptographic theory. Graham has suggested utilizing technologies such as digital time-stamping (DTS), which uses one-way cryptographic hashing techniques,[77] but recognizes that there are likely to be other solutions.[78]

The importance of intellectual preservation for the future of scholarly communication cannot be overemphasized. Without some enduring way of ensuring the authenticity of digital documents over time, it is possible that networks will ultimately be unable to support some of the basic requirements of scholarly communication.

Licensing and Intellectual Property Rights

The growth in provision and use of digital information resources (including e-serials published by commercial or learned society publishers) has resulted in fundamental changes in the way information is owned. The information content of printed serials has been usually purchased outright by subscription, either directly from the publishers or through subscription agents. The organization or individual that purchases a serial will then normally retain physical custody of the artifact (a volume or issue) for as long as it is required. Assuming that this artifact is kept in an appropriate environment and safeguarded against disaster (e.g., fire and flood), it should last for a long time. Given the fact that printed serials are normally subscribed to by more than one organization, a distributed "canonical archive" of scholarly serials is built up in this way. Long-term preservation and access is essentially a by-product of this process and does not require specific initiation.

The situation of digital information resources is quite different. The "purchaser" of a digital resource such as an e-serial (unless it is a physical artifact, e.g., a CD-ROM) does not necessarily retain "physical custody" over it. Concerns over copyright mean that commercial publishers tend to license the use of information to customers, thus ensuring that contract law rather than copyright law governs the use of the information.[79] A license for a commercial electronic serial would normally give a "subscriber" specific rights over the use of a particular serial, or group of serials, only for a limited amount of time. This is where the position becomes problematic. What happens when the subscribing institution decides to cancel its subscription? Would all access rights to that serial, including those back issues already "paid for," then be removed? What would happen if the serial itself is no longer published or if the publisher is taken over or ceases trading? Research organizations and libraries might then find that they have no direct control over which particular e-serials can be preserved as part of the "canonical archive" of scholarly communication. Because most licenses are time limited, Okerson has argued that they are a flexible way of ensuring that libraries' concerns about ongoing access can be addressed in the agreements negotiated between libraries and publishers.[80] However, if publishers commit to providing continued access to serial back issues after termination of the license, this may have cost implications for the publisher.[81] It is possible that some digital publications will disappear before all licensing problems are resolved.

Responsibility for Preservation

Borgman has written that scholars, as both authors and readers, "expect access to publications long after the documents' authors are dead, the serials in which they appeared have ceased to be published, or the publishers have been acquired by an international conglomerate or otherwise ceased to exist."[82] In the print world, the task of preserving the published scholarly record has historically fallen to research libraries. In a world of e-serials and e-print archive services it is by no means clear that libraries will have exactly the same role. Who, then, should be responsible for preserving the scholarly record in digital form?

Several different answers are possible. Some, including the CPA/ RLG task force, argued for a decentralized approach. The task force report suggests that digital information creators, providers, and owners should have the initial responsibility for archiving, while certified digital archives would be given the legal rights and duties to exercise an aggressive fail-safe rescue function.[83] For serials, this suggests that the responsibility for the preservation of the scholarly record would lie initially with the publishers of e-serials or with the providers of institutional e-print archives.

In the short term, some commercial and learned society publishers might welcome a decentralized approach because they would have a commercial interest in controlling user access to the content of e-serials. In this scenario, publishers would maintain and migrate the digital versions of papers themselves until such time as the serial is no longer of economic value.[84] So, for example, the storage hardware might need to be periodically upgraded, sometimes delivery formats would change, but the serial itself need never go "out of print." The most critical time will come when the publishers no longer have any economic interest in keeping a serial going, or when the publisher is taken over or otherwise ceases trading. It is at this point that some kind of fail-safe mechanism would need to be activated. This type of approach, inevitably, would include a level of risk and would require good leadership and coordination from information professionals.[85] There is evidence to suggest that some publishers are aware of their preservation responsibilities and are sensitive to libraries' concerns.[86] Elsevier Science, for example, declares in licenses its intention to maintain the digital files of ScienceDirect in perpetuity, and commits itself to transferring them to another depository if it is unable to do so.[87]

A second and more traditional approach would be to adapt the more centralized models that have been used to maintain the existing printed scholarly record. Under this model, national libraries and some of the larger research libraries store and maintain large collections of printed serials. In order to perpetuate this system, many national libraries use some kind of legal deposit legislation to ensure that all relevant published works are collected and preserved. A few countries have successfully extended legal deposit legislation to cover digital publications, but this does not always include online publications such as e-serials. This situation, however, is slowly changing. For example, the report of a recent U.K. Working Party on Legal Deposit recommended that e-serials that have additional information content beyond the print original and those that are available only in digital form should be considered as suitable candidates for future legal deposit legislation.[88]

The products of self-archiving initiatives offer some different challenges. In the same way as serial publishers, centralized services such as the Los Alamos e-print archive or PubMed Central definitely do have an interest in maintaining access to the papers that are stored on their systems.[89] Some advocates of self-archiving go further. One of the Public Library of Science group's justifications for insisting that publishers transfer digital copies of papers to services such as PubMed Central after six months is that such services will be able to continue the preservation role traditionally undertaken by research libraries. Little thought appears to have been taken about the long-term implications of this. Addeane S. Calleigh, the editor of *Academic Medicine,* has argued that many of those who have called for services such as PubMed Central have "not recognized the expertise and long-term difficulty of assuming the role previously played by libraries as the science community's archivists."[90] The position is even more problematic when authors self-archive papers only on institutional e-print servers. The institutions that host such services will somehow need to be made aware that they have the primary responsibility for the long-term preservation of all papers stored in the service. It is far from clear at the moment how this could be coordinated.

In practice, the system that is most likely to evolve will be neither completely centralized nor decentralized. Preservation in the short term will probably become part of the responsibility of publishers or of some centralized e-print services, as well as becoming part of the continuing role of some national and research libraries. New types of third-party services may also develop, and Anderson has suggested that librarians should attempt to shape their development.[91] One danger is that some players in the scholarly communication process may just assume that existing libraries will be able to continue to preserve scholarly communication without first ensuring that they have the necessary technical, legal, and financial means to do so. Another possible problem is that many preservation decisions might be made with regard to short-term commercial interests rather than in the wider public interest.[92] There is a need to make all participants in the scholarly communication process more aware of digital preservation issues. In addition, there is a need for effective cooperation between publishers, libraries, and all of the other stakeholders in the scholarly communication process. Boyce says that all of these will have to work together in order to preserve access to digital information.[93] Organizations such as the Digital Library Federation (DLF) and the Council for Library and Information Resources (CLIR) in the United States and the U.K. Digital Preservation Coalition may have a role in helping to foster this cooperation.[94]

One significant recent effort has been the development of the Andrew W. Mellon Foundation's e-journal archiving program. The foundation is funding several major U.S. libraries to undertake the development of practical e-journal repositories that meet specific requirements identified by the DLF together with CLIR and the Coalition for Networked Information (CNI). While some of the participating libraries are concentrating on the development of tools or solutions for dynamic serials, Yale, Harvard, and the University of Pennsylvania have chosen to work with individual publishers. For example, Yale University Library has announced that it will collaborate with Elsevier to create a digital repository for all of the serials published by Elsevier Science.[95] These types of initiatives provide models for publisher and library cooperation, as well as offering the opportunity for some practical experiences with digital preservation.

Selection for Preservation

Deciding what needs to be preserved could be another problem. As digital storage devices become cheaper and more compact, the temptation may be to suggest that everything should be kept. Little is known about the economics of digital preservation over a long period of time, but both emulation and migration strategies are likely to be expensive in terms of both time and technical expertise. In normal circumstances, some kind of selection before preservation will be necessary.

For scholarly electronic serials, this process may be made easier by the reliability mechanisms that already exist, such as peer review. Peer-reviewed serials would be obvious candidates for preservation, as would less formal, newsletter-type publications issued by learned societies and other organizations. However, it may be harder to assess articles "published" in e-print services. The nature of digital information also means that any such appraisal would have to take place very early in its life cycle. It will not be useful to wait until the information has become unavailable before deciding on preservation; no copies may remain in existence to be preserved. Instead, the identification of suitable resources for preservation should be made close to their issue or publication dates, and rights for their long-term preservation should also should be negotiated at the same time. In addition, it may be useful in some circumstances if selection and appraisal become continuous processes.

Another problem is that there is no clear idea as to which particular file format should be seen as the definitive version for preservation. Many e-serial publishers have created SGML-based files that are used to generate PDF or HTML versions for delivery over the Web. Which one of these formats should be preserved? Also, where printed versions also exist, should these be kept as well? What about those papers that include embedded multimedia, software, and data sets, or contain hyperlinks to other documents, or are otherwise dynamic? What preservation strategies should be adopted for these types of information? Decisions on these issues will have to be made on a title-by-title or, possibly, a paper-by-paper basis.

CONCLUSION

This chapter has attempted to outline some of the problems that need to be confronted to ensure the continued existence and accessibility of the information content published in scholarly e-serials. Other important issues have not been discussed here, most notably the likely economic implications of long-term digital preservation. Librarians, publishers, archivists, computer scientists, and others with an interest in digital preservation are currently investigating many of these issues. It is important to realize that many of the problems will only be solved with the practical experience of ensuring the preservation of digital information, and with practical cooperation between publishers, libraries, scholars, and other stakeholders in scholarly communication.

One more point needs to be considered. In the past, the preservation of the canonical archive of scholarly communication was considered a specialist activity within the library and information professions. With the advent of digitally based scholarly communication, digital preservation might become one of the basic functions of the digital research library. Indeed, all other digital library activities, including resource discovery and access, may ultimately become dependent upon interested parties solving the digital preservation conundrum.

NOTES

1. F. W. Lancaster, *Toward Paperless Information Systems* (New York: Academic Press, 1978).

2. Donald Waters and John Garrett, eds., *Preserving Digital Information: Report of the Task Force on Archiving of Digital Information* (Washington, DC: Commission on Preservation and Access, 1996), <http://www.rlg.org/ArchTF/> (viewed May 14, 2001).

3. Michael Alexander, "Virtual Stacks: Storing and Using Electronic Journals," *Serials* 10(2) (1997): 173-178.

4. Peter Leggate and Mike Hannant, "The Archiving of Online Journals," *Learned Publishing* 13(4) (2000): 246-250.

5. John Feather, *Preservation and the Management of Library Collections* (London: Library Association Publishing, 1991), 2.

6. Margaret Hedstrom, "Digital Preservation: A Time Bomb for Digital Libraries," *Computers and the Humanities* 31 (1998): 189-202.

7. Charles M. Dollar, *Archival Theory and Information Technologies: The Impact of Information Technologies on Archival Principles and Methods* (Ancona, Italy: University of Macerata, 1992), 66.

8. David Bearman, *Archival Methods*, Archives and Museum Informatics Technical Report, 3(1) (Pittsburgh, PA: Archives and Museum Informatics, 1989), 17-27.

9. Maurice B. Line, "The Publication and Availability of Scientific and Technical Papers: An Analysis of Requirements and the Suitability of Different Means of Meeting Them," *Journal of Documentation* 48(2) (1992): 201-219.

10. Andrew M. Odlyzko, "Tragic Loss or Good Riddance? The Impending Demise of Traditional Scholarly Journals," *International Journal of Human-Computer Studies* 42 (1995): 71-122.

11. Fytton Rowland, "Who Will Buy My Bells and Whistles? The True Needs of Users of Electronic Journals," *Serials* 13(2) (2000): 73-77.

12. Dennis P. Carrigan, "Research Libraries Evolving Response to the 'Serials Crisis,'" *Scholarly Publishing* 23(3) (1992): 138-151.

13. Michael Buckingham, "Where Is the Revolution?" *Nature* 311 (September 27, 1984): 309-310.

14. Brian Shackel, *BLEND-9: Overview and Appraisal*, British Library Research Paper, 82 (London: British Library, 1991).

15. Fytton Rowland, Cliff McKnight, Jack Meadows, and Peter Such, "ELVYN: The Delivery of an Electronic Version of a Journal from the Publisher to Libraries," *Journal of the American Society for Information Science* 47(9) (1996): 690-700.

16. Cliff McKnight, *Electronic Journals: What Do Users Think of Them?* Paper presented at ISDL '97: International Symposium on Research, Development and Practice in Digital Libraries 1997, Tsukuba, Ibaraki, Japan, November 18-21, 1997, <http://www.dl.ulis.ac.jp/ISDL97/proceedings/mcknight.html> (viewed May 14, 2001).

17. Fytton Rowland, "Print Journals: Fit for the Future?" *Ariadne* 7 (January 1997): 6-7, <http://www.ariadne.ac.uk/issue7/fytton/> (viewed May 14, 2001).

18. Fytton Rowland, Cliff McKnight, and Jack Meadows, eds., *Project ELVYN: An Experiment in Electronic Journal Delivery* (London: Bowker-Saur, 1995).

19. Clifford Lynch, "The TULIP Project: Context, History and Perspective," *Library Hi Tech* 13(4) (1995): 8-24.

20. Charles Oppenheim, Clare Greenhalgh, and Fytton Rowland, "The Future of Scholarly Journal Publishing," *Journal of Documentation* 56(4) (2000): 361-398.

21. Kenneth Frazier, "The Librarians' Dilemma: Contemplating the Costs of the 'Big Deal,'" *D-Lib Magazine* 7(3) (March 2001), <http://www.dlib.org/dlib/march 01/frazier/03frazier.html> (viewed May 14, 2001).

22. Leah Halliday and Charles Oppenheim, "Developments in Digital Journals," *Journal of Documentation* 5(2) (2001): 260-283.

23. Robert Bley, "NESLI: A Successful National Consortium," *Library Consortium Management: An International Journal* 2(1) (2000): 18-28.

24. Sarah C. Michalak, "The Evolution of SPARC," *Serials Review* 26(1) (2000): 10-21.

25. Ronald E. LaPorte, Eric Marler, Shunichi Akazawa, Francois Sauer, Carlos Gamboa, Chris Shenton, Caryle Glosser, Anthony Villasenor, and Malcolm Maclure, "The Death of Biomedical Journals," *BMJ* 310 (May 27, 1995): 1387-1390.

26. Stevan Harnad and Matt Hemus, "All or None: No Stable Hybrid or Half-Way Solutions for Launching the Learned Periodical Literature into the Post-Gutenberg Galaxy," in *The Impact of Electronic Publishing on the Academic Community*, ed. Ian Butterworth (London: Portland Press, 1998), <http://tiepac.portland press.co.uk/books/online/tiepac/session1/ch5.htm> (viewed May 14, 2001).

27. Ann Okerson and James O'Donnell, eds., *Scholarly Journals at the Crossroads: A Subversive Proposal for Electronic Publishing* (Washington, DC: Association of Research Libraries, 1995), <http://www.arl.org/scomm/subversive/index.html> (viewed May 14, 2001).

28. Harnad and Hemus, "All or None."

29. Stevan Harnad and Jessie Hey, "Esoteric Knowledge: The Scholar and Scholarly Publishing on the Net," in *Networking and the Future of Libraries 2: Managing the Intellectual Record*, eds. Lorcan Dempsey, Derek Law, and Ian Mowat (London: Library Association Publishing, 1995), 110-116.

30. Stevan Harnad, "The Self-Archiving Initiative," *Nature* 410 (April 26, 2001): 1024-1025.

31. Paul Ginsparg, "First Steps Towards Electronic Research Communication," *Computers in Physics* 8(4) (1994): 390-396.

32. Steven B. Giddings, quoted in Gary Stix, "The Speed of Write," *Scientific American* 271(6) (December 1994): 72-77.

33. Harold Varmus, *PubMed Central: An NIH-Operated Site for Electronic Distribution of Life Sciences Research Reports* (Bethesda, MD: National Institutes of Health, August 30, 1999), <http://www.nih.gov/welcome/director/pubmedcentral/pubmedcentral.htm> (viewed May 14, 2001).

34. Arnold S. Relman, "The NIH 'E-biomed' Proposal—A Potential Threat to the Evaluation and Orderly Dissemination of New Clinical Studies," *New England Journal of Medicine* 340(23) (June 10, 1999): 1828-1829.

35. Edward J. Valauskas, "Waiting for Thomas Kuhn: First Monday and the Evolution of Electronic Journals," *First Monday* 2(12) (December 1997), <http://www.firstmonday.dk/issues/issue2_12/valauskas/> (viewed May 14, 2001).

36. Andrew Odlyzko, "The Economics of Electronic Journals," *First Monday* 2(8) (August 1997), <http://www.firstmonday.dk/issues/issue2_8/odlyzko/> (viewed May 14, 2001).

37. Richard J. Roberts, Harold E. Varmus, Michael Ashburner, Patrick O. Brown, Michael B. Eisen, Chaitan Khosla, Marc Kirchner, Roel Nusse, Matthew Scott, and Barbara Wold, "Building a 'GenBank' of the Published Literature," *Science* 291 (March 23, 2001): 2318-2319.

38. "Public Library of Science," <http://www.publiclibraryofscience.org/> (viewed May 14, 2001).

39. Stevan Harnad, "On-Line Journals and Financial Fire Walls," *Nature* 395 (September 10, 1998): 127-128.

40. Christine L. Borgman, *From Gutenberg to the Global Information Infrastructure: Access to Information in the Networked World* (Cambridge, MA: MIT Press, 2000), 91.

41. Jack Meadows, "Scholarly Communication and the Serial," in *Scholarly Communication and Serials Prices*, ed. Karen Brookfield (London: Bowker-Saur, 1991), 5-14.

42. Barrie T. Stern and Henk C. J. Compier, "ADONIS: Document Delivery in the CD-ROM Age," *Interlending and Document Supply* 18(3) (1990): 79-87.

43. Steve Hitchcock, Leslie Carr, and Wendy Hall, "A Survey of STM Online Journals, 1990-95: The Calm Before the Storm," in *ARL Directory of Electronic Journals, Newsletters and Academic Discussion Lists*, Sixth Edition (Washington, DC: Association of Research Libraries, 1996), 7-32, <http://journals.ecs.soton.ac.uk/survey/survey.html> (viewed May 14, 2001).

44. Judith Wusteman, "Electronic Journal Formats," *Program* 30(4) (1996): 319-343.

45. Mark Bide and Associates, *Standards for Electronic Publishing: An Overview*, NEDLIB Report Series, 3 (The Hague: Koninklijke Bibliotheek, 2000), 7.

46. Paul Tyers, "Roman Amphoras in Britain," *Internet Archaeology* 1 (1996), <http://intarch.ac.uk/journal/issue1/tyers_index.html> (viewed May 14, 2001).

47. Richard Entlich, Lorrin Garson, Michael Lesk, Lorraine Normore, Jan Olsen, and Stuart Weibel, "Testing a Digital Library: User Response to the CORE Project," *Library Hi Tech* 14(4) (1996): 99-118.

48. Cliff McKnight, Jack Meadows, David Pullinger, and Fytton Rowland, *ELVYN: Publisher and Library Working Towards the Electronic Distribution and Use of Journals*. Paper presented at Digital Libraries '94: The First Annual Conference on the Theory and Practice of Digital Libraries, College Station, Texas. June 19-21, 1994, <http://csdl.tamu.edu/DL94/paper/mcknight.html> (viewed May 14, 2001).

49. Michael E. Lesk, "Electronic Chemical Journals," *Analytical Chemistry* 66(14) (1994): 747A-755A.

50. Mark Bide and Associates, *Standards for Electronic Publishing*, 17.

51. Peter Murray-Rust and Henry S. Rzepa, "Chemical Markup, XML, and the Worldwide Web: 1. Basic Principles," *Journal of Chemical Information and Computer Sciences* 39(6) (1999): 928-942.

52. Peter Murray-Rust, "The Globalization of Crystallographic Knowledge," *Acta Crystallographica* D54 (1998): 1065-1070.

53. CLIC is an acronym made up from the four organizations involved in the project: the Royal Society of Chemistry; the University of Leeds; Imperial College of Science, Technology and Medicine, London; and the University of Cambridge.

54. David James, Benjamin J. Whitaker, Christopher Hildyard, Henry S. Rzepa, Omer Casher, Jonathan M. Goodman, David Riddick, and Peter Murray-Rust, "The Case for Content Integrity in Electronic Chemistry Journals: The CLIC Project," *New Review of Information Networking* 1 (1995): 61-69.

55. Omer Casher, Gudge K. Chandramohan, Martin J. Hargreaves, Christopher Leach, Peter Murray-Rust, Henry S. Rzepa, Roger Sayle, and Benjamin J. Whitaker, "Hyperactive Molecules and the World-Wide-Web Information System," *Journal of the Chemical Society: Perkin Transactions* 2(1) (January 1995): 7-11.

56. Margaret Hedstrom, "Preserving the Intellectual Record: A View from the Archives," in *Networking and the Future of Libraries 2: Managing the Intellectual Record*, ed. Lorcan Dempsey, Derek Law, and Ian Mowat (London: Library Association Publishing, 1995), 180.

57. John C. Mallinson, "On the Preservation of Human- and Machine-Readable Records," *Information Technology and Libraries* 7 (1988): 19-23.

58. Maynard Brichford and William Maher, "Archival Issues in Network Electronic Publications," *Library Trends* 43(4) (1995): 701-712.

59. Neil Beagrie and Daniel Greenstein, *A Strategic Policy Framework for Creating and Preserving Digital Collections* (London: South Bank University, Library Information Technology Centre, 1998), <http://www.ukoln.ac.uk/services/papers/bl/framework/framework.html> (viewed May 14, 2001).

60. Seamus Ross, "Consensus, Communication and Collaboration: Fostering Multidisciplinary Cooperation in Electronic Records," in *Proceedings of the DLM-*

Forum on Electronic Records, Brussels, 18-20 December 1996 (Luxembourg: Office for Official Publications of the European Communities, 1997), 330-336.

61. Seamus Ross and Ann Gow, *Digital Archaeology: Rescuing Neglected and Damaged Data Resources* (London: South Bank University, Library Information Technology Centre, 1999).

62. Mary Feeney, ed., *Digital Culture: Maximizing the Nation's Investment* (London: National Preservation Office, 1999), 42.

63. Cliff Lynch, "Canonicalization: A Fundamental Tool to Facilitate Preservation and Management of Digital Information," *D-Lib Magazine* 5(9) (September 1999), <http://www.dlib.org/dlib/september99/09lynch.html> (viewed May 14, 2001).

64. Jeff Rothenberg, *Avoiding Technological Quicksand: Finding a Viable Technical Foundation for Digital Preservation* (Washington, DC: Council on Library and Information Resources, 1999), <http://www.clir.org/pubs/abstract/pub77.html> (viewed May 14, 2001).

65. David Bearman, "Reality and Chimeras in the Preservation of Electronic Records," *D-Lib Magazine* 5(4) (April 1999), <http://www.dlib.org/dlib/april99/bearman/04bearman.html> (viewed May 14, 2001).

66. Waters and Garrett, *Preserving Digital Information*, 6.

67. Hedstrom, "Preserving the Intellectual Record," 185.

68. Ross, "Consensus, Communication and Collaboration," 331.

69. Stanford University Libraries, *HighWire Press Ensures That Online Publications Don't Get Lost in Cyberspace* (Stanford, CA: Stanford University, February 4, 2000), <http://www.stanford.edu/dept/news/pr/00/000204highwire.html> (viewed May 14, 2001).

70. Vicky Reich and David S. H. Rosenthal, "LOCKSS (Lots of Copies Keep Stuff Safe)," *New Review of Academic Librarianship* 6 (2000): 155-161.

71. Michael Day, "Issues and Approaches to Preservation Metadata," in *Guidelines for Digital Imaging* (London: National Preservation Office, 1999), 73-84, <http://www.rlg.org/preserv/joint/day.html> (viewed May 14, 2001).

72. Lynch, "Canonicalization."

73. Consultative Committee for Space Data Systems, *Reference Model for an Open Archival Information System (OAIS)*, CCSDS 650.0-R-1 (1999), <http://ssdoo.gsfc.nasa.gov/nost/isoas/ref_model.html> (viewed May 14, 2001).

74. Titia van der Werf, *The Deposit System for Electronic Publications: A Process Model*, NEDLIB Report Series, 6 (The Hague: Koninklijke Bibliotheek, 2000).

75. Kelly Russell, Derek Sergeant, Andy Stone, Ellis Weinberger, and Michael Day, *Metadata for Digital Preservation: The Cedars Project Outline Specification* (Leeds: Cedars Project, 2000), <http://www.leeds.ac.uk/cedars/metadata.html> (viewed May 14, 2001).

76. Clifford A. Lynch, "Integrity Issues in Electronic Publishing," in *Scholarly Publishing: The Electronic Frontier*, ed. Robin P. Peek and Gregory B. Newby (Cambridge, MA: MIT Press, 1996), 133-145.

77. Hashing techniques use algorithms that convert the arrangement of all characters, symbols, graphics, etc., within a particular document into a unique hash value that can be stored and retrieved as metadata. Any change (however small) to the document will produce a different hash value when it is converted using the

same algorithm. The process is described as "one-way" because there is no means of recreating the original document from its hash value.

78. Peter S. Graham, "Long-Term Intellectual Preservation," in *Digital Imaging Technology for Preservation*, ed. Nancy E. Elkington (Mountain View, CA: Research Libraries Group, 1994), 41-57.

79. Ann Okerson, "What Academic Libraries Need in Electronic Content Licenses," *Serials Review* 22(4) (1996): 65-69.

80. Ann Okerson, "Copyright in the Year 2010: No Longer an Issue for Scholarly Electronic Publishing," *Serials Review* 25(4) (1999): 33-35.

81. Sally Morris, "Archiving Electronic Publications: What Are the Problems and Who Should Solve Them?" *Serials Review* 26(3) (2000): 64-68.

82. Christine L. Borgman, "Digital Libraries and the Continuum of Scholarly Communication," *Journal of Documentation* 56(4) (2000): 412-430.

83. Waters and Garrett, *Preserving Digital Information*, 21.

84. Morris, "Archiving Electronic Publications," 67.

85. Margaret Hedstrom, "Electronic Archives: Integrity and Access in the Network Environment," in *Networking in the Humanities*, ed. Stephanie Kenna and Seamus Ross (London: Bowker-Saur, 1995), 77-95.

86. Ellen Finnie Duranceau, "Archiving and Perpetual Access for Web-Based Journals: A Look at the Issues and How Five E-Journal Providers Are Addressing Them," *Serials Review* 24(2) (1998): 110-115.

87. Karen Hunter, "Digital Archiving," *Serials Review* 2(3) (2000): 62-64.

88. Geoff Smith, "The Legal Deposit of Non-Print Publications: The 1998 Working Party on Legal Deposit," *Serials* 12(2) (1999): 125-129.

89. Richard E. Luce, "E-Prints Intersect the Digital Library: Inside the Los Alamos arXiv," *Issues in Science and Technology Librarianship* 29 (winter 2001), <http://www.library.ucsb.edu/istl/01-winter/article3.html> (viewed May 14, 2001).

90. Addeane S. Caelleigh, "PubMed Central and the New Publishing Landscape: Shifts and Tradeoffs," *Academic Medicine* 75(1) (2000): 4-10.

91. Rick Anderson, "Is the Digital Archive a New Beast Entirely?" *Serials Review* 26(3) (2000): 50-52.

92. David Haynes and David Streatfield, "Who Will Preserve Electronic Publications?" *Serials* 10(3) (1997): 345-351.

93. Peter B. Boyce, "Who Will Keep the Archives? Wrong Question!" *Serials Review* 26(3) (2000): 52-55.

94. Neil Beagrie, "The JISC Digital Preservation Focus and the Digital Preservation Coalition," *New Review of Academic Librarianship* 6 (2000): 257-267.

95. Yale University Library, *Yale Library to Plan Digital Archives with Elsevier Science* (New Haven, CT: Yale University Library, February 23, 2001), <http://www.library.yale.edu/Administration/newsreleases/elsevier_release.html> (viewed May 14, 2001).

PROJECTS AND INNOVATIONS

Chapter 12

Interactive Peer Review in the *Journal of Interactive Media in Education:* Processes, Tools, and Techniques for Managing Persistent Discourse

Tamara Sumner
Simon Buckingham Shum
Simeon Yates

INTRODUCTION

Where and with whom is the interpretation taking place in a multimedia document?

Ricki Goldman-Segall, 1995

Why would somebody manipulate someone else's discourse? It already happens all the time. In written texts, writers often use snippets of other people's discourse to support, guide, or influence the reader's interpretive process. Academics and researchers use quotes from other people's articles (such as ours from Ricki Goldman-Segall)[1] to contrast with, or lend support to, their own ideas or theories. Reporters take excerpts from recorded interviews and use them in print articles or newscasts, often resulting in "sound bites" with interpretations the original speaker may find surprising.

The influence these discourse snippets have on readers' interpretive processes can stem from several factors, including the perceived authority of the person whose discourse is being used or the juxtaposition the writer has intentionally created between the discourse snippet and the primary text. Such juxtapositions or interconnections between texts are termed "intertextuality."[2] Intertextuality can range from "manifest" to "latent," with a continuum in between. An example of manifest intertextuality would be quotes in newspaper articles. An example of latent intertextuality would be the styling of a film or book in mimicry of an existing film or book. Intertextual links often mark the key relationships between different texts and help to situate texts within a social and cultural context.

In scientific and academic publishing, Web-based digital communications media are changing both the possibilities for and the practices surrounding scholarly discourse and article intertextuality. In his studies of scientific publishing, Latour analyzes the influential role of bibliographic citations (a prominent form of manifest intertextuality) in establishing credibility for the research being published within a disciplinary community.[3] He argues that authors often use citations to create the illusion of a crowd of proponents and supporters behind their research. Recently, technical systems have been created for certain disciplines (e.g., computer science) that can automatically link bibliographic references to online versions of the article being cited.[4] In effect, the cited articles are now only one or two clicks away, making it much easier for interested readers to decide for themselves if the prior literature does indeed support the new research.

Journal peer reviewing is an area of scholarly discourse where the Web offers an incredible opportunity for experimentation. Historically, journal peer reviewing has consisted of a closed process where reviewers and editors act as anonymous status-judges charged with evaluating scholarly work.[5] In this article, we describe our experiences designing and implementing an innovative, interactive peer review process for the *Journal of Interactive Media in Education* (JIME). One of our key goals was to design a process and supporting technology that (1) transformed peer review into an open process promoting constructive dialogue between participants and in turn (2) reified this surrounding discourse and embedded it back into the scholarly articles themselves to provide a visible trace of the articles' history and intellectual lineage. With this enriched context readily available and integrated into the document form, readers are in a better position to interpret for themselves the work's relevance and quality. Thus, a chief outcome of our approach is to render "practically persistent," i.e., visible and accessible, those previously invisible discourses (the reviews and editorial commentary) and their intertextual relationships with each other and the scholarly article.

In the remainder of this chapter, we begin by laying out a number of related definitions of discourse and persistence that we shall deploy in the presentation of JIME. We then present how persistent discourse is being explicitly captured and managed in JIME to influence the reader's interpretive process, namely to provoke them to consider multiple perspectives, question assumptions, and raise new issues. In particular, we examine the role of editorial mediation and the specific "discourse management" activities that editors engage in. We then look into the future and consider various emerging hypermedia technologies and analyze the intertextuality practices that these technologies support.

DISCOURSE AND PERSISTENCE

"Discourse" is a widely used term in the social sciences.[6] Contemporary uses derive from two broad sources. First, the term has been used by linguists and those working in areas such as conversation analysis. In this case "discourse" denotes verbal interactions (spoken or written) that maintain a syntactic, semantic, narrative, or pragmatic coherence over time. Such discourses form essentially complete texts—where a text is defined as a socially and contextually complete utterance, interaction, or communication.[7] Under this definition, a book, a film, a short phone conversation, and an e-mail interaction can all be viewed as texts. It is the fact that the text makes "sense" as a whole over time that defines it as a discourse. In this case, discourse analysis explores how the text makes "sense"—this might involve considering how turns were taken in a conversation or how specific linguistic markers guide the reader through the narrative of a novel. For the purposes of this chapter we will call this definition of discourse *micro-discourse*.

Second, the term "discourse" is used by sociologists and those working in the field of cultural studies to denote the intersection of a system of knowledge, related texts from a range of media and the related material and social practices which generate and are generated by these texts. This second model of discourse is tied to the work of Foucault and other poststructuralist writers.[8] In this model discourses consist of:

- statements (texts) about a specific topic (e.g., information technology (IT) in education, academic journals);
- socially constructed rules that prescribe ways of talking or thinking about these topics;
- subjects (people and objects) which personify or characterize aspects of the discourse (e.g., educators, types of educational technology);
- systems of authority that mark out this knowledge as truthful, valid, or reliable; and
- social (discursive) practices that produce and reinforce the above texts, rules, subjects, and systems of authority (e.g., journal review processes).

Within this article, we term this definition *macro-discourse*. Discourse analysis in this case means analyzing the form, content, and functioning of these five elements of macro-discourse, and pointing out the specific intertextual links between texts produced by discursive practices. Clearly texts formed from micro-discourses are themselves part of macro-discourses. Some discourse analysts have married these two levels in order to explore how the macro-discourses both produce and are produced by the micro-discourses of day-to-day interactions.[9,10]

The second key concept we need to consider before presenting our case is "persistence." In thinking about the ways in which new digital technologies engender "persistent discourse," the focus is often upon micro-discourses (e.g., considering how computer-mediated communication [CMC] technologies make e-mail interactions persistent). Here, we will expand "persistence" to consider both micro- and macro-discourses and their interdependencies. Consider the distinction between persistent texts and transitory texts. Speech is the archetypal transitory text. Though we have memories of a spoken interaction, there is no material record—unless we made a recording. Persistence is in part therefore a product of the medium. Tape recordings, printed texts, photographs, etc., make a text persist that would otherwise be transitory. However, in addition to material persistence, there is also cultural persistence. The Bible and the Koran are classic examples of texts that are culturally persistent. Even though the original material texts do not exist, a complex set of cultural and material practices maintain the existence of the texts. In effect, materials can capture micro-discourses, but additionally, practices play a key role in maintaining macro-discourses.

We also distinguish between "permanent persistence" and "practical persistence." Many libraries keep copies of newspapers, and media companies keep archives of footage, making these texts persistent. However, access to these persistent texts is limited or difficult, making them inaccessible to all but a few motivated people. On the other hand, an archived Usenet discussion can be practically persistent in a manner in which a TV news interview is not. Thus, practical persistence is less about permanence and more about the capturing of texts and their intertextual connections in accessible ways.

The following discussion of JIME highlights the ways in which macro- and micro-discourses are rendered practically persistent by Web-based technologies. In this case, micro-discourses related to a key central text are being captured. At the same time, the journal itself is embedded in a macro-discourse, and previously transitory elements linking the micro- and the macro-discourses, such as the intertextual links and discursive practices (e.g., comments by reviewers), have also become persistent, visible, and accessible.

Our discussion begins with general background information on the journal's goals and the organizations involved. Then we describe the central text and analyze the supporting discourse and intertextual discourse relations. Finally, we discuss the overall journal management process and analyze the roles and activities involved in managing and transforming the persistent discourses in the journal site.

JOURNAL OF INTERACTIVE MEDIA IN EDUCATION

JIME is a freely available e-journal targeted at researchers and practitioners interested in educational technology, both in school and workplace settings.[11] It is published by the Open University, and two of this article's authors (Sumner and Buckingham Shum) are founding editors. JIME was founded with three goals in mind. First, as with most journals, it is intended to be a forum for innovative work in its field (educational technology). Second, rather than simply reading about interactive media, we wanted to make it possible for readers to directly experience the systems and techniques being described. Third, we believed that a multidisciplinary field could best be advanced by bringing together people reflecting the field's multiplicity of perspectives. Thus, we wanted to foster discussions between participants from diverse backgrounds (e.g., researchers, educators, system designers, and policymakers) and distant geographic locations.

Central Document

With these goals in mind, we created the document interface shown in Figure 12.1. The rationale and human-computer interface considerations that went into this design are fully described elsewhere.[12,13] The document (i.e., journal article) is the central artifact and is shown in the left pane. Referring back to our earlier definitions of discourse, the journal sits within two macro-discourses—the system of knowledge related to JIME's specific contents (the field of interactive media in education) and the system of knowledge related to academic journals (how they operate, their basis for authority, the roles of participants such as authors, reviewers, and editors, etc.).

Discourses and Discourse Relations

Most of the review process takes place using the document interface, with supplements, from e-mail. The discourse (i.e., discussions between readers, authors, reviewers, and editors) is shown in the right pane. A key aspect of our design is the integration between the document and the discourse, where links to the discourse are embedded directly into the document form itself (e.g., the comment icons at the start of every section heading). We refer to this form of explicit sup-

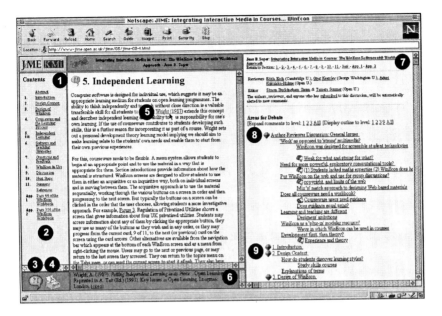

FIGURE 12.1. Document-Centered Discourse Interface. On the left is the Article Window, on the right the Commentaries Window showing the outline view of review discussion Key: (1) Comment icon embedded in each section heading displays section-specific comments; (2) active contents list; (3) iconic link to display top-level discussion outline; (4) iconic link to download PDF version; (5) citation is automatically linked to entry in references, displayed in footnote window; (6) reverse link to citation(s) in the text; (7) links from discussion back into article; (8) general heading for discussion; (9) headings for section-specific comments.

port for discourse intertextuality as "document-centered discourse." Thus, the technology supports the micro-discourse of journal reviewing practices. At the same time it captures this review discourse and makes it persistent and visible to others. In doing so, these previously hidden aspects (themselves micro-discourses) of the production of academic macro-discourse (in this case of IT for education) become persistent and visible. This document-centered discourse interface is very link-rich, making the publication of documents with associated discourse time and effort intensive. To make the publication of these documents tractable, we created the D3E toolkit to automate large parts of the mark-up and publication process. To date, we have used this toolkit to create document-centered discourse sites in numerous contexts, including two e-journals,[14] a national policy debate,[15] and an academic conference making innovative use of digital and face-to-face communication modes.[16] Our experiences across these sites indicate that the technology alone is insufficient to ensure (1) that discourse occurs and (2) that it serves the desired goals. By far the most important factor is the redesign of practices, specifically the roles and processes whereby discourse takes place and is captured, managed, and transformed to achieve organizational goals.

Processes and Issues

In the case of JIME, this redesign of practices entailed rethinking and redesigning the journal peer review process and participant roles (Figure 12.2). When an article is received and judged to be relevant to the journal, the publisher (often the same person as the editor) uses the D3E toolkit to create a secret review site for that article, resulting in the document-centered discourse interface. The editor solicits re-

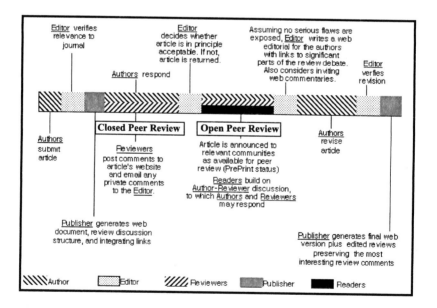

FIGURE 12.2. The JIME Review Life Cycle. The figure shows the closed and open peer-review periods, and the active stakeholders at different points.

viewers, and when all reviewers (usually three) are arranged, the editor uses e-mail to introduce the participants (authors and reviewers) to each other and brief them on the review process.

Next, for a one month "closed review" period, reviewers and authors discuss and debate the article. Although reviewers may choose to remain anonymous, journal policy is to encourage named review and, with only a couple of exceptions, all reviewers to date have done so. During this period, editors support the debate process in many ways. For instance, we may need to answer questions participants have about the process or the technologies. Often, we need to remind authors that they are not only allowed, but encouraged, to participate. Based on the outcome of the closed review period, the editor decides whether or not the article is in principle acceptable and should move to the open review period. If so, the secret site containing the submitted article and review debate is made available to the public for a one-month open review period. During that period, readers are also able to join the discussion.

After the open period, the editor performs a metareview of the article, summarizing the reviewers' points, adding additional comments, and formulating required and suggested changes to the article. These editorial comments are made directly into the review debate, and additionally all people subscribed to that article (minimally the authors and the reviewers) also receive these comments in their e-mail and are free to respond. Authors can use this opportunity to challenge and negotiate the change requests suggested by the editor by responding in the review discussion area.

An important form of editorial comment concerns suggesting and promoting new forms of "hypermedia literacies." For instance, as shown in Figure 12.3, we try to demonstrate and promote interlinking between: (1) the article and its associated review debate and (2) other articles. Sometimes, instead of requesting authors to modify part of their article in response to a comment, the editor will instead ask authors to respond in the review debate and suggest linking to this part of the debate in the article itself. Figure 12.4 shows how authors link from within their published article back to a particularly interesting thread in the article's review discussion. Such linking enables authors to use the review discussion as a form of "amplifying footnote." In this way, the narrative flow of the central document is preserved, but

One concerns the question of "cueing" as raised by the comments of Koschmann. See my comments at:

http://www-jime.open.ac.uk/Reviews/get/bryce-reviews/32/1/2.html

Another issue is the perceived benefit in a number of the student's minds associated with the absence of the patient:

http://www-jime.open.ac.uk/Reviews/get/bryce-reviews/31/1/2.html

FIGURE 12.3. Editorial Demonstrations of "Threaded Hypertext Literacy." This example shows contributions to online peer-review debates with citation and cross-linking from one review discussion to another.

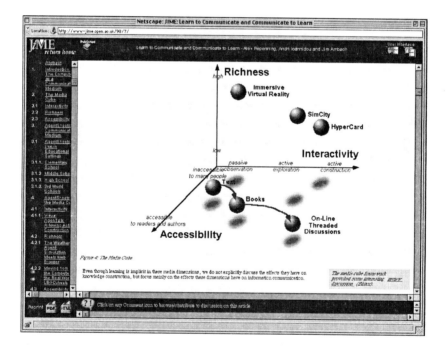

FIGURE 12.4. The persistence of the review discussion makes it a resource for authors or editors to point readers to. This screenshot shows a figure from a published JIME article that provoked much discussion among the reviewers. The editors have inserted a link (lower right corner) in the final text taking the reader to this discussion, thus incorporating it into the final publication, and making it available for readers to respond to.

the intellectual effort invested in the review process is re-used by drawing readers' attention to the availability of this secondary resource.

The authors then modify the article in response to the review debate and the editorial metareview. When the editor receives the final article and judges the modifications to be acceptable, the editor then edits the review debate to determine which parts will be published with the final article. Low-level comments pertaining to writing style or syntax are removed since these should have been addressed in the rewrite. Likewise, comments suggesting how to change parts of the article that have been addressed are also removed. Essentially, the editor culls the review debate to make sure the context that the comment pertained to still exists. If it does not, the comment is removed. Sometimes the editor will ask reviewers if they wish to modify a specific comment or add another one in light of changes in the article. Often the comments left after this culling are those related to broader theoretical or methodological issues, related experiences or systems, ancillary questions, etc. Thus, the review discussion is not persistent in the sense that comments are archived forever. Instead it is "practically persistent" in the sense that comments are accessible and inspectable for the duration of the context in which they are meaningful.

Discourse Management and Editorial Mediation

Using technology and process redesign, we have transformed journal reviewing from a one-way, hidden exchange of transitory monologic statements to a multiway open dialogue between participants. By doing so, we hope to support readers to judge documents by taking into account the multiple perspectives within the field of educational technology, and hence to consider the multiple possible interpretations.

Specifically, JIME tries to do this in several ways. First, the policy of named participation urges participants to take ownership of their point of view that, in turn, helps readers to trace the perspective that comments are based on. Second, the "practical persistence" of the debate makes the review process, and the multiple perspectives, open and inspectable to all participants and the public. Thus, the multiplicity of perspectives and opinions is preserved and visible, which is quite different from traditional journals where the final article embodies a single (and supposedly united) perspective coming out of the editorial process. Third, and most importantly, JIME editors play an active role in managing and transforming the micro-discourses (the review process) and mediating the macro-discourses (particularly the discourse of academic journals).

At the micro level, the editor manages the discursive process by setting the time limits and guiding participants through the closed and open review periods. The editor also takes active steps to manage and actively transform the discourse itself, taking what steps seem necessary to preserve comments' contexts or relationships with the document as the document is rewritten during the publishing process. These steps include culling out comments that may no longer be appropriate, rearranging comments if the document is reorganized, and sometimes seeking additions or changes to comments from the original commenter.

At the macro-discourse level, for participants to successfully enact the new review process, editors must take active mediation steps to change participants' systems of knowledge about practices surrounding academic journals. In effect, editors engage in "technology-use mediation" which Orlikowski et al. define as a set of activities that are deliberate, explicit, ongoing, and organizationally sanctioned interventions within the context of use that can significantly influence the effectiveness of computer conferencing technology.[17,18] These mediation activities help to adapt new communication technology to the context of use, and to adapt or configure users to both the new context and the features of the new technology (e.g., reminding authors to participate in the closed review, guiding participants through the two review periods, suggesting to authors and other participants new ways to take advantage of hypermedia).

DISCUSSION

In the case described, the editorial organization managed digital texts in order to support or influence the interpretation of a key document. In doing so, the editors captured elements of a macro-discourse, producing in turn a micro-discourse that itself became a persistent element of the original macro-discourse. Table 12.1 summarizes the key

TABLE 12.1. Key Points from JIME

Issue	JIME
Organization	Educational institution
Goals	Supporting new models of academic publishing
Technology	Specialized Web and CMC environment
Central document	Academic article
Macro-discourse	IT in education, academic journals
Micro-discourse	Structured review discussion between authors, reviewers, editors, and readers that is tightly linked to the journal article
What is persistent?	Intentionally captures the micro discussion and attempts to alter and record the macro-discourse of the journal reviewing process
Role of management	Discourse management to support varied interpretations

points from JIME. The organizational goals lead to a particular type of *remediation.* "Remediation" is the process whereby new media refashion or re-represent earlier media to achieve their cultural significance.[19] Bolter and Grusin note that "much of the current World Wide Web also remediates older forms without challenging them," a type of re-representation or remediation they refer to as "transparent immediacy." However, there is another type they term "hypermediacy"—a fascination with the medium itself—whereby new media refashion earlier media (e.g., by recontextualizing snippets or creating new juxtapositions). Here, JIME practices a form of explicit hypermediacy as shown in the model in Figure 12.5. The final outcome is a much more open discourse in which the previously hidden communicative relationships within the academic review process become overtly visible. The remediation role here is one of supporting the presentation of competing interpretations of the central document and keeping open the opportunity for further interpretations. The dialogical discourses of debate and conflict are also captured and remain persistent. In the same manner that printing made individual texts practically fixed and persistent, new digital technologies may make the intertextual relations of macro-discourses practically persistent.

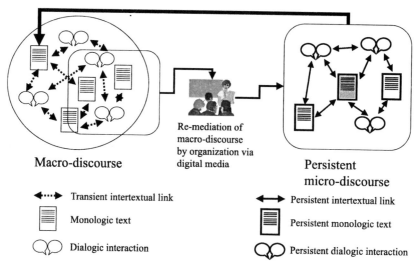

Macro-discourse   Re-mediation of
                   macro-discourse
                   by organization via
                   digital media   Persistent
                                                   micro-discourse

◀┈┈▶ Transient intertextual link   ◀━━▶ Persistent intertextual link

▤ Monologic text   ▤ Persistent monologic text

◖◗ Dialogic interaction   ◖◗ Persistent dialogic interaction

FIGURE 12.5. Managing Persistent Discourse

Two important points become clear in developing this model. First, the persistence provided by digital technologies differs from that provided by other communications technologies. In previous work, the term "fixity" has been used to describe the ability of printed text to materially fix acts of communication.[20,21] As we have argued elsewhere, digital technologies threaten the material basis upon which fixity and its cultural uses are based.[22] As we noted, new cultural practices can compensate for such developments, essentially providing digital texts with fixity.

Many technological innovations can be used to control interpretation and discourse (as seen with some political Web sites),[23] or to open up discussion to allow a multiplicity of perspectives (as with JIME). In the case of current digital technologies (e.g., Web-based hypermedia), one important affordance is the ability to capture both the texts and their intertextual relationships and to make these links both visible and interactive. As we have tried to demonstrate in this chapter, it is not simply the affordances of the technology but the combination of these affordances with associated cultural practices and institutional goals that provide "open discourse." In the remainder of this chapter, we review the affordances of future hypermedia technologies and illustrate how these technologies could be deployed to achieve very different organizational goals; i.e., to either encourage or discourage the articulation of multiple perspectives.

LOOKING TO THE FUTURE

The Web uses a very simplistic hypermedia model compared to hypermedia systems that have been built over the last decade. The Web's obvious strength—its sheer scale—is attributable to a large extent to this simplicity, but the absence of a number of key features is making Web authoring and reading/searching increasingly difficult. A number of "next generation" hypermedia features are beginning to emerge that have implications for the forms that persistent discourse may take in the future, and how they may be managed.[24] To illustrate, we take three significant technical developments on the Web, introducing each, and considering its implications for managing discourse: semantically encoded hypertext, open hypermedia, and network visualization.

Semantically Encoded Hypertext

Until very recently, as far as computational agents (e.g., Web servers, browsers, search engines) were concerned, the Web comprised undifferentiated documents and links. Without the addition of special analytical capabilities that would allow it to analyze the text in a document, an agent could not distinguish one *type* of document or relational link from another because no information about them was made explicit. Adding explicit information about the function or meaning of a link or document creates a richer semantic hypertext network, which in turn enables new varieties of computer support for interpretation (see Box 12.1). This can be implemented in a number of ways that are still being developed. Metadata initiatives (data about data) are one of the most significant efforts, aiming to provide standard, structured information about a document's content and links (for example, Dublin Core).[25] The kind of metadata provided is determined by the information that a user community will find most valuable to use when searching for documents. Since metadata schemes only work if a critical mass of major players in a given community or disci-

BOX 12.1. Possibilities for Using Semantically Encoded Hypertext

Use to *discourage* multiple interpretations and debate	Use to *encourage* multiple interpretations and debate
A site concerned with controlling interpretation could design a metadata scheme that supported their worldview (i.e., their ontological position). By defining the concepts and interrelations "that count," one can convince others of the rigor of one's position, unless they are able to challenge either the ontology, or the way in which it has been instantiated. *Example:* A political party could introduce the reader to a metadata scheme, implemented in its Web site, of "the key process for tracking manifesto promises": for every *promise,* there must be *evidence.* Visual maps could be provided to show the mapping between promises and evidence; users could search for *evidence: employment* to focus only on evidence.	A semantic hypertext defined by an ontology that assumes from the start a multiplicity of perspectives and definitions provides the building blocks for different stakeholders to contest meaning. *Example:* In a real debate, one would expect to be able to *agree* and *disagree,* to explore *pros* and *cons,* to post *questions* about *solutions* and *claims.* The whole tenor of the ontology that is set up for discourse is different.

pline adopts them, and information that is not in a metadata scheme will remain "invisible," defining a scheme is like defining an ontology—a structured view of the critical concepts in the field. Other initiatives are using knowledge modeling schemes to add "ontological tags" to Web documents, and knowledge-based software agents to search for and reason about document interrelationships. Elsewhere, we have explored the trade-off between providing a very rich, expressive semantic scheme, and the added complexity for users.[26]

Open Hypermedia

At present, Web links are embedded in the content of documents. To add or change a link, you need authorial access to the document. However, at a technical level in hypertext, document content and interdocument relationships are in principle separable, and next-generation Web systems make it possible for "linksets" to be stored on "link servers," specifying source and destination addresses.[27] Using such a system, one views a Web site and can then view different linksets overlaid on the Web site's pages; that is, words become links to wherever the linkset has specified. This effectively wrests some authorial control from the document's authors, since they can no longer predict how words are linked and hence how the whole document is interpreted (see Box 12.2).

External link servers are a key component of what are termed "open hypermedia systems" which aim to enable "anything to be linked to anything." Such functionality has been available for non-Web environments for a while (e.g., Microcosm), but have been developed for the Web only recently.[28]

Site Mapping and Visualization Tools

An extremely common finding in hypermedia research is that a well-designed visual map of the key parts of the network is a powerful navigational aid for users, particularly if it shows where they currently are and where they have been. Unless intentional disorientation of users is a goal, there is no reason for any Web site not to seek to aid navigation. An interesting development is the ability to generate a Web site map automatically with tools that analyze the site's link

BOX 12.2. Possibilities for Using Open Hypermedia	
Use to *discourage* multiple interpretations and debate	Use to *encourage* multiple interpretations and debate
External link bases are difficult to conceive as a technology for controlling interpretation, since their purpose is explicitly to enable multiple layers of links, and linking to and from Web sites to which one does not have any other form of authorial access. One can envisage sites devising a way to block access to link servers if they do not wish other groups to impose their linksets. Such a site could use an internal open hypermedia system as a publishing tool to *generate* their site, since such tools provide useful facilities for managing links.	Different link layers can be added by anyone, taking readers to different interpretations of texts. *Example:* In JIME, one could switch between links that amplify and support the author, and those which challenge.

structure, and even the content and similarity of documents, and then render these structures visually.[29] Such tools provide a way to see "behind the scenes," that is, behind the carefully constructed map provided by the publisher, and perhaps beyond the hypertext links to conceptual links between documents that are otherwise unlinked (Box 12.3). This represents another possible way to change the discourse from that intended by the authors of the primary document(s).

CONCLUSION

Scholarly publishing and communications are undergoing rapid and far-reaching change. More journals are going online, and the Web is becoming increasingly embedded in the practice of scholarship. It remains to be seen if society can make the most of these changes: will electronic journals improve the dissemination of scholarly products, or will they be used to fundamentally transform scholarly practices to encourage new forms of participation in scholarly endeavors? Although the former would be beneficial, our work is focused on the latter ideal. The challenge is one of design: we need to reconceptualize electronic journals as tools that can actively support inquiry, perspective taking, and community building, and try to design them accordingly.

Toward this end, we have created a specially designed computer-meditated conferencing technology to realize an innovative peer review model within an academic e-journal—the *Journal of Interactive Media in Education*. A key element of our approach was to pay careful attention to rethinking the social processes around this new tech-

---

BOX 12.3. Possibilities for Using Site Mapping and Visualization Tools

Use to *discourage* multiple interpretations and debate	Use to *encourage* multiple interpretations and debate
Provide a static, crafted map of the site that emphasizes its coherence and draws attention to particular documents and relationships.	Provide users with active maps that allow one to see the current threads and activity hotspots in the site, which is constantly evolving through open discourse.

nology, i.e., the peer-review process and editorial mediation activities. It is only through this integrated redesign of social processes and technical products that we are able to achieve our organizational goals: to shift reviewing from a closed process centered on evaluating scholarly work to an open process promoting constructive dialogue between participants.

NOTES

1. Ricki Goldman-Segall, "Deconstructing the Humpty Dumpty Myth: Putting It Together to Create Cultural Meaning," In *Contextual Media: Multimedia and Interpretation,* eds. Edward Barrett and Marie Redmond (Cambridge, MA: MIT Press, 1995): 27-52.

2. Graham Allen, *Intertextuality*, ed. John Drakakis (London and New York: Routledge, 2000).

3. Bruno Latour, *Science in Action: How to Follow Scientists and Engineers Through Society* (Cambridge, MA: Harvard University Press, 1988).

4. Lee Giles, Kurt Bollacker, and Steve Lawrence, *Citeseer: An Automatic Citation Indexing System.* Paper presented at the 3rd ACM Conference on Digital Libraries, Pittsburgh, PA, June 23-26, 1998.

5. Harriet Zuckerman and Robert K. Merton, "Patterns of Evaluation in Science: Institutionalisation, Structure, and Functions of the Referee System," *Minerva* 9(1) (January 1971): 66-100.

6. M. Wetherell, S. Taylor, and S. J. Yates, *Discourse Theory and Practice: A Reader* (London: Sage in association with the Open University, 2001).

7. M. Halliday, *Language As Social Semiotic: The Social Interpretation of Language and Meaning* (London: Edward Arnold, Ltd., 1978).

8. Michel Foucault, *Discipline and Punish: The Birth of the Prison,* trans. Alan Sheridan (London: Penguin, 1979).

9. Norman Fairclough, *Discourse and Social Change* (Cambridge, MA: Polity Press, 1992).

10. Margaret Wetherell and Jonathan Potter, *Mapping the Language of Racism: Discourse and the Legitimation of Exploitation* (New York: London: Harvester Wheatsheaf, 1992).

11. *JIME: Journal of Interactive Media in Education,* <http://www-jime.open. ac.uk/> (viewed May 1, 2001).

12. Tamara Sumner and Simon Buckingham Shum, *From Documents to Discourse: Shifting Conceptions of Scholarly Publishing.* Paper presented at the Conference on Human Factors in Computing Systems (CHI '98), Los Angeles, CA, April 18-23, 1998.

13. Tamara Sumner and Simon Buckingham Shum, *A Toolkit for Publishing Web Discussion Documents: Design Principles and Case Studies.* Paper presented

at the Asia Pacific Computer Human Interaction 1998 (APCHI 98), Shonan Village Center, Japan, July 15-17, 1998.

14. Simon Buckingham Shum and C. McKnight, eds., "World Wide Web Usability: Special Issue," *International Journal of Human-Computer Studies* 47(1) (1997): 1-222.

15. *Dearing Report Discussion Site*, <http://d3e.open.ac.uk/Dearing/> (viewed June 25, 2001).

16. *Learning.Org*, <http://www.learning.org> (viewed June 25, 2001).

17. Tamara Sumner, Simon Buckingham Shum, Michael Wright, Nathalie Bonnardel, Aline Chevalier, and Annie Piolat, "Redesigning the Peer Review Process: A Developmental Theory-in-Action," in *Designing Cooperative Systems: The Use of Theories and Models,* eds. Rose Dieng, A. Giboin, L. Karsenty, and G. De Michelis (Amsterdam: IOS Press, 2000): 19-34.

18. Wanda Orlikowski, JoAnne Yates, Kazuo Okamura, and Masayo Fujimoto, "Shaping Electronic Communication: The Metastructuring of Technology in the Context of Use," *Organization Science* 6(4) (1995): 423-444.

19. Jay David Bolter and Richard Grusin, *Remediation: Understanding New Media* (Cambridge, MA: MIT Press, 1999).

20. Jay David Bolter, *Writing Space: The Computer, Hypertext, and the History of Writing* (Hillsdale, NJ: Lawrence Erlbaum Associates, Inc., 1991).

21. B. Anderson, *Imagined Communities: Reflection on the Origin and Spread of Nationalism* (London: Verso, 1983).

22. Simeon Yates and Tamara Sumner, *Digital Genres and the New Burden of Fixity*. Paper presented at the Hawaiian International Conference on System Sciences (HICCS 30), Wailea, Hawaii, January 7-10, 1997.

23. Simeon Yates and Jane Perrone, *Politics on the Web*. Paper presented at the International Conference on Internet Research and Information in the Social Sciences, Bristol, U.K., March 25-27, 1998), <http://www.sosig.ac.uk/iriss/papers/paper46.htm> (viewed June 25, 2001).

24. M. Bieber, F. Vitali, H. Ashman, V. Balasubramanian, and H. Oinas-Kukkonen, "Fourth Generation Hypermedia: Some Missing Links for the World Wide Web," *International Journal of Human-Computer Studies* 4(1) (1997): 31-65.

25. *Dublin Core Metadata Initiative,* <http://dublincore.org/> (viewed May 1 2001).

26. S. Buckingham Shum, A. MacLean, V. Bellotti, and N. Hammond, "Graphical Argumentation and Design Cognition," *Human-Computer Interaction* 12(3) (1997): 267-300.

27. L. Carr, D. De Roure, W. Hall, and G. Hill, "The Distributed Link Service: A Tool for Publishers, Authors and Readers," *World Wide Web Journal* 1 (winter 1995).

28. Steve Hitchcock, Leslie Carr, Steve Harris, Wendy Hall, Steve Probets, David Evans, and David Brailsford, "Linking Electronic Journals: Lessons from the Open Journal Project," *D-Lib Magazine* 1998, <http://www.dlib.org/dlib/december 98/12hitchcock.html> (viewed June 25, 2001).

29. C. Chen and M. Czerwinski, *From Latent Semantics to Spatial Hypermedia: An Integrated Approach*. Paper presented at the 9th ACM Conference on Hypertext, Pittsburgh, PA, June 24-24, 1998.

Chapter 13

Science's Knowledge Environments: Integrated Online Resources for Researchers, Educators, and Students

Nancy R. Gough

DEVELOPING THE KNOWLEDGE ENVIRONMENT CONCEPT

The American Association for the Advancement of Science (AAAS) established a collaboration with Stanford University Libraries (SUL) and the Center for Resource Economics/Island Press (Island Press) in 1996 to help scientific researchers and nonprofit organizations harness the power of the Internet and electronic publishing. At that time, only a handful of journals were available through the Internet, and the World Wide Web was in its infancy. It was clear, however, that the Web could transform the ways in which scientists gathered and shared information as part of research efforts. The collaborative recognized that Web-based technologies could enhance access to data based information and greatly improve the effectiveness of information transfer and the creation of new knowledge. Development work on the project began in early 1998 after the collaborative received a grant from the Pew Charitable Trusts to create a prototype of the Web-based electronic networking tools we envisioned.

Knowledge environment (KE) describes the collection of electronic networking tools that have been and continue to be developed. Knowledge environments use practical, production-quality tools to systematize the consensus knowledge within a scientific domain, and to facilitate users' access to that knowledge. Predicted users include researchers, educators, and students. In a KE, access occurs through searching, browsing, and current awareness features combined with user-friendly graphical interfaces. KEs combine primary and review literature with more interactive functions and gateways to dispersed sources of information. Specific electronic tools that facilitate the entry of information into the underlying databases are also being developed as part of the concept.

Science's Signal Transduction Knowledge Environment (STKE) is the first implementation of the KE concept and has laid the foundation for two additional KEs at *Science* and AAAS: one focused on AIDS science and one focused on the science of aging. The initial development of Science's STKE was aimed at the researcher; however, the STKE continues to reach out to new audiences, and additional features are being developed to allow the STKE to meet the needs of undergraduate and graduate educators and students. Continued support for the STKE project has come from the Charles A. Dana Foundation to further the work on the prototype development and testing. In 2000, the STKE received additional support from the National Science Foundation (NSF) as part of the Biosci Ed Net project. The NSF funds have been used to develop features that will enhance the usefulness of Science's STKE for undergraduate biology education.

GOALS OF KEs

The overarching goal of the KE project is to identify and develop a mix of tools and approaches (algorithms, schemas, programs, and human organizational structures) that are stable, scalable, interoperable, and cost-effective across a wide range of disciplines. The defining goals for the KE project are to save the researchers, educators, and students time in the information-gathering process, to increase the likelihood of the scientist making new connections between facts from discrete sources, and to support educational, collaborative, and community-building efforts. An additional goal of the project is to better understand the tools and organizational structures scientific authorities need when they attempt to systematize a domain's knowledge.

SIGNAL TRANSDUCTION:
THE PARADIGM FOR KEs

Signal transduction (ST) is the study of how cells control their own and each other's behaviors through chemical signals. ST research is an intensely active field of biomedical research and is of interest to a broad array of scientists and undergraduate and graduate biology educators. Science's STKE should be useful to the scientists who specialize in ST, as well as the many scientists who need to follow and apply the current findings of this field even though their primary interest may not be in ST mechanisms themselves. ST research was selected for the prototype KE because

- the characteristics of the potential user base permits testing many of the electronic tools that are central to the KE concept;
- the user population is an interdisciplinary group; therefore, tools specifically designed to facilitate communication across disciplines and to filter information in order to present material relevant to the user's interest can be tested;
- information about ST is well suited for organization into a hierarchical database allowing the testing of a graphical interface to access and display data from the database maintained by experts;
- the users would benefit from management tools developed to organize and collate the primary literature, because no single journal serves as the main source of ST information; and
- the informal exchange of information within this research community is also fractured because ST researchers do not all belong to one scholarly society.

FEATURES OF SCIENCE'S STKE

Experienced editors from *Science* worked with software developers from HighWire Press to develop the prototype, which includes information management tools that ST researchers indicated they needed. The prototype was launched in September 1999 with a subset of the proposed Science's STKE content available. Since the launch, all of the sections of the STKE have been implemented and continue to grow and evolve. Science's STKE emphasizes information vetted by authorities in the field, prudently supplemented with automated functions where appropriate. The high editorial standards that have been the benchmark for *Science* are applied to selection of material for the original content published at Science's STKE. In addition to AAAS, seventeen publishers have agreed to include full-text access to ST content from their journals in the prototype. The STKE is also an electronic journal, updated weekly with original articles. The content of the STKE can be divided into four categories: literature, community resources, online resources, and the connections map database. Each of these categories will be described in more detail.

Literature

The STKE publishes solicited articles categorized as perspectives, reviews, or protocols. Original STKE content can be cited just like any other published paper using the URL as its unique identifier. The editors provide weekly summaries in the "This Week in Signal Transduction" (TWIST) section of especially interesting and important articles published in the primary literature during the previous week. This function features articles published in the virtual journal and serves as an information management tool for the ST researchers who must scan numerous sources to stay abreast of current advances. The STKE also serves as a digital library through the virtual journal, which provides full-text access to papers published in the field of ST from forty-five publications from eighteen different publishers. The integration of TWIST with the virtual journal allows the full text of many of the featured articles to be available directly through the STKE.

The virtual journal represents one place where the STKE has been a leader in the development of tools and software for information management and integration, as well as outreach into the publishing community. The articles in the virtual journal are located and added to the database through an algorithm designed to identify ST-related literature. The editors review the articles included and have a mechanism by which to add or remove articles as needed. However, the virtual journal represents a major tool for ST researchers and educators by collating ST literature into one location from many different journals. Furthermore, the STKE has worked hard to promote the virtual journal concept within the online publishing industry. Technical hurdles remain in that all of the participating publishers have their online journals with HighWire Press. The STKE would like to be able to include journals located with other vendors in the participating publishers group, providing a more complete set of primary literature for the ST community.

Perspectives provide an opinion or viewpoint of the author(s) on a particular subject and as such are not peer reviewed. These can be focused on recent papers from the primary literature, reviews of recently published books, or reports from scientific meetings. Reviews are more comprehensive documents that provide new insights, as well as summarize the information currently available. The best reviews reflect the unique viewpoint of the author and show how new findings alter current thinking about major issues in a particular field. Reviews are evaluated by peer review for scholarship, accuracy, clarity, and effectiveness of presentation. Protocols are a completely separate type of document; they provide detailed instructions and descriptions of methods for experimental techniques particularly useful in the study of signal transduction. Protocols are grouped under the following categories: (1) molecular genetic techniques, (2) biochemical methods and assays, (3) cells, microscopy, and microinjection techniques, and (4) biophysical methods.

Each of these three types of original content (perspectives, reviews, and protocols) can be linked to other resources on the Web, such as animations or related databases, and all are available in a downloadable PDF format. The STKE has created animations to accompany perspectives and reviews and to utilizes this feature of online publishing to enhance the Connections Maps. Although the STKE art staff have created some of the animations, frequently the authors or connections maps authorities have provided the animations or movies. This demonstrates that the users and contributors are enthusiastic about the multimedia aspect of online publishing, which enables the dynamic nature of cellular signaling to be presented and highlighted in a manner that cannot be achieved in print journals.

Community Resources

Community resources include the White Pages (a user-populated directory of people, laboratories, and institutions involved in ST research and teaching), the Q&A discussion forums, and Letters. The STKE has experienced very limited success with the Q&A forum and the Letters features. Two types of Q&A forums have been launched: focused discussions, which are accompanied by opening statements and moderated by a leading scientist in the topic under discussion, and open forums loosely oriented around broad topics, which are monitored by the editors. To increase participation in the focused Q&A forums, the editors have used e-mail invitations to scientists in the field. However, despite this personal and direct promotion of the Q&A forums, only a handful of people have submitted responses to these threaded discussions. Participation in Q&A forums as they are currently focused may be limited because the scientific community has other mechanisms by which to communicate. These include listserves, e-mail, meetings, online bulletin boards, and old-fashioned telephone calls and correspondence. Thus, it is not clear yet whether Q&A moderated threaded discussions are resources that the community needs at this time. The open forums have been more successful and continue to provide an avenue for communication among the ST community. The STKE users have not utilized the Letters function. This may be due to a lack of visibility of the Letters in the current site design and represents one of the challenges in considering how to best make the various features and functions available and accessible to the user.

The White Pages are well populated and there is an easy user interface for submission of information to this database. The only caveat has been that the STKE relies on the honor system for users to enter certain White Pages information, such as laboratory or institution affiliation. This has sometimes created problems when a user lists an association with an inappropriate place or, in many cases, multiple places. However, feedback from the STKE member responsible for maintaining the laboratory or institution has allowed the technical staff to track these problems and correct them, as well as institute a twice-yearly check on the database to look for anomalous entries. Thus, the White Pages have been a successful interface for the ST community, and they have presented the STKE with challenges for quality control and user presentation. The STKE hopes to improve the user experience by providing the information in a variety of browsable formats, including by geographical location and topic.

Online Resources

Current online resources include: (1) access to Science Careers job search interface, (2) an editorially created set of links to ST-related meetings and conferences called Events, and (3) an editorially reviewed and organized set of links to other resources on the Internet called ST on the Web (STOW). To increase and promote user participation, STOW has an interface where the user can submit a site for inclusion. The ST community has submitted many of the sites included in STOW. The editors review each of the submissions to determine if the site is sufficiently current, useful, and related to ST to include in this list of related Web sites. As a result of user submissions, STOW has been reorganized to include a section called Signal Transduction Labs and People, which allows members of the ST community to have a link to their lab homepage. Another new section of STOW that was added as a result of STKE's participation in the BEN project is Sites for Educators. (BEN stands for the Biosci Ed Net Collaborative, which is a group of professional societies and coalitions for biology education. BEN received a two-year grant from the National Science Foundation to be part of the Digital Libraries Initiative. The BEN project is specifically aimed at the development of a digital library and portal for online teaching resources for the instruction of undergraduate biology.) The STOW section and the interface for user submissions is one of the STKE successes in encouraging user feedback and interaction with the site to improve and enrich the information available. As such an interactive resource, STOW blurs the line between online resources and community resources, demonstrating one of the challenges of how to present the integrated information available at a KE in the most intuitive manner.

Based on the success of the STOW submission interface, the STKE is developing a similar interface for the submission of entries to the events list and for submission to the BEN resources at the STKE. Users have used the regular feedback mechanism to send information about upcoming meetings or conferences. However, an interface that easily allows the user to enter all the relevant data would encourage users to submit entries and would allow a single location for all of the required information to be supplied. Just as with the STOW interface, the submissions would be reviewed by the editors prior to inclusion in the events list. The BEN submissions would be editorially reviewed, as well as peer-reviewed online, for educational value and appropriateness.

CONNECTIONS MAPS AND CONNECTIONS MAPS AUTHORITIES DATA ENTRY SYSTEM (CMADES)

These two interrelated features are the most innovative and challenging pieces of the STKE project. The challenges have been both technical and community related. The Connections Maps are a graphical representation of a database of information about the molecules involved in cellular signaling cascades. CMADES is the software that allows the scientists (called Authorities) to enter the information about the components involved in ST and then organize the information into linear pathways. The first implementation of CMADES was as a Java applet that operated through an Internet browser. This implementation created problems as browser software was updated. Each Authority had a different set of specifications, and thus the software required individualization for each Authority. A major goal of 2001 was the release of a new version of the CMADES software as a stand-alone application that is browser independent. CMADES automates many of the functions involved in adding data into the Connections Maps database, such as references and descriptors, as well as allowing the Authorities to indicate the relationships between the components in the pathway through the use of a graphing tool. The latest version (released in May 2002) is an enhanced version of the stand-alone application. It allows for multiple authority groups for the pathway authorities and more detailed contributor information to be displayed to the STKE user. In addition, a new display for the graphical portion of the Connections Maps is now available, allowing the STKE user to zoom and to move the display.

The ST community has been very receptive and willing to participate as Authorities. The editorial staff currently selects each Authority with recommendations from the editorial board and suggestions from the current Authorities. To facilitate the Authorities' ability to use CMADES independently, a user manual was written to explain the underlying data structure for the database, as well as the specific instructions for how to use the CMADES software. Each new Authority presents questions and issues to consider in terms of how best to design a database and a user display with sufficient flexibility and yet structure to allow organization and integration of the complex information being supplied. The technical team has been very responsive to the requests and suggestions by the Authorities, which have substantially improved the database and CMADES functionality. Some of the automated functions come from the use of controlled vocabularies for the Authorities to use to enter information into particular fields in the database. The Authorities have been responsive to using these defined terms and willing to help in the construction and addition of depth to the vocabularies. Furthermore, as more Authorities have worked to build pathways that interconnect, the database is serving as a community-building tool. The scientists are using the database to interact through an Authority Notes field in the database to communicate as they work to organize knowledge in their field and think about how their entries in the database should be connected to the existing entries created by other scientists.

The Connections Maps are completely dynamic and are created when a user selects a pathway to view. This allows the data in the database to be continuously updated without any lag in the update of the information on the site. One of the challenges for the STKE is to develop a more "cellular" context for the graphical display of the pathways. A second goal is to use the information in the database to allow the users to access the data through various mechanisms of organization, such as viewing all of the components from a particular organism or tissue.

AAAS and the STKE continue to work toward the goal of transforming the Connections Maps database into a sophisticated bioinformatics tool. To promote this goal, Science's STKE is investigating collaborations with other groups interested in creating databases of ST information, such as the Alliance for Cellular Signaling. Future development of the Connections Maps database will be aimed at the creation of tools and interoperability standards for performing pathway finding and sophisticated searching that spans across more than just the Connections Maps database.

PERSONALIZATION (MY STKE)

As an online publication and resource, the STKE is equipped with tools that the user can apply to personalize his or her STKE experience. The STKE has an Alert function set by the user that sends an e-mail message when STKE content is updated that meets the user's specified parameters. Filters is another personalization tool that allows the user to have presented only material that is new since the last visit. Folders provide a method for the user to store and organize STKE content for future reference. The Related Resources function allows the users or the editors to provide a link between multiple pieces of STKE content to further personalize the view and organization of the STKE. Additional tools are under development and include browsing functions, more filter settings, and the ability to save searches. These features are a major benefit to the user: the management tools were one of the main goals of the KE project.

FUTURE CHALLENGES FOR AAAS
AND THE KE CONCEPT

The STKE is currently facing challenges related to increasing the ease of utility of the KE tools and features and improving the intuitiveness of the site organization. As part of this challenge, the STKE and AAAS are embarking on an overall redesign of the STKE. The method being used for the redesign is an expandable and modifiable template that can be adapted to fit the needs of additional *Science* KEs and that can allow easy transition for users among the various *Science* online products. User feedback, as well as experience gained from the development of other sites similar to the AAAS KEs by HighWire, are driving the redesign strategy.

Another major challenge faced by the STKE, and other KEs to come, is the development of a viable and sustainable business model. Several approaches are being pursued for the STKE and include applying for continued grant funding, marketing for advertisers, obtaining corporate and philanthropic sponsors, charging modest subscription fees to individuals and institutions, and licensing fees for the Connections Maps database.

As for specific goals, the STKE intends to reach out to the ST community to encourage participation in the community and interactive parts of the STKE. This is a great challenge. The experience gained so far indicates that the community is not as prepared or comfortable with online discussions (Q&A forums) or Letters as expected. The editors hope that a more intuitive user interface for some of these community features will promote user participation. That aspect of encouraging participation has been addressed during the redesign process. A partial redesign has been completed. Expanded personalization features were expected to be ready by summer 2002. These should enable more user interaction and customization of the site. Promotion of the interactive features through advertisements, e-mail notices, and homepage announcements will also be strategies used to gain broader acceptance and comfort for these interactive aspects of online publishing.

Another challenge the STKE faces is in the implementation of the site's contributions to the BEN collaborative. This project is specifically intended to be an interactive community resource. The STKE and the BEN partners will require easy-to-use contributor, editorial, and reviewer interfaces. The ultimate intention of the BEN collaborative is to enable instructors to submit material for inclusion in BEN online and provide for peer review online, as well as editorial review and production online. This project requires promotion and acceptance by the educator community. This represents an expansion of the STKE target audience, which was primarily the ST research community.

A final challenge that KEs face is the ability to interoperate with other sites and databases. The STKE faces this challenge in several aspects: participation in the BEN collaborative, expanding the participating journals and publishers in the virtual journal, and linking and interoperating with other ST databases through the Connections Maps database. These are technical challenges that will require extensive cooperation among the various participants to develop protocols and establish standards that allow the current participants, as well as future groups, to interact online without having to develop and redevelop unique processes and solutions for each partner. An adaptable and expandable system of interoperability is important for solving these issues.

Chapter 14

Serials Solutions: A Method for Tracking Full-Text Electronic Journals in Aggregated Databases

Peter McCracken

INTRODUCTION

Librarians are familiar with the challenges of determining which journals are present in database aggregators such as ProQuest, JSTOR, Lexis-Nexis, Project Muse, and many others. The full-text journals in the large aggregators vary based on the aggregators' agreements with journal publishers, and with as many journals as they have, content can literally change on a daily basis. When libraries subscribe to one of these services, they and their patrons suddenly have access to a wealth of resources. Managing and tracking these resources, however, presents significant new challenges. Not knowing where to find information about a database's content is terribly frustrating; librarians know there is a chance that a journal article might be available through some of the many available electronic resources, but they do not have the time to search through each database to figure out where they can find the particular article they seek. Most libraries have access to between 7,000 and 10,000 full-text journals, and some have access to many, many more. Given the cost of these resources, it is important that librarians make the most of what is available and *know* what is in these resources.

BACKGROUND AND PROBLEM

As a reference librarian, I have long been frustrated by not knowing which journals are available in these databases. At one institution, we added content notes to our online catalog for those journals available through JSTOR, but we did it only once. We also never updated the information, either with new journals that became available through JSTOR, or with changes to the available content dates. I started to notify our cataloging department about the resources that were now available, but I realized I would need to provide the specific information on each title—sending a URL with the information would not suffice—and because of staffing situations in cataloging, even then there was only a minimal chance that the changes would be incorporated. And what would we do when future changes appeared? Would I need to notify them again and again? How could we keep track of the changes in the largest aggregated collections? What about the smaller ones?

One print product provided information on which journals were available through which aggregators, but we certainly did not have access to all of the aggregators listed in the journal, and the product did not list all of the aggregators that we could access. It came out in print once or twice a year, so content changes ensured that it was incorrect the day it was published, and became more so with each passing week. Librarians could not use it unless they were physically at the reference desk; students could not use it unless they knew it existed. Finally, the idea of recording electronic holdings through a print resource seemed counterintuitive—why not use the most appropriate technology, namely, the technology that was originally being used to provide the resource?

Attempting to determine the content of these databases can try anyone's patience. Librarians feel they cannot rely on aggregators to provide continuous access to specific journals, and aggregators do add and drop journals at seemingly random intervals. Librarians often lament these problems and direct their anger at the aggregators themselves. This complaint, however, ignores the business model by which the major general-subject journal aggregators create their databases. Librarians should not vilify database aggregators on these points. Libraries sign contracts with publishers such as ProQuest, EBSCO, InfoTrac, Wilson, and others on an annual basis, and they sign a contract for access to the database as a whole, not to the individual titles within the database. The presence of multiple major databases, plus the testimony of anyone who has attempted to negotiate contracts with aggregators, provide ample evidence that this is a challenging, fiercely competitive market. No monopoly exists in the marketplace, and every aggregator is trying its utmost to provide the best product at the best price.

Aggregators, therefore, must try to find the optimum balance between price and content. In addition to negotiating contracts with libraries, they negotiate contracts with publishers, paying each publisher a set price for rights of inclusion of the publisher's content in the database. If a publisher feels disadvantaged by the sale of its product through an aggregator, and the publisher and aggregator are unable to come to a suitable agreement, then the publisher can rescind reprinting rights with little or no warning. Lacking rights to the content, the aggregator has no choice but to remove it from the database. This may mean that no additional articles are added to the database, or that *all* content, past and present, from the particular publisher or journal must be removed. Seeking to repair such damage to a database's material, the aggregator will attempt to add content from sources similar to those recently lost. Or if aggregators can add other content inexpensively, they may jump at the chance to increase the number (if not the quality) of the journals in the database.

Publishers, too, are not specifically to blame in this environment. Publishers earn much less per individual user through aggregated databases than through traditional print or direct electronic subscriptions. Several publishers are becoming increasingly hesitant about distributing their content through aggregators and are demanding more money for reproduction rights. The result, again, is that aggregators may lose content from reputable publishers with little or no prior notification.

Although the process is admittedly irritating, it is important that librarians understand the reasons for and causes of these variations in databases from major aggregators. When librarians pay for access to specific journals, as they do through electronic publishers such as Elsevier, CatchWord, and similar publisher-directed databases, they have every reason to expect that access to the journals will be prompt, accurate, and reliable. If they so choose, librarians can easily catalog this content with some assurance that it will still be available next month. In the case of general-subject databases, however, librarians must recognize and accept that variations in the content of these databases are inevitable.

Given the existing situation, content will continue to change, often without warning. Large aggregators such as Lexis-Nexis and Pro-Quest may have literally hundreds of monthly changes to the content in their databases. Trying to track these changes is too expensive, irritating, and time consuming for librarians to do on their own.

SOLUTIONS

Overview

So how can we as librarians know, in a timely fashion, what is available in these databases? I realized there must be a better possible solution, so I spent some time thinking about it and developed ideas about how it could be done. I realized that someone would eventually market the solution, and I expected they would be quite successful. The model I saw was similar to copy cataloging: libraries allow another reliable service provider to do most of their cataloging for them; they catalog just the new or challenging or locally specific items themselves. If someone could do this for aggregator holdings, and provide it to all libraries at a reasonable price—certainly much lower than the cost of doing it themselves—then everyone would win. By creating a database that tracks all of the full-text titles in nearly all the English-language databases available today, one company can do inexpensively for all what would cost each a great deal.

As I explored the possibilities of developing this product, I found that nothing like it was available. Jake (http://jake-db.org), the "jointly administered knowledge environment," offered something somewhat similar, but not with the simplicity and specificity that I felt was required. Jake acts more as a reference tool for librarians; it is often difficult for patrons to understand what the results mean. Generally, jake's results reflect the presence of a journal in all databases that are included in jake's master database. It is possible to configure jake so that its results are limited to those accessible to the institution's patrons, but the programming for that is a challenge to many potential users. I envisioned a resource in which an organization delivered a final product, with no need for complicated installation, configuration, or maintenance to make it work. This product would also be something that the average patron could be expected to utilize remotely, without a librarian's explanation.

Ideally, each journal would receive a complete record in the library's online catalog, informing users of the availability of the journal's contents. Of course, the work of individually importing or creating so many records, with the knowledge that access to them may be lost next year when subscriptions to aggregators change, or next week when the aggregator is forced to pull the journal from the database, makes this an impossible task. Doing this work for content that librarians cannot easily track or control may seem self-defeating at times. Some content providers list all the journals available in their databases, and some libraries have taken to downloading that data and processing it themselves for addition to the catalog. But updating these records in a prompt manner, given all the other demands on a librarian's time, is difficult and expensive to sustain.

Serials Solutions

Intelligent outsourcing seemed to make the most obvious sense, and Serials Solutions has created a service to do just that. As we began this project, our first step was to collect the data we would need to share with libraries. In order to create this massive database of holdings, we had to (and still must) collect accurate data from aggregators and publishers. As aggregators come to understand our business model, and the benefits it brings to them and their clients, they increasingly support our project. In essence, we promote their product to their current clients. We are now publicizing our agreements with publishers, so librarians can know that publishers and aggregators recognize and support the valuable role we play between the content distributors and the content users.

Librarians have expected title lists since they began comparing databases, and major aggregators have been posting content information on their Web sites since the mid-1990s. In some cases, it is simple for us to download the data and process it slightly before adding it to our master database. Several aggregators provide us with specialized reports or download sites where we can more easily and quickly access the metadata that describes their content. These are the easy ones. Other databases are more difficult, and the work required to prepare the data can vary dramatically. Sometimes it may consist of collecting and collating appropriate data, and other times it can consist of reviewing a list of several thousand entries, and deleting inappropriate or irrelevant entries. Lexis-Nexis's Academic Universe, for example, contains hundreds of journal "supplements" which by rights should be incorporated into the entry for the journal title. Too many titles in Academic Universe have just one or two issues in the database, hardly justifying the appearance of the journals in a library's list. We believe that the current variations and inconsistencies in the Lexis-Nexis title lists require that a librarian review all entries on a case-by-case basis. This cannot be done for every database, of course, but for one with as much market saturation as Lexis-Nexis has, and for one with as many content variations as they list, we feel it is vital that we review this data by hand.

We collect information about all of these databases and update our own master database monthly. We also need to collect information about the subscribing libraries. Because every report is specific to a subscribing library, we need to know which databases the library's patrons can access. We also collect information about every individual subscription available through services such as CatchWord, ingenta, Elsevier, and other electronic publishers and distributors. Many libraries have access to only a specific collection of journals from these publishers, rather than all journals the publishers offer. Some institutions, in fact, ask that we add a list of their print serial holdings to their reports, and this quickly provides an even more complete overview of the journals their patrons can access. We collect this data and add it to our database.

Libraries also provide us with information about the URLs their patrons use to access these resources. Our database allows a wide variation of URLs, from journal-specific URLs (where available) to library-specific redirect URLs that lead the user through an additional server. Because our information resides on the library's server and within the institution's IP range, IP-based access is in no way limited. Serials Solutions' database can accommodate proxy servers and other institution-specific URL data. Once we have collected data on the library's databases, individual subscriptions, and URL requirements, we are able to sort the data within our own database and produce a library-specific report.

Serials Solutions' Product

The final product is a print or HTML report that lists, in alphabetical order, all of the journals that patrons at a particular library can access in electronic format, including coverage dates. Many libraries like having the print report: it is good to have on hand at the reference desk, and is easy and quick to consult. Others prefer the HTML report, which immediately provides access for distance education students. We update all reports every other month, so they are kept current, with minimal additional work. Whenever possible, the HTML report includes links directly to the journal's Web page. At times, it is necessary to provide a link to the database home page, but as aggregators' linking technology improves, we will incorporate journal-specific links into the reports we provide to our clients.

Other formats are also available: many libraries have created their own solution to this problem, and when this is the case they can purchase raw data from us and then adapt it to the format they need to replace the content of their existing database. Apart from the dramatic savings in time, this usually results in better data than they previously had because we are able to collect information regarding even the smallest databases, which might not otherwise be worth a librarian's investment in time. The result for patrons is a familiar interface, but with more accurate and complete data.

The Serials Solutions product is clearly efficient and cost-effective: for less than the cost of many individual journals, a library knows exactly what is available through all its full-text aggregators. Locating specific journals not held in print is suddenly a project of just a minute or two, rather than hours of searching through perhaps a dozen or more database title lists, and only when those lists are actually available and accurate. The cost savings alone are significant; at a session at the American Library Association's 2000 Annual Conference in Chicago, one interlibrary loan librarian was quoted as saying that in their research, nearly 40 percent of all requested English-language articles were available through the aggregators to which the institution's patrons already had access. Reductions in interlibrary loan costs, plus dramatically increased delivery times for patrons, show obvious examples of the value of this product.

IMPLEMENTATION AND ENHANCEMENTS

We have designed Serials Solutions' reports for use in a variety of settings. Libraries can keep our print report at a service point; we do not have any limits on the number of photocopies of that report they can make. Libraries can post the HTML report on their Web site, so that students and patrons—regardless of their location—have a single location to check for information about journals available electronically. We also provide this information in Excel, XML, and other formats, as needed by libraries. In addition, we produce a MARC product designed to be incorporated into a library's online catalog.

Libraries have requested full MARC records of these titles, and we have responded, combining a complete database of CONSER-created MARC data from the Library of Congress with our own knowledge of aggregator holdings. We provide the MARC records in whatever format libraries want: either a single record for each aggregator's holdings, so a journal that appears in four full-text sources will be represented by four separate MARC records, or a record that reflects all four sources on the same MARC record.

Anyone just beginning to work with the metadata surrounding full-text database contents will quickly recognize that there is little or no standardization of titles between the title lists. We feel lucky if the aggregator includes an ISSN; in most cases title lists contain wide variations regarding the use of articles, ampersands, and variant titles. We felt it was critical that we create a database of accurate content. Through use of the CONSER-created database of MARC serials records, we are beginning to provide accurate and reliable cataloging records. We combine our holdings data with Library of Congress-created cataloging data, and the result is reliable, useful MARC records.

Finally, as of this writing (May 2002), we have completed development of technology that brings us to our original vision of incorporating this information into the library's online catalog. We combine our holdings data with CONSER MARC records to provide complete catalog records for the journals available through database aggregators. All electronic manifestations of a specific journal appear in a single MARC record, with separate 856 fields for each electronic version of the journal. As with our HTML and print reports, these records show the dates of coverage in each database. We update these records regularly, in a format that allows easy loading and overlaying of existing Serials Solutions records.

DEVELOPMENTS AND IMPLICATIONS

We have discovered an interesting side benefit to the Serials Solutions product. Subscribers often notify us of apparent errors in our reports. Now that libraries can easily know what aggregators claim is in their databases, librarians are discovering that these claims are not always accurate, and they come to us with this information. It is now easier for librarians to identify specific examples of missing data, which they then share with us. We base our data on what the aggregators provide to us, but as we receive this information, we become a nexus for data about the true content of the databases.

When we learn of errors in aggregators' title lists, we contact them and ensure that their content is what they say it is. It may be that they are not accurately representing what they are selling, or perhaps they have previously unknown database access or content problems. Perhaps the aggregators, for example, are not receiving the content they are expecting. In the end, all parties benefit. These errors will continue to appear for months to come, but the process of reporting them to Serials Solutions improves the accuracy of reports for all who use the databases, and empowers librarians in their abilities with and knowledge of these products.

CONCLUSION

Serial Solutions' product is by a librarian, for librarians. Librarians know best what they need to do their job most effectively, and Serials Solutions is dedicated to listening to librarians and responding to their concerns. Rather than just telling a vendor what we wanted to see and waiting for several years for perhaps half of what I had hoped for, I decided to do it myself. It is certainly a challenge, but it is also very fulfilling to see it come to fruition. As a result of my experience as a librarian, Serials Solutions aims to operate in a manner librarians would like to see from vendors. For example, we place all relevant information on our Web site and in our literature. Librarians work best with knowledge, and we make a point to provide as much as possible at the outset.

Our clients include major public library systems, corporate libraries, community college libraries, small private colleges of just a few hundred students, Association of Research Libraries (ARL) institutions with nearly 30,000 students, and all types and sizes in between. Much to the chagrin of our accountant, we continue to provide a significant consortial discount, because we believe strongly in the value of libraries working together to achieve common goals. Regardless of pricing and the presence or absence of consortial purchases, all our client libraries continue to receive individualized reports, as each library is unique.

Although there are clearly more areas for Serials Solutions to expand into and better products for us to provide in the near future, we believe that our current product goes a long way toward solving one of the more vexing problems facing libraries and librarians today. We are excited about the reception of our product to date, and we look forward to further improving the access I expect at the reference desk every day.

Chapter 15

Building Dspace to Enhance Scholarly Communication

Eric Celeste
Margret Branschofsky

INTRODUCTION

The MIT Libraries have built a durable digital document repository called DSpace to house the digital output of our faculty's research. DSpace will be a home for the digital documents our faculty want to share with their colleagues around the world. DSpace also expresses the ferment in scholarly communication, and the potential shift away from the journal as the primary means of disseminating research findings. This chapter takes a brief look back at where scholarly communication has been, describes how it may now be changing, shares our vision of how DSpace fits into that picture, and glances at the impact DSpace will have on our faculty and library.

BACKGROUND

Scholarly communication has not significantly changed since the middle of the seventeenth century when the Royal Society of London launched its *Philosophical Transactions* (1665). This development marks the beginning of the scholarly journal, whose original purpose was to formalize and regularize the exchange of information between scholars, replacing the heavy exchange of correspondence previously required to keep abreast of developments in the world of learning. Learned societies continued to be the primary publishers of scholarly journals until well into the twentieth century, providing services to members of the society and to universities, while relying on the support of scholars and universities to maintain financial security. The society journal offered scholars a vehicle for disseminating their work and ideas, while also providing them with a means of learning about others' endeavors. Authors contributed to the advancement of journals in their disciplines by providing editorial and reviewing services gratis. Development of the peer review system provided universities with an evaluation system for rewarding faculty through advancement and tenure. Universities contributed to the support of society journals through subscriptions paid by their libraries.

It was not until after World War II, when government funding of science and technology resulted in a huge increase in the numbers of journals published, that this model changed. As more authors submitted articles to be published, and as disciplines became more specialized, many more journals were created. University libraries were well funded and bought these journals to keep up with demand from faculty. Such a climate of demand made it possible for commercial publishers to step into the journal market, gradually raising prices in order to make profits. The continuous rise in the price of journals came to a head during the 1980s when university library budgets were no longer able to keep up with the inflation of prices.

Informal means of communication have always accompanied the more formal print outlets. Scholarly communication occurs at conferences, through correspondence, and through the exchange of prepublication information within a discipline. An informal network of communication between the top scholars in a discipline, called the "invisible college," often provides the primary means of communication between established scholars. Because of the long time lag between the submission of an article for publication in a print journal and the actual publication date, a practice of exchanging preprints became a part of the communication culture within several scientific disciplines.

For a period of six years beginning in 1961, an early experiment to develop a centralized method of disseminating preprints via the Information Exchange Groups in the biomedical sciences was supported by the National Institutes of Health. Also during the 1960s, the Stanford Linear Accelerator Center (SLAC) took an early lead role in collecting and cataloging preprints in the field of high-energy physics (HEP), thereby supporting a preprint culture in that field.[1] It was in HEP that the first preprint server was established at Los Alamos National Labs in the early 1990s.

SHIFT

Scientific advance supported by peer-reviewed publishing in the journal literature has come under pressure from two fronts. On one front, librarians have been concerned about the business model of journals, particularly the fact that journals have been getting too expensive for library budgets. Observers on the other front have feared that the pace of journal publishing cannot keep up with the pace of innovation. Pressures from both fronts may squeeze scholarly communication apart into its component services, ready to realign into a new system.

Herbert Van de Sompel[2] has drawn from and expanded on the work Roosendaal and Geurts[3] in order to propose six basic services which comprise scholarly communication: registration, awareness, certification, archiving, rewarding, and accessibility. Since these are not common terms, they deserve some definition. Registration (such as submitting a paper to a journal) is the service which takes in a scholar's work and acknowledges it as his or her own. Certification (such as peer review) declares the work to be of a certain scholarly value. Other individuals learn of the work's existence through awareness services (such as advertising). Accessibility services (such as library lending) make the work available to others. Archiving preserves the work for future scholars. Finally, rewards (such as tenure) encourage scholars to keep contributing to the system.

In the journal publishing model, registration, certification, and awareness are all typically provided by publishers, archiving and accessibility are typically provided by libraries, and institutions usually do their own rewarding through systems such as tenure. But as many respected journals fall months and even years behind the pace of innovation in their fields, new technological approaches are pulling these services out of their comfortable contexts. Preprint servers such as arXiv.org e-Print archive (now housed at Cornell) provide registration of new works, new forms of open certification are emerging on the Internet, and accessibility is easier to provide than ever, thanks to the Web. However, participation in this new model is limited to a few scholarly disciplines and the depth of commitment to their new roles by some of the players is uncertain. Still, new technologies offer the opportunity to redefine scholarly communication, allow faster dissemination of works, and revise business models.

As these scholarly communication services are squeezed apart and realigned, new players can take responsibility for each role. We have already seen examples such as arXiv.org emerge, dedicated to improving communications within particular disciplines. This makes a certain amount of sense, since the allegiance of faculty is often at least as great toward their discipline as it is to the institution housing them at any given moment. Still, institutions have a great deal of interest in the output of their faculty, and may have more consistent resources available to sustain digital repositories over the long haul. Institutions also have an interest in capturing output from all disciplines, not just those with a cultural predisposition toward sharing.

Although the MIT Libraries certainly do not intend to replace the journal publishing model, we do want to play a part in providing some of the component services of scholarly communication in the digital age. In particular, we do not see others systematically capturing and providing access to the digital output of our research process, output in which we have a large vested interest. As models realign, we think it is vital that libraries step up to such a challenge.

RESPONDING WITH DSPACE

In 1999, the MIT Libraries decided it was time to take some action on behalf of our institution to capture the digital output of the research that happens at MIT. The transformation of scholarly communication under way and the emergence of a community dedicated to making it possible to sew together the contents of a diverse universe of open electronic archives constituted a ripe environment for this kind of experiment. Most importantly, a corporate partner with an interest in this kind of tool came to light: Hewlett-Packard (HP).

Hewlett-Packard Laboratories, the research arm of HP, was interested in learning what it takes to start up and manage a digital repository and how the market (in this case the MIT community) would respond to the availability of such a repository of research output. Such repositories of digital content are a key aspect of the future, and in academe HP has found a partner ready to experiment with that future today. HP Labs also wanted a test bed for further research initiatives in the capture, storage, management, and dissemination of digital documents.

MIT's view that it was important to attempt an institutional approach to collecting digital output of research found some quick confirmation. In the fall of 1999 the MIT Libraries received an invitation to participate in the Universal Preprint Server (UPS) meeting sponsored by a wide array of library organizations and the Research Library of the Los Alamos National Laboratory.[4] The main thrust of this meeting was the development of the "open archives protocol" and the formation of what became the Open Archives Initiative. We agreed in the now superseded Santa Fe Convention to a framework to support the basic interoperability of electronic print archives.[5] Of great interest to MIT was the tacit acknowledgment by such a wide array of participants that there were two ways to build such archives: in disciplinary stovepipes or as institutional repositories. At this point we had already begun our negotiations with Hewlett-Packard to develop an institutional repository, and in Santa Fe we found that MIT was the only organization moving ahead with a real-world test of the feasibility of setting up an institutionally bound repository.

DEFINING DSPACE

DSpace is intended as a home for completed works resulting from research at MIT, works ready to be shared with colleagues. DSpace does not house works in progress or other works not yet fit for broad exposure. DSpace offers producers the option of superseding a work with a corrected or enhanced edition, but the older editions remain on the system for the record. Producers submit work to DSpace only if their intent is to share that work with the world. Certain conditions may prevent our ability to fully share a particular work at a particular time, but such sharing should be the intent of the producer of the work.

In order to fulfill our desire to take responsibility for the registration, accessibility, and archiving services of scholarly communication with respect to MIT's own digital output, we required that DSpace primarily serve as a reliable repository. To ensure that the services we provide could tie into those offered by other players, we would also have to take advantage of existing and future protocols. Building a sustainable system would require that others adopt DSpace as a solution to similar challenges, which in turn would require that we understand business models which are able to support such a system. These, and learning to work with a corporate partner such as HP, were the essential goals with which we embarked on the project.

A reliable repository of digital works at MIT must cope with producers from a wide variety of disciplines. Supporting these disciplines requires a variety of submission paths with differing assumptions about metadata schemas, work flow, and approval. A professor of physics will come to DSpace with very different requirements than a researcher in genetics. DSpace will have to allow them to use appropriate language to describe their works and employ separate approval paths to move the works out for public access.

In return for submitting their work to DSpace, faculty and researchers (our producers) will acquire a persistent URL which they can share with colleagues and cite, knowing that it will not change or become a dead link. They will benefit from preservation services which will enable future researchers to retrieve documents even if the format in which they were originally submitted is no longer supported by common tools of the day. They will find that their work becomes part of a greater body of work which will attract scholars and increase the exposure of all the material within it. They will not have to worry about maintaining their own high-visibility presence on the Web.

We intend for DSpace to participate in the emerging economy of open digital archives worldwide. Support for the Open Archives Protocol is a first step in this direction. As other standards emerge for the interchange of information among archives, DSpace will take advantage of them.

One indicator of DSpace's success will be its adoption by other academic research institutions. The Andrew W. Mellon Foundation is supporting our adoption efforts by funding positions within the project aimed at discerning what might be appropriate business models for DSpace. In order to be able to sustain DSpace over the long haul, or to convince others that they can and should implement a DSpace of their own, we must understand how we can support the long-term effort of managing this repository. Part of the DSpace effort is understanding what it costs and how we will pay for it.

IMPACT ON FACULTY

Another indicator of success will be the extent to which faculty participate in contributing content to DSpace. Faculty responses to the project have fallen into two distinct categories depending upon the publishing conventions and "cultures" within their disciplines.

In disciplines where it is established practice to submit one's papers to electronic preprint archives, such as physics and mathematics, faculty expressed no concerns regarding peer review, nor were they concerned about jeopardizing their chances of publishing in established journals. These faculty roundly dismissed journals that reject articles based on previous appearance on a Web site. Some faculty claimed that the feedback they get from dissemination on the preprint server is more valuable than comments made by the limited number of reviewers provided by publishers. They claimed that preprint servers were more important than traditional journals. On the other hand, these faculty did not see a strong need for an MIT-based system, since they already have adequate facilities for preprint dissemination through their disciplines. We were assured, nevertheless, that many of them would also contribute to DSpace, as long as we made the submission process simple. Ideally, they would like to be able to submit to their discipline-oriented e-print sites and DSpace using exactly the same procedure, preferably in one step.

In most other disciplines, where there is not a strong e-print culture, faculty expressed a strong belief in the peer-reviewed publishing process and also expressed strong concerns about the quality of DSpace's content. Many also expressed concern about copyright transfer agreements they sign with publishers that preclude or limit the right to display articles on personal or institutional Web sites.

Others mentioned that their need for timely dissemination of research results was already being met by publishers' preprint sites, where accepted-but-not-yet-published articles are displayed.

Faculty in all disciplines were interested in using DSpace to display images, datasets, and video and audio files that they do not publish in established journals. Many expressed dismay at the mounting "page charges" required by publishers, especially for color graphics and images. As more and more research is being expressed in rich-media formats, DSpace will offer faculty a means of publishing an unlimited amount of digital information in formats that are not usually handled by traditional publishers.

IMPACT ON LIBRARIES

An organization which has focused on combing the world's resources and selecting that which best serves its host institution is instead asked to share its host institution's output with the world. An institution which prides itself on proper application of metadata is instead asked to facilitate the input of metadata by novices. In some ways DSpace turns the library inside out. Yet the mission of an academic research library is to facilitate the teaching and research of its host institution. DSpace will serve an important role in meeting this mission over the coming decades. A close look at the architecture of DSpace reveals a structure not so far removed from what we know as a library today.

Our task of selection, of sorting through the world's bounty for that most beneficial to the work of MIT, inverts with DSpace. Our selectors today work closely with faculty to understand their interests, learn what journals they consult, and anticipate the requirements of new courses they plan to teach. DSpace asks us to draw out of our faculty and researchers what they wish to share with colleagues around the world. We must work with faculty not only to discern their needs, but also to discover what they have to offer. We become not just one of their sources, but also one of their destinations.

Today we manage a considerable budget, balancing needs as expressed by our faculty and students, and deploying acquisitions agents and catalogers to bring the material here to MIT and make it visible to our community. With DSpace we will be deploying some portion of our budget to make the work of MIT visible to the world. Yesterday the assets we managed were those items we brought to MIT; today in DSpace the assets are the output of MIT itself, the fruit of its labor.

Our organizational skills, until now deployed to tame a collection of foreign objects so that they would be useful to the institution, will have to be trained also on our own work. In fact, much of the metadata generation will be done by the producers themselves. Our task is shifting from creating the metadata itself to building systems that help others supply appropriate descriptions and classifications of information.

Still, in some ways, DSpace does not differ all that much from the traditional library. We found as we applied the language of the Open Archival Information System (OAIS) [6] to DSpace that the same mapping exercise applied to the traditional library revealed many similarities and helped clarify the roles that librarians may play as DSpace enters production. The OAIS model does not require that the tasks it identifies be resolved electronically, so it applies quite nicely to both the digital and the physical realms of libraries.

For example, today's creators of submission information packages (catalogers) might find an appropriate role specifying the submission information package contents for DSpace. Those who manage our current catalog media and management might find a similar role managing DSpace's database. Librarians who help our community form queries that successfully retrieve information from our current systems will help consumers of the DSpace system as well. Although DSpace turns us inside out in some respects, in others it will further leverage the expertise already present in the libraries.

CONCLUSION

The DSpace project team is currently hard at work developing the system that will fulfill these promises. DSpace began beta-testing with a few early adopters on campus during the spring of 2002. A full rollout at MIT should follow in the fall of 2002. Once the MIT implementation is firmly established, we expect to start sharing DSpace software with a small select set of academic research libraries interested in adopting it as a way to capture the output of their institutions. When DSpace has been successfully implemented at one or two other research institutions, it will be available for adoption by any interested party. We are developing DSpace as an open source effort, both to reduce barriers to adoption and to increase the pool of expertise devoted to its development. Our Web site at <http://www.dspace.org> provides more details about DSpace and an opportunity to sign up for periodic updates on the effort.

Much work lies ahead in the implementation and adoption of DSpace. The MIT Libraries expect plenty of surprises and challenges. We look forward to the lessons we will learn by making this effort, and to the partners we will get to know on the journey.

NOTES

1. James E. Till, "Predecessors of Preprint Servers," *Learned Publishing* 14(1) (January 2001): 7-13.

2. Herbert Van de Sompel, *Preview of the Open Archives Metadata Harvesting Protocol,* Paper presented CNI Fall 2000 Task Force Meeting, San Antonio, Texas, December 8, 2000.

3. Hans E. Roosendaal and Peter A. Th. M. Geurts, "Forces and Functions in Scientific Communication: An Analysis of their Interplay," *CRISP 97 Cooperative Research Information Systems in Physics,* eds. M. Karttunen, K. Holmlund, and E. R. Hilf (1997), <http://www.physik.uni-oldenburg.de/conferences/crisp97/roosendaal.html> (viewed May 31, 2001).

4. Open Archives Initiative, "First Meeting of the Open Archives Initiative," Santa Fe, New Mexico, October 21-22, 1999, <http://www.openarchives.org/ups 1-press.htm> (viewed May 31, 2001).

5. "The Santa Fe Convention for the Open Archives Initiative," <http://www. openarchives.org/sfc/sfc_entry.htm> (viewed June 25, 2001).

6. CCSDS, *Reference Model for an Open Archival Information System (OAIS): Red Book,* May 1999, <http://ssdoo.gsfc.nasa.gov/nost/isoas/ref_model.html>. In order to describe DSpace with some efficiency, we will use the terminology of the OAIS model. This model is proving to be a reasonable common language when discussing digital archiving projects, and is helpful in this regard. However, DSpace will differ in some fairly significant architectural ways from the OAIS model, so our use of this terminology should not imply an adoption of the whole model.

INDEXING

Chapter 16

Indexing Electronic Journals

Cathy Rentschler

In 1995, *Library Literature and Information Science* (formerly *Library Literature*) became the first H. W. Wilson index to include electronic journals. Five years later, our procedures are established, and the staff and I have become familiar with the new skills required. We have increased our coverage from three electronic titles to nine, and we have seen the migration from electronic mail to the Web.

THE SELECTION PROCESS

Studying journals to be indexed in *Library Literature and Information Science* usually means sitting around a large table piled with stacks of sample issues. The journals are passed around, examined, and evaluated against the criteria for inclusion. In contrast, the examination process for electronic journals means that members of the in-house selection committee sit in front of their computers looking at titles on the screen. The *Directory of Electronic Journals, Newsletters and Academic Discussion Lists*, published by the Association of Research Libraries, is still a valuable resource for identifying titles to examine.[1] *Library Literature and Information Science* itself is another resource, and we note titles that have been mentioned in the literature of the field. Our first criterion for electronic journals is archiving of published issues. We do not want to index ephemeral material that is not being archived, and we need to look at issues that have been "published," rather than subscribe and wait for issues to appear. Our second criterion (one used for print titles as well) is articles of reference and research value. We also exclude titles with invalid addresses and titles with only one archived issue. Print publications must hve published several issues, ideally at least one volume, before they are considered for *Library Literature and Information Science.*

SUBSCRIPTIONS

Once a journal has been selected for indexing, the next step is to subscribe to it. For print titles, we enter subscriptions through our serials vendor or request a complimentary subscription. When we first began to index electronic journals, "subscribing" was handled via electronic mail. Subscribers would receive an e-mail message notifying them whenever an issue was published. Subscribers then requested the contents, also via e-mail. The staff learned how to set up the subscriptions and to save the confirmation message explaining listserv commands. Although several of the electronic journals we index still send out e-mail notification, all of them have now migrated to the Web. We have bookmarked the URL for each title, and a staff member checks them regularly to see if a new issue has appeared. At the same time, the "masthead" or introductory page is checked for changes in publication schedules, content, etc. In one or two cases the URL has changed and the new address is bookmarked.

PROCEDURES AND SYSTEM SPECIFICATIONS

We had considered doing all of the indexing and keyboarding on a personal computer that would be connected to our data entry system. In 1995, there was only one personal computer in the department. (Our work is normally done on dumb terminals connected to a mainframe.) We decided to print a hard copy of each issue, which an indexer would index just like any print publication, and give it to a data entry clerk for keyboarding. We have now moved to data entry by indexers and have connected the departmental PCs to the mainframe, so it is not necessary to print a hard copy of each issue. We still print the table of contents as part of the serial check-in function. Indexers index by switching back and forth between the journal Web site and the Wilson Company data entry system. They give me printouts of their previous day's work, whether print or electronic. I check the indexing and give the printouts to a reviser to release into the *Library Literature and Information Science* database (LIB).

When we first decided to include electronic titles, we realized that the citations would not look like those for a print publication. We also knew that the bibliographic records in the LIB database had to be MARC-compatible. We looked at style manuals for electronic citations to determine what elements were usually included. A print publication normally has a volume and/or issue number, an issue date, and paging. This information, along with the author's name and article title, allows a user to locate that article. Electronic journals, in turn, have retrieval methods, server addresses, file sizes, article addresses, and archive sites. They may in fact have multiple retrieval methods and addresses. At the time we decided to include electronic journals, the MARC fields and the citation styles were still in development. Fortunately, there are staff members at the Wilson Company who monitor these developments and could advise me. We had to consider fields for the Wilson Journal File[2] as well as the LIB database.

Since electronic journals are in fact computer files, we include the general material designator (GMD) in each bibliographic record. We keyboard paging as given by the journal. In many cases no paging is noted, so we use the number of lines or bytes, as cited by the journal. Electronic addresses for a particular article are also keyboarded in each bibliographic record. We found that articles might have an e-mail, ftp, gopher, telnet, or Internet address as their retrieval method; some articles had multiple methods. Later, we began to see separate addresses for ASCII and HTML versions of an article. We included all the retrieval methods at first, but now find that most have only a URL. We decided to use only HTML addresses, and to ignore archival site addresses.

In the Wilson Journal File, print publications have publisher name and address fields. No change was needed for the publisher name field, but we substituted retrieval methods (electronic addresses) for the usual street address, city, etc. All retrieval methods, including gopher, are included in the Journal File record, but most have only a URL today. Subscription instructions, such as "send the message SUBSCRIBE PACS-P to the listserv address," would be included in a note field.

PROBLEMS AND DEVELOPMENTS

Excluding questions about subject headings and matters of style, problems with indexing print publications usually involve typographical errors or missing issues. Our problems with electronic journals have followed the same pattern, but the methods of solving them have been different and can be carried out more quickly.

One of our first problems was a minor one, an apparent typographical error. For a print journal we would have waited to see if a correction appeared in a subsequent issue. If it were a serious error we might try to alert our users, perhaps by adding "[sic]" in a title, for example. In this case, I e-mailed the editor. She replied immediately, was grateful for my alerting her to the problem, and made an online correction to the article.

A subsequent problem was more serious. We received one issue by e-mail when we had not received the previous issue. The problem occurred because the journal's server changed. This explained why no subscriber activity was being recorded on the server. The editor gave me the new address and sent the missing issue by e-mail.

As time went on, we began to realize that our electronic journals were establishing Web sites. This meant we did not have to "subscribe" or to wait for e-mail messages, but could periodically check the Web for new issues.

We have bookmarked the Web sites of our electronic journals. When an additional PC was installed in our department, another problem was identified. In transferring the bookmarks to the new PC we discovered that one of the addresses was no longer valid. We instituted a new procedure of testing the URL for each site on a regular basis. When a change occurs, the Journal File record is updated, just as we update addresses for print publications. We also update the bookmarks on our personal computers. A staff member also regularly checks the "What's New" section of journal Web sites for possible changes.

We still find it more convenient to print a hard copy of the journals for indexing and data entry. We have experienced an occasional problem with missing lines of text or lines running off the screen or the page. Modifying printer commands and an e-mail query to the journal editor did not resolve the problem. We have found that printing the Web version has worked better. We also learned that other subscribers had not reported any problems, leading the journal editor and myself to believe that most users are migrating from e-mail to the Web site.

It was exciting to be editor of the first and only H. W. Wilson index to include electronic journals, but that is no longer the case. *Education Index* now includes an electronic journal, and I expect other Wilson indexes will follow suit. Our staff served as a resource for the staff of *Education Index* and will do the same for other departments. As Wilson indexes become available through WilsonWeb, there will be the opportunity for users to link directly to an article by clicking on the address included in the *Library Literature and Information Science* citation. We also expect that more electronic journals will be included in the future. The number of electronic journals indexed has already grown from three to nine active titles, and whenever we study the index we will be looking for new titles that meet our criteria. In the early 1980s, the H. W. Wilson Company began offering its indexes in electronic formats through Wilsonline. Later, CD-ROM versions and magnetic tape formats were added. Original abstracts are being created for many products and full-text options are under way. Wilson products have certainly entered the digital age. The company celebrated its centennial, "Celebrating the Future, Commemorating the Past," in 1998. Today its mission remains the same: to give its users the information they want in the way that they want it.

NOTES

1. Dru Mogge and Diane K. Kovacs, *Directory of Electronic Journals, Newsletters and Academic Discussion Lists*, Seventh Edition (Washington, DC: Association of Research Libraries, 1997).

2. The Wilson Journal File is the company-wide database of all journals indexed by H. W. Wilson Company indexes. The database includes such information as journal title, publisher, frequency, price, etc. It also includes who indexes what (e.g., *Journal of Academic Librarianship* is indexed in *Library Literature and Information Science* and in *Education Index*), along with start and end dates. Title changes, cessations, etc., are also available. At the beginning of May 2002, there are over 7,000 records in the file, of which nearly 5,200 are active titles. The full file is available only in electronic format.

Chapter 17

Uniform Resource Identifiers and Online Serials

Leslie Daigle
Ron Daniel Jr.
Cecilia Preston

INTRODUCTION

The publication of serials online is of considerable current interest. Numerous experiments are being conducted and some systems have been deployed, but widespread use of such publication systems still seems to be a few years away. Ultimately, the shape online serials take in the world will be the result of compromises between many communities. By virtue of its (near) ubiquity and popularity, the Internet is the de facto standard network for use by online publications with an eye to global accessibility. To date, the application software infrastructure of the Internet and the World Wide Web have not been sufficient to meet the needs of serious online serial publications. This chapter outlines the work that is being done to address some of those issues, in particular in the area of providing general infrastruc-

The authors would like to thank Patrik Fältström, Michael Mealling, and Renato Ianella for their cooperation on an earlier paper, parts of which provided the basis for this chapter's discussion of URN abstract architecture.

ture for robust Internet identifiers for online resources. This is a revision of a chapter that was published in the first edition of this book in
1998. The standards development that was described as "in progress"
then has played out as expected; this revision includes some additional material describing initiatives that apply the standards described herein, as well as some initiatives that approach the problem
from the traditional publishing community's point of view.

Publishers form one of the most obvious communities involved in
the shaping of online publication systems. They are particularly concerned about the ease of copying digital works, and are loath to provide much of their content until rights management systems can offer
solid protection. Companies such as ContentGuard, Sealed Media,
InterTrust, and IBM are actively developing and marketing digital
rights management products to publishers to address these concerns.[1,2]
The International DOI Foundation's Digital Object Identifier initiative was established specifically to bridge the gap between publishers' needs and the electronic medium for accessing and trading in digital objects. But publishers do not operate in a vacuum. They rely on
customers—readers and librarians. While publishers might wish to im-
pose extremely strong licensing and/or copyright management systems that charge for even trivial access to a document, readers and librarians will reject solutions that are too expensive or cumbersome.
This is not a problem that will be solved by Internet technology, but the
appropriate infrastructure must be available to support solutions that
are adopted by the publishing community.

Scholars and archivists are another community with legitimate
concerns about the online publication of serials and the impact on the
long-term integrity of the literature. Procedures for storing paper over
long periods of time are well understood; storing digital data over
such time scales is an area of current investigation.[3] The desires of
scholars and archivists for very strong guarantees on the longevity
and integrity of the literature have a downside—cost. The cold fact of
the matter is that most century-old articles are rarely accessed, making it difficult to justify a massive infrastructure for their preservation. Instead, an approach to preservation that is less expensive than
the current model for physical works is needed. This may imply that
fewer sites will store copies of a work, and other sites that access the
work will pay to do so. These, too, are important issues that must be

resolved in order for online publications to gain the stature and respect of their physically published counterparts. Again, the solution must come from the interested communities, and the technical advancement of the Web infrastructure must be such that it can support the practices that these communities promulgate.

The rest of this chapter focuses on the specific issues of Internet infrastructure for one component of the technological solution—resource identifiers. Our premise is the same one that has motivated all Internet infrastructure standardization—that whatever community-specific or proprietary systems are built to function appropriately on the Internet are best supported by open and extensible standard infrastructure. This is as true at the so-called applications layer as it is in the nitty-gritty layers of Internet working.

ONLINE PUBLISHING AND THE WEB—TODAY

The integrity of citations between articles is one strength of the serial. The hyperlink mechanism of the Web is the natural way for referencing one article from another. Linking mechanisms will also be used for including figures in articles (including animation, video, audio, and links to the underlying data sets, for example), obtaining articles from a table of contents, and returning articles that meet search criteria. In fact, these links are the heart of the Web. Currently, these links are implemented using Uniform Resource Locators (URLs), the "addresses" of resources on the Web. URLs provide a "compact representation of the location and access method for a resource available on the Internet."[4] This compact representation for protocol-specific information made it very easy to build the Web from the bottom up, and to incorporate a great deal of information that already existed in ftp and gopher sites. The Web simply could not have been created any other way.

This low barrier to entry has downsides as well. Since it is so easy to start providing resources on the Web, very little advance planning is needed. Longevity of links has not been a major consideration of most providers of Web resources. As a consequence, all users of the Web are familiar with the problem of broken links. The brief history of the Web already provides numerous examples—including the seminal documents on the origin of the Web itself. Initially, these documents were all provided from the CERN Web server, and consequently were identified using URLs of the form <http://info.cern.ch/> and were widely cited. When the World Wide Web Consortium (W3C) was formed, the documents were moved off CERN's machines. For about a year CERN provided a forwarding service, but now, old links to those documents are broken. If you happen to know that almost all those documents are available at <http://www.w3.org/> then it is easy to find them again. However, no software currently exists that will perform that mapping without the participation of the site that originally provided the document repository that has moved.

The Web has been in general use for less than a decade. We are concerned about the availability of Web resources over much longer time scales—on the order of a century. As Tim Berners-Lee notes, much of the fragility of Web links is due to poor choice of identifiers.[5] But we are confronted with a trade-off. Embedding particular access technology information, such as protocol, host, port, and path in an identifier makes it easy to resolve but limits its lifetime. Identifiers without such information can have long lifetimes, but require extra steps to resolve. The simple fact of the matter is that using identifiers based on technologies of the late twentieth century, such as HTTP, DNS, and HTML, is a high-risk strategy to achieve long-lived identifiers. Using the Web to publish online serials requires the development of an identification system and resolution mechanism that avoids the use of such potentially transient information. Of course, half of that requirement already exists. Numerous bibliographic identification systems, such as ISBNs, ISSNs, SICIs (Serial Item and Contribution Identifiers), Library of Congress Control Numbers, and SuDoc numbers are currently in use. These identifiers do not display the dependence on specific technology which typical URLs do. The remainder of this chapter discusses how such identifiers might be resolved, and the issues that arise.

DEVELOPMENT OF INTERNET IDENTIFIERS

Broken links are not the only problem that can be attributed to the use of retrieval information as an identifier. Since URLs often incorporate domain names, common practice is to contact the first machine that is associated with that name. This results in overloaded servers and duplicated intercontinental traffic. All these problems became apparent very early in the development of the Web. The Internet Engineering Task Force (IETF) is the de facto standards body for defining the necessary technology infrastructure for the Internet. In 1992, it established a working group on Uniform Resource Identifiers (URI) that was to standardize various URL schemes that were emerging at that time, as well as to consider what could be done about other related problems. That working group developed a model that allows resources to be identified by a Uniform Resource Name (URN), which would be a persistent identifier for a resource, independent of information such as protocol, host, port, etc. One of the requirements placed on URNs by the working group was that URNs be able to utilize existing forms of identifiers such as ISBNs, ISSNs, LC control numbers, etc. URLs and URNs were defined to be the two classes of URI.

To obtain a copy of a resource, a URN would be mapped to a set of URLs that are the current locations of the resource. The browser or other client software would then pick one URL from the set and use it to fetch the resource. This would add a measure of fault tolerance to obtaining resources. If the first server was down, the client could use one of the other URLs in the list. Replicating a resource could be achieved by copying the resource to a new location, then adding the URL for that new location to the list. Moving a resource to a new location would be like replicating it, followed by deleting the old URL and resource instance.

The data structure for mapping URNs to URLs was called the Uniform Resource Characteristics (URC). This name was given because, in addition to the URN and URL information, the URC was to be a carrier for information about the format of a resource at a particular URL, bibliographic information on the resource, and perhaps a digital signature to ensure that the resource had not been tampered with. The URC proposals ultimately became a generalized metadata structure for a resource.

Following on the work of the URI group, the IETF URN working group was formed with the consensus viewpoint that no single naming scheme would suit all needs. Although bibliographic resources are the primary focus of this paper, it is important to recognize that other types of electronic resources (e.g., programming elements, transaction data) also need persistent identification systems. The requirements of these identification systems are sometimes at odds with standard bibliographic practices. What was needed was a technical infrastructure, or framework, that would support many different schemes. This chapter describes the outcome of the work of that group in some detail.

A URC-WG was not formed in the IETF, but many of the people involved in the URC effort have participated in follow-up efforts. The Resource Description Framework (RDF) specified by the W3C is the closest intellectual successor of URCs, and it defines the framework for more community-specific metadata specifications such as PRISM (Publishing Requirements for Industry Standard Metadata).[6]

This original model is described in the IETF documents RFC 1630, RFC 1737, and RFC 1738.[7,8,9] As pieces of the puzzle were defined and standardized, understandings of the concepts evolved as well—so these documents do not necessarily reflect the current state of thinking. Work is underway to publish a roadmap of the IETF documentation and provide an overview of the documents that are considered current.[10] In particular, URIs were originally intended to be subdivided into URLs and URNs. Years of debate in the technical forums failed to yield an adequate differentiation between the two classes. Today, "URI" is used to refer to the general class of identifiers (which may behave more like addresses or names, depending on how the scheme is defined), "URN" is a specific URI scheme defined by the IETF, and "URL" is still the common term used to refer to any URI that does not use the URN scheme.

Today, URNs have been standardized and provide one mechanism for persistent, location-independent identification. However, other schemes have been developed to address some or all of the same goals. Today, the term "URI" is used to refer to any scheme, "URN" refers to a particular scheme standardized by the IETF to meet the requirements laid out in RFC 1737, and "URL" has been deprecated in the technical literature (replaced by "URI"), although it is still the commonly recognized term.

Urns AND THE INTERNET INFORMATION INFRASTRUCTURE

URN work within the IETF was initially plagued by circular discussions and consequently no development progress. These early efforts attempted to solve both the Internet technical infrastructure issues and all the related problems raised by the different end-user communities (publishers, network-level software developers, etc.). Indeed, many of the original proposals for URN systems featured resource-naming structures that were tightly coupled to a resolution mechanism that was geared to solve one community's needs. From the IETF's perspective, the critical step was to focus strictly on finding the technical infrastructure for Internet identifiers that would provide persistent identifiers and support the solutions such communities developed within their own frameworks of discussion. To achieve this, two important things were needed: a separation of the structure of the name (identifier) from the resolution mechanics, and a resolution infrastructure that is multitiered and permits distributed information management at all levels.

There are three primary reasons why the separation of the name from the particulars of the resolution process is necessary. The first is only underscored by the success of the Web—there is a real need for Internet identifiers that are not dependent on resource location and that have some capacity for persistence. This alone would reduce the frequency with which resources "disappear" because the file name is changed, or the machine on which a resource resides is changed, and so forth. Beyond that, resource access robustness would be improved considerably by providing access to a particular resource from one of several suggested locations. URNs are meant to address all of these issues. Therefore, the temptation is to start by proposing specific techniques to solve these Web-general problems. Extensions can be made to servers, registration services can be added to already popular services, and there are several companies offering services today to cache or optimize delivery of content.

However, the second reason for which the separation between identifier and resolution process is necessary stems from the very fact that different communities have very different resolution needs. The technical infrastructure for URNs must be capable of supporting the resolution mechanisms developed by those individual communities, and not just for specific application software. Two key requirements for which the solutions are often in opposition are speed of access and strongly authenticated security mechanisms. Taking a minute to locate a deeply archived document anywhere in the world can be considered fast. Then, having located that document, it would probably be important to authenticate that it is indeed the expected resource (through a signing or certification of the resource itself, the URC referencing it, or even the URN referring to it). That part of the process takes time. On the other hand, various networked systems rely on the ability to consistently refer to configuration data or other resources that are stored and maintained at remote locations. These resources may be created, used, and destroyed in a period of less than an hour, which is a lifetime for machine accesses. While it might be reasonable to take a day to assign an appropriate identifier to a book, and thirty seconds to verify access rights and account information to view it, speed (of assignment as well as of resolution of identifiers) may take precedence over ability to charge for access to one of these network resources. No single end-to-end resolution mechanism can solve all such communities' needs.

The third reason for the separation of the name and resolution process is simply to allow resolution systems to evolve. As part of the effort to recognize the naming needs of different communities, and to allow the reuse of existing names, URN identifiers are divided into "namespaces." In rough terms, a namespace is a collection of identifiers that are related through some externally defined relationship. ISBNs form a namespace in that they are assigned through a known process, and the initiated eye can extract information from the string of digits. The collection of HTTP URLs could be considered a namespace, in that they refer to the set of Web-accessible resources available at an instant in time. A "URN namespace" is now defined as an existing or new namespace that has a well-defined mapping to the URN syntax and is registered with the Internet Assigned Number Authority (IANA), by the process defined in RFC 2611 and currently under revision.[11,12] Typically, URN namespaces will have support systems for resolution using the URN infrastructure. The support systems may change over time. Different URN namespaces have been, and will continue to be, proposed for identifying different types of resources and different assignment policies. Proposals to date range from identifiers for booklike documents (ISBNs) to protocol elements (Object Identifiers [OIDs], Virtual Reality Modeling Language [VRML] objects). Individual communities will establish resolution systems that are tailored to their needs, but there is nothing inherent in the identifier that precludes the use of other resolution systems.

Dividing URNs into different namespaces is the first step in supporting the second important infrastructural goal of the URN work: a multitiered resolution infrastructure with distributed information management. This is important because centralizing information away from its caretaker tends to lead to lags in updating and other errors. The resolution services for a URN must be provided by parties responsible for maintenance of the information about that URN (directly or through arrangement with another party). Since the resources named by a URN may change ownership over time, the resolution services for a URN must be able to change without modifications to the URN itself. The URN system abstract description outlines a method of handling URN identifiers with these necessary modular layers of information management. In addition to accommodating differences across namespaces, this approach is also designed to distribute authority in such a way as to keep all information maintenance close to the responsible entity. For example, if a resource location changes, only the final level of resolution needs to be made aware of the change.

While the namespace itself can also be used to distribute the load of resolution work to servers nearest the resource, some namespaces will not want to publish details of the structure of their names. Such namespaces can either opt to include other indications of subauthorities in translating their names into URN representations, or these will fall into the category of URNs that are handled by a single external resolution system for the entire namespace.

Rules for individual namespaces are determined by the registrants of the namespace before they are registered as URN namespaces. Authority of assignment of individual names within the namespace is also dependent on the individual namespace, and is not part of the URN resolution framework.

From the standpoint of client software, this distributed authority also means that sites may have local procedures to follow. As an example, consider a user working for a corporation whose library has licensed *Books in Print* on CD-ROM. If that user were to click on a link that used an ISBN-based URN, it would be feasible to send the resolution request to software at the library that could search the CD-ROM and return bibliographic information on the book, instead of requiring access to the global Internet to interact with a remote resolver service.

OUTPUT OF THE URN WORKING GROUP

The previous section explained the basic principles that formed the foundation of the IETF's URN working group efforts. The final versions of the documents were produced and approved in May 2002, and within three months after that the working group was to close and the documents were to be published as RFCs.

Syntax

The first standards-track document from the URN-WG defines the syntax for URNs, RFC 2141.[13] As described in RFC 3044, an example URN would be:

urn:ISSN:1560-1560[14]

This example illustrates two important points. First, URNs are structured into three components that are delimited by the colon character: a literal string "urn," the namespace identifier (NID), "ISSN" in this case, and the namespace specific string (NSS). The NSS is a legal identifier from the namespace identified by the NID. In this example, the string "1560-1560" is a valid ISSN. The URN shown above illustrates the use of identifiers from existing standards, with only minor recoding to get them into a unified syntax.

The URN-WG has not defined the one true method for resolving URNs. Instead, there is a proposal for a method that can be used as a "fallback" if local methods fail, or if no local method is defined for a particular URN namespace. This solution is based on a two-step resolution procedure. The first step is to locate a resolver, which can map from URIs to information about the resources the URIs identify (e.g., through a database or some other mechanism). The second step is to communicate with the resolver to find out about a particular URI. Those steps are discussed in the next two sections.

Resolver Discovery

The URN-WG has recommended one particular approach to resolver discovery. Originally described in RFC 2168, this approach has been generalized and is now referred to as the "Dynamic Delegated Discovery System" (DDDS), documented in published and forthcoming RFCs.[15,16,17,18] A general resolution discovery system, the first document describes the architectural approach, and the other two describe a particular implementation that is used for resolving URNs. This uses a special DNS resource record, called the NAPTR (Naming Authority PoinTeR) record, which carries the rule stating how to extract parts of a URI and rewrite those parts into a domain name. There are some questions as to whether the DNS-based approach will scale in operational contexts. No serious issues have been unveiled since its initial publication four years ago. However, the architecture of the resolution system defined in a forthcoming RFC is independent of DNS, and another database approach can be defined and deployed when there is sufficient operational experience to appreciate fully what the performance and scaling issues truly are.[19] Also, the nature of the approach to URNs is such that this whole system can be replaced with a more suitable one when the operational requirements are understood through experience, without perturbing the then-existing URNs.

Here we will illustrate the DDDS/NAPTR process with a simple example of how ISSNs might be handled. Recall that our example ISSN-based URN looks like:

urn:ISSN:1560-1560

The first step in the NAPTR method is to discover the rewrite rule(s) for the namespace. To do this, the NAPTR method specifies that there be an apparently centralized site, urn.arpa, which registers the rewrite rules for all namespaces. The process of finding a resolver begins by extracting the NID, "ISSN" in this example, and asking the

Domain Name System for any NAPTR records associated with the name issn.urn.arpa. The DNS might return a NAPTR record that told clients the next domain name to query was bib.urn.issn.org, that they could expect to find a resolver at that name, and that they could use either the Z39.50 or the HTTP protocol to talk with that resolver. Finally, the NAPTR record might tell the clients that the URN resolver could provide information about the resource identified by the URN, but that the resource itself would not be available from that site.

As an alternative example, consider

URN:ISBN:0-395-36341-1

The proposed ISBN URN namespace suggests that resolution will mostly be handled by ISBN group agencies, which govern the assignment of ISBNs and are typically associated with national libraries.[20] These hold the bibliographic information for registered ISBNs. Using the DDDS resolution infrastructure, resolution can be directed to the individual group agency responsible for the particular ISBN.

The details of the NAPTR record, and how it encodes all the information above, are not germane to this chapter. We refer any interested readers to the DDDS specification for those details as well as additional examples.[21,22,23] One point that must be underscored here is the fact that the owner of a namespace does not have to be the entity that manages operation of the resolution system directly; that can be delegated (subcontracted) under the authority of the namespace registrant.

The information at the namespace_identifier.urn.arpa level can be quite minimal. Also, it only appears to be centralized. The design of the DNS is such that the administrators of urn.arpa do not have to be the administrators of namespace_identifier.urn.arpa.

Use of one and only one protocol to communicate with the resolver is not necessary. The example mentioned that either Z39.50 or HTTP could be used to query the resolver. Any other protocol can also be used. This is one way that NAPTR accommodates future developments.

Resolvers will have different information available, and will be prepared to answer different types of requests. Some resolvers will have the resources themselves, and could answer requests for the resources with their data. Other resolvers might have only bibliographic information, or a single URL for the resource. These different forms of requests types, known as resolution services, are described further in RFC 2483.[24]

Communicating with a Resolver

The previous section discussed how a client could use the DDDS procedure to find a resolver and determine the protocol to use and the queries to ask when speaking with the resolver. The URN-WG has approved one proposal for such a resolution protocol for experimental use. That proposal is a simple convention for encoding resolution service requests and responses as HTTP requests and responses. Known as THTTP (Trivial HTTP), it was developed with the intention of being easy to retrofit onto existing HTTP servers and is documented in RFC 2169.[25]

Resolution services, such as mapping an Identifier to a Resource (I2R), an Identifier to a URL (I2L), or an Identifier to a (URC [Uniform Resource Characteristics]) description of the resource (I2C), are encoded as HTTP GET requests. All of HTTP's features for format negotiation are available. The THTTP specification has also been developed to use some of the special capabilities of HTTP in order to make life easier for users. For example, the I2L request returns the URL in a Location: header. This makes the browser automatically try to fetch the resource for the common case of a simple citation to a resource using a URN.

Other protocols can be used for communicating with a resolver— encodings in Z39.50, LDAP (Lightweight Directory Access Protocol), and CORBA IIOP (Common Object Request Broker Architecture Internet Interoperability Object Protocol) are all possibilities. The Los Alamos experimental system used the Handle resolution protocol from the Corporation for National Research Initiatives (CNRI).

URN IMPLEMENTATION STATUS

Currently the two most popular Web browsers, Netscape Navigator and Microsoft's Internet Explorer, do not offer native support for URNs. It is logical to ask how URNs can be deployed. The Netscape browsers have offered special treatment of URIs that begin with "urn:" for quite some time. These are sent to the HTTP proxy. This means that organizations with firewalls can modify their proxy server to understand URNs, and all the Netscape browsers behind the firewall will instantly gain URN support. This forms the basis of current URN demonstrations. Starting with version 4.0, Internet Explorer offers the ability for custom "protocol handlers" to be downloaded and installed. This feature can be used to add URN support in situations where there is no proxy, or modifying it is infeasible. A prototype implementation is available.[26]

Beyond the client issues, URN deployment software is in good shape. The NAPTR resource record has been part of the last few years' releases of BIND (Berkeley Internet Name Demon), the de facto standard DNS server distribution. Support for the THTTP protocol is easy to develop using (Common Gateway Interface) CGI scripts.

ISSUES IN URNs

While the previous sections of the chapter have presented URNs as a possible technology to use in the publication of online serials, there are still open issues about how URNs should evolve. At this time, the thorniest issues involve namespaces. In addition, there are operational concerns about the migration of resources and the consequent maintenance of information in the resolution system(s).

The last issue facing the URN-WG concerned namespaces and namespace identifiers. As discussed previously, a namespace is a system for assigning identifiers according to a particular scheme. The scheme may imply delegation of authority when binding an identifier to a work, such as in ISBNs. There may be even more freedom in the choice of identifiers, such as the Domain Name System.

One of the problems the URN-WG has had to deal with is the result of the IETF's bitter experience with the top levels of the Domain Name System. Until relatively recently, the .com, .edu, .org, and .net domain registrations were operated as a monopoly by Network Solutions Inc. Because that company had the sole right to assign names in those domains, it became the target of an antitrust suit. This and other issues led to the creation of the Internet Corporation for Assigned Names and Numbers (ICANN). This same sort of battle occurs at the root of the domain tree. Currently, it is not possible for anyone to create new top-level domains (such as .web, .biz, .lib, or .realestate) without explicit approval from ICANN. Coming up with a scheme that will allow new top-level domains to be created in a controlled manner has occupied much of the efforts of ICANN's Board of Trustees. These same sorts of problems may arise in registries of URN namespaces.

From a technical standpoint, there is also a certain tension between easily conceived hierarchies and stable systems. For example, a hierarchy of names based strictly on geographic boundaries is subject to the very real external events of countries that split and/or change boundaries.

For these reasons, the URN-WG defined a registration process for establishing new namespaces (registering Namespace IDs, NIDs). This was originally defined in RFC 2611, and has been revised in a forthcoming RFC.[27]

As with the deployment of the Web and URLs initially, some of these issues will best be exposed through the adoption and use of URNs. The basic architecture for URNs is now set; operational experience will guide future refinements.

ILLUSTRATIONS OF URIs IN ONLINE PUBLISHING

There are three important steps to consider in the use of URNs for online serials publishing—the creation or adoption of a URN namespace (and the maintenance of it), the publishing of a resource with a URN, and the resolution of the URN into the desired resource, once it has been published. The URN becomes the focal URI in this process, with URLs and URCs supporting the operations.

As mentioned previously, a URN namespace may be constructed from an already-existing namespace, such as ISSNs. In that case, the only necessary step is the formalized registration of the namespace and any necessary mappings into URN syntax and structure—see RFC 3044.[28] Alternatively, an organization may choose to develop its own namespace—see RFC 3085.[29] In either situation, creation of a

URN namespace implies a certain commitment, undertaken directly or delegated to another party, to reliably assign identifiers to resources, and possibly provide the ability to resolve published URNs to resources. If resolution is to be provided, it must be in the context of a reliable service that will be available for the duration of the use of the namespace and its identifiers (possibly outstripping the original proposing organization's intentions). Consideration of the necessary resources to provide these services must be given before the serious undertaking of creating a new URN namespace where an existing one might suffice. Indeed, whenever possible, it is desirable to use an existing namespace rather than creating a new one for each publishing activity.

The envisioned publishing process using URNs is not so different from standard "Web publishing" as it stands today. However, it is expected that publishers will provide (or delegate) resolution services to access the resources they publish with URNs. Thus, a published resource must have a name assigned to it (through the namespace's particular name assignment process—e.g., the standard ISSN assignment process), and the resource and its information must be made available to the service that will provide resolution to the resource.

Finally, the consumer of the URN—the reader of the online serial—will encounter URNs in citations and references from other online material. Resolution, carried out by a browser or intermediary software, will entail the iterative lookup described in previous sections. The user (or the user's agent) may select a particular copy of a resource based on availability, proximity, quality of reproduction, etc. It is this step that is most heavily supported by the proposed URC concept—standardized metadata describing the various locations, costs, and characteristics of the desired resource. The final resolution step, of course, is still achieved through a URL that indicates current locations of the resource and the protocol(s) needed to access it.

WHERE FROM HERE?

There is a growing list of registered URN namespaces. These are registered with the Internet Assigned Numbers Authority (IANA), and the registry is visible at IANA's registration Web page.[30] Formally registered namespaces today include: IETF (RFC 2648), ISSN (RFC 3044), and NEWSML (RFC 3085), with more in the pipeline for publication and registration (ISBN, National Bibliography Number). Several more are under discussion for application in specific protocol contexts, underscoring that the URN framework is viewed as meeting a broad range of identification requirements.

The next phase of URN (and URI) evolution will no doubt focus on more operational issues and support services.

OTHER WORK

Other initiatives are underway that have specific impacts on the publication and management of online serials and the use of uniform resource identifiers.

ISSN International Centre Project

For some time, the ISSN International Centre (ISSN IC) has been exploring an experimental URN-based service for ISSNs. The role of the ISSN in online serials publication and the URN work are described in a recent article by Françoise Pellé about ISSN evolution.[31] The present implementation at the ISSN IC includes a centralized resolution system that allows direct access to electronic resources by using the ISSN identifiers as URNs within an ISSN namespace. The resolution software provided by the ISSN IC is intended to be able to translate a given ISSN URN into electronic locations:

- Location of the bibliographic description or metadata
- Location of the periodical itself (if it is in electronic form)

Clearly, this project has important relevance for online serials publication as a potential leading identifier for the serial publication. Being focused on the bibliographic aspect of the serial publication, this identifier and resolution service may be of primary use for librarians and those maintaining the catalogs.

Sicis and Uniform Resource Names—DIEPER Project

Derived from Issns, Sicis are used to refer to specific items in serial publications. As part of the work done in the European Union's DIEPER (Digitized European PERiodicals) project, Juha Hakala describes the potential for using the ISSN database as a way station for resolving SICI-based Urns.[32]

Digital Object Identifier (DOI)

The International DOI Foundation was created in 1998 with the goal of supporting the needs of the intellectual property community in the digital environment by the development and promotion of the Digital Object Identifier system as a common infrastructure for content management.[33] Much of the work that has been done in the DOI development has been focused on addressing important questions of management of access to (digital) intellectual property. These questions are of course of prime importance in the consideration of developing successful online serial publications. However, the DOI approach is specifying one system, tied to the International DOI Foundation, and this solution may not be the approach of choice for all online serial publications. The DOI itself is not incompatible with the URN standard described in this chapter; what is still missing is a link (e.g., namespace registration) between the DOI system and the general URN infrastructure.

CONCLUSION

Online serials publication, in the context of today's Internet, relies heavily on the use of the Internet's identifier infrastructure. Although it has not previously been robust enough to adequately support the real-life needs and requirements of commercial publishers, steps are being made through the definition and nascent deployment of URN systems. Clearly, issues remain, and operational shortcomings will be illustrated only through usage. The URN infrastructure is timely, and support for more exploration of operational issues will lead to more robust, flexible systems for the future.

NOTES

1. International Business Machines, "Cryptolopes," <http://www-4.ibm.com/software/security/cryptolope/about.html>.

2. "InterTrust," <http://www.intertrust.com>.

3. Clifford A. Lynch, "The Coming Crisis in Preserving Our Digital Cultural Heritage," in *To Preserve and Protect: The Strategic Stewardship of Cultural Resources, Library of Congress Bicentennial Symposium, Washington, DC, October 30-31, 2000.* Available from: <http://www.loc.gov/bicentennial/abstracts/preserve/lynch.html> (abtract), <http://lcweb.loc.gov/locvideo/preserve/lynch.ram> (cybercast).

4. Roy Fielding, "Relative Uniform Resource Identifiers," RFC 1808, Internet Engineering Task Force, June 1995. Available from: <http://www.ietf.org/rfc/rfc 1808.txt>.

5. Tim Berners-Lee, "The Myth of Names and Addresses," *World Wide Web Design Issues*, <http://www.w3.org/DesignIssues/NameMyth.html>.

6. "PRISM: Publishing Requirements for Industry Standard Metadata," <http://www.prismstandard.org>.

7. Tim Berners-Lee, "Universal Resource Identifiers in WWW," RFC 1630, Internet Engineering Task Force, June 1994. Available from: <http://www.ietf.org/rfc/rfc1630.txt>.

8. Karen Sollins and Larry Masinter, "Functional Requirements for Uniform Resource Names," RFC 1737, Internet Engineering Task Force, December 1994. Available from: <http://www.ietf.org/rfc/rfc1737.txt>.

9. Tim Berners-Lee, Larry Masinter, and Mark McCahill, "Uniform Resource Locators (URL)," RFC 1738, Internet Engineering Task Force, December 1994. Available from: <http://www.ietf.org/rfc/rfc1738.txt>.

10. Leslie L. Daigle, "Uniform Resource Identifiers: Comprehensive Standard," Internet Engineering Task Force (forthcoming).

11. L. Daigle, D. van Gulik, R. Iannella, P. Fältström, "URN Namespace Definition Mechanisms," RFC 2611, Internet Engineering Task Force, June 1999. Available from: <http://www.ietf.org/rfc/rfc2611.txt>.

12. L. Daigle, D. van Gulik, R. Iannella, P. Fältström, "URN Namespace Definition Mechanism—Revised," Internet Engineering Task Force (forthcoming).

13. Ryan Moats, "URN Syntax," RFC 2141, Internet Engineering Task Force, May 1997. Available from: <http://www.ietf.org/rfc/rfc2141.txt>.

14. S. Rozenfeld, "Using the ISSN (International Standard Serial Number) as URN (Uniform Resourse Name) Within an ISSN-URN Namespace," RFC 3044, Internet Engineering Task Force, January 2001. Available from: <http://www.ietf.org/rfc/rfc3044.txt>.

15. Ron Daniel Jr. and Michael Mealling, "Resolution of Uniform Resource Identifiers Using the Domain Name System," RFC 2168, Internet Engineering Task Force, June 1997. Available from: <http://www.ietf.org/rfc/rfc2168.txt>.

16. M. Mealling, "Dynamic Delegation Discovery System (DDDS)," Internet Engineering Task Force (forthcoming).

17. M. Mealling, "A DDDS Database Using the Domain Name System," Internet Engineering Task Force (forthcoming).

18. M. Mealling, "URI Resolution Using the Dynamic Delegation Discovery System," Internet Engineering Task Force (forthcoming).

19. M. Mealling, "Dynamic Delegation Discovery System (DDDS)."

20. J. Hakala and H. Walravens, "Using International Standard Book Numbers as Uniform Resource Names," RFC 3187, Internet Engineering Task Force, October 2001. Available from: <http://www.ietf.org/rfc/rfc3187.txt>.

21. Mealling, "Dynamic Delegation Discovery System (DDDS)."

22. Mealling, "A DDDS Database Using the Domain Name System."

23. Mealling, "URI Resolution Using the Dynamic Delegation Discovery System."

24. Michael Mealling and Ron Daniel Jr., "URI Resolution Services Necessary for URN Resolution," RFC 2483, Internet Engineering Task Force, January 1999. Available from: <http://www.ietf.org/rfc/rfc2483.txt>.

25. Ron Daniel Jr., "A Trivial Convention for Using HTTP in URN Resolution," RFC 2169, Internet Engineering Task Force, June 1997. Available from: <http://www.ietf.org/rfc/rfc2169.txt>.

26. See "Verisign PIN Pilot," <http://pin.research.netsol.com/>.

27. L. Daigle, "URN Namespace Definition Mechanisms—Revised."

28. S. Rozenfeld, "Using The ISSN (International Serial Standard Number) As URN (Uniform Resource Names) Within an ISSN-URN Namespace."

29. A. Coates, D. Allen, and D. Rivers-Moore, "URN Namespace for NewsML Resources," RFC 3085, Internet Engineering Task Force, March 2001. Available from: <http://www.ietf.org/rfc/rfc3085.txt>.

30. Internet Assigned Numbers Authority registry of URN namespaces is available at <http://www.iana.org/>.

31. Françoise Pellé, "ISSN: An Ongoing Identifier in a Changing World," *The Serials Librarian* 41 (forthcoming 2002).

32. Juha Hakala, "Linking Articles and Bibliographic Records with Uniform Resource Names," *The Serials Librarian* 41 (forthcoming 2002).

33. International DOI Foundation, "The Digital Object Identifier," <http://www.doi.org>.

Chapter 18

Citing Serials:
Online Serial Publications
and Citation Systems

Janice R. Walker

Electronic serial publications pose unique citation problems, whether these are digital versions of print publications or uniquely electronic ones. Many of the existing formats for scholarly citations fail to take into account the structure of electronic publications or to address adequately some of the specific issues prompted by online serial publications. This chapter examines the problems inherent in the formats proposed by the Modern Language Association (MLA) and the American Psychological Association (APA) for citing online serial publications and outlines the tenets of an alternative format, Columbia Online Style (COS), an expansion of the Walker/ACW Style for citation of electronic sources. Further, it examines the specific structures of some common online serial publications and shows how these elements can be translated using COS to fit the purpose of scholarly citations for both print and online publications.

THE MODERN LANGUAGE ASSOCIATION

For over fifty years, the Modern Language Association has been *the* authority for writing in English and literature subject areas. In 1995, the MLA committee recognized the need to include formats for citing publications accessed by computers, attempting to address two important considerations: (1) how to locate the text again, and (2) how to ensure that the text consulted will still be available for verification. According to Phyllis Franklin, the problem of locating Internet sources is primarily one of infrastructure:

> A reader who wishes to locate a book can take a few pieces of information—such as the author's name and the title—to a library or bookstore in this country and many others and readily determine whether the volume is available. Publication practices, copyright laws, and the organization of libraries provide an infrastructure that makes locating print publications a relatively simple matter. Consequently, references to print sources can be brief. Because no comparable infrastructure yet exists for electronic publications, citations of them must provide more information than references to print sources normally contain.[1]

However, MLA's initial answer to this problem in the fourth edition of the *MLA Handbook for Writers of Research Papers* was to include the word "Online" as the publication medium, followed by the "name of the computer network," e.g., "Internet." The *Handbook* further suggested that the writer *may* want to include the electronic address used to access the document, preceded by the word "Available," as supplementary information only.[2] By allowing the omission of electronic addresses, MLA defeated its own goal of providing sufficient information to locate the source again.

Franklin notes that "the rules for citing electronic material that the MLA committee established are not presented as definitive, and they will surely change as the technology and practices governing electronic communication evolve."[3] And change they did. The fifth edition of the *MLA Handbook,* released in 1999, presents a format that, although it rectifies the problems in the previous edition by including Internet addresses and no longer requiring the nebulous denominator "Online," introduces new ones.[4]

In order to distinguish between the Internet address and other information, especially end punctuation, in a bibliographic entry, MLA opted to add angle brackets ("<" and ">") around the Internet address. Not only is the use of these characters unnecessary and confusing, it does not solve the problem it purports to address. Most modern word processors recognize WWW and e-mail addresses and automatically format them as hypertextual links, even within for-print documents. Corel's WordPerfect, for example, includes the last angle bracket (but not the first) in the address link. For documents that are read online (that is, on a computer), as many now are, this means that the functionality of the link created by the software application is impaired—the link will not work because of that pesky angle bracket. Microsoft Word's default settings automatically delete the angle brackets entirely, recognizing them for what they are—an error. Thus, it is entirely possible that an author trying to follow MLA's format for citing online sources would not be able to do so—his or her word processor would simply not allow it. MLA's answer to this dilemma (currently available only on its Web site[5]) is to instruct authors to change their word processor's default settings in order to accommodate a format that serves no purpose.

For authors publishing their work on the World Wide Web, angle brackets may cause additional problems since they are considered "reserved characters" in HTML (HyperText Markup Language). That is, text enclosed within angle brackets in HTML documents will not show up on the page at all, since these characters are used to designate HTML tags or command sequences. In order to circumvent this problem, angle brackets used as typographical characters must be designated using ASCII/ISO codes. For example:

Author's Name. Title. Date of Pub. Date of Access. <http://whatever.edu>.

This would appear on the Web page as:

Author's Name. Title. Date of Pub. Date of Access. <http://whatever.edu>.

Most newer HTML editors will automatically insert these codes for authors. However, Internet addresses are often formatted as hypertext links (which usually means they are blue and underlined in both HTML and word-processed files), so we end up with Internet sources set apart by color and underlining—and by angle brackets. Why add such complexity if it serves no purpose?

MLA justifies its decision to surround Internet sources with angle brackets by noting that it helps readers to be "certain about where it [the Internet address] begins and ends,"[6] citing the authority of the Internet Engineering Task Force (IETF). However, the IETF document cited is a Request for Comment (RFC) only, not an accepted standard.[7] In addition, the RFC calls for the use of delimiters (angle brackets, quotation marks, or white space) only in *plain text* documents. Plain text documents do not allow for the use of various fonts, underlining, boldface, italics, colors, or any of the other features we typically expect to find in word-processed documents nowadays; plain text files also do not include the capability to link documents and files. Moreover, according to the RFC that MLA cites, "For robustness, software that accepts user-typed URI [Uniform Resource Identifiers] should attempt to recognize and strip both delimiters [i.e., angle brackets] and embedded whitespace."[8] While the RFC is most likely appealing to developers of browser software to include this robustness (the IETF, which publishes the RFC, is composed primarily of "network designers, operators, vendors, and researchers concerned with the evolution of the Internet architecture and the smooth operation of the Internet"[9]), nonetheless, stripping these delimiters is exactly what Microsoft Word does when it deletes the erroneous angle brackets—and exactly what MLA would have authors circumvent by changing the default settings.

If the only justification for including angle brackets around Internet addresses is to avoid confusion with punctuation, then following the guidelines set forth in *The Columbia Guide to Online Style*[10] would solve the problem without adding to the technological complexities of document production. Columbia Online Style (COS) places the date of access in parentheses following the URL (Uniform Resource Locator, or Internet address), thus avoiding both the problem with the default settings in word processors and the problem with end punctuation. MLA instead places the date of access immediately after the date of publication, without clearly designating which date is which. COS, on the other hand, encloses the date of access in parentheses, clearly setting it apart from the date of publication or last revision; the date of access is not part of the document being cited, so citing it parenthetically only makes sense.

Another key sticking point for MLA is the ability to ensure the availability of a text. Although they recognize the fluidity of many electronic publications, they see this fluidity as problematic. Attempting to ensure the verifiability of a writer's sources, while a worthwhile goal, entails additional problems, including those of limited computer resources and sometimes lack of sufficient knowledge of protocols, which could preclude the ability of many authors to provide a reliable means of archiving or accessing texts. Librarians, too, have recognized the need to find a way to archive important information published electronically, but discouraging the use of such information is not a viable option. MLA, however, continues to do just that—discourage the use of electronically published information by its privileging of print-based forms instead. As Joseph Gibaldi notes, the MLA recommendations are aimed primarily at those who "use ideas and facts from electronic sources to *complement* those derived from traditional print sources" (emphasis added).[11]

MLA's suggestions, as well as those proposed by other major styles such as the American Psychological Association, continue to reflect a vision of electronic documents as print-based, available through technological means, rather than work published electronically that may or may not translate into print. This conception of electronic publications has precipitated much of the confusion over citation formats. Thus, the formats recommended by all of the major styles fail to follow the same logic as that used for citation of print sources, and add to the marginalization of electronic publications, the complexity of citing them, and the confusion of scholars who would use (and create) them.

THE AMERICAN PSYCHOLOGICAL ASSOCIATION STYLE

The fourth edition of the *Publication Manual of the American Psychological Association,* released in 1995, recommends that scholars follow the guidelines first proposed by Xia Li and Nancy Crane in their groundbreaking work, *Electronic Style: A Guide to Citing Elec-*

tronic Information,[12] the first widely disseminated attempt to codify a system of documentation specifically for electronic sources. Li and Crane's work, while laudable, is marred by problems. The initial format they developed, as included in the APA *Publication Manual,* presents the following format for citing online serials:

Author's Last Name, Initials. (Date of publication). Article title [number of paragraphs]. *Journal Title* [Medium], *Volume Number* (Issue Number). Available [Protocol]: Specify path[13]

APA includes models for subscriber-based online serials and for general-access online serials available through ftp or e-mail protocols. Obviously, without specific models for online serials available on the World Wide Web, this model is inadequate, but the time frame for Li and Crane's work and for publication of the fourth edition of APA's *Publication Manual* precluded these works from addressing the more recent proliferation of online, and especially WWW, resources. Thus, these models could not and do not reflect the breadth and variety of electronic sources, or the moves toward standardization, we are now seeing.

Problems with Li and Crane's/APA's guidelines for citing online publications include their suggestion that, if an online file does not include a date of publication or last revision, the researcher should substitute the date of access, which could confuse a reader—if only one date is given, how is the reader to know whether it is the date of publication or the date of access? Additionally, the use of the word "available" is misleading: an online source may *not* be available at any given time; all the researcher can safely attest to is that at the time he or she last visited the site it was. Specifying the medium, i.e., "Online serial," is also problematic. I am not certain exactly what the word "Online" refers to—one can be "online" when one is connected to a local area network (LAN) or to a wide area network (WAN) such as the Internet, to a local bulletin board service or chat room, or to a subscriber-based service such as America Online. One is "online," as a matter of fact, whenever one is using a computer at all, even if it is *not* connected to a network. And the same electronic publication or software application may be available on CD-ROM, on diskette, or installed on a hard drive, so citing the publication medium may be not only unnecessary but confusing.

One interesting idea Li and Crane propose is the use of paragraph numbers in a work to designate location or length. However, counting the number of paragraphs in lengthy works can be extremely tiresome and sometimes impossible. Further, with search features found in most word processing and browser programs, it is just plain unnecessary. Li and Crane also add to the confusion about the nature of listservs on the Internet, citing a listserv posting by including the statement "Available E-mail: listname@address" in their citation. This would seem to imply that one can simply send an e-mail to the address cited and receive a copy of the referenced work. Of course, this is not how online discussion lists work: most discussion lists require sending a subscription request to a separate address to join the list, and messages may or may not be archived, depending on the software and the decision of the list owner. Further, even when messages are archived, they are generally available only by sending certain specific commands to a listserv, listproc, or majordomo address, not to the list address itself, or they may be available at a separate WWW, ftp, or gopher site. Messages sent to the discussion list address itself (if allowed) will be distributed to all members of the list and will not provide the sender with the archival copy, even if there is one. Li and Crane also insist that the e-mail address be included for authors of e-mail, for both the sender and the recipient of personal e-mail messages, which is analogous to including the home addresses or phone numbers for senders and recipients of "snail mail" cited in publications—not only is it unnecessary, it could also be construed as an invasion of privacy. Last, but certainly not least, in order to avoid confusion with the online address of a source, Li and Crane opted to eliminate the end punctuation from their formats—there is *no* period at the end of a bibliographic entry.

Some of these problems were addressed in Li and Crane's updated edition released a few years later, parts of which have been published on the World Wide Web.[14] In their update, they included the date accessed as a separate element in both formats, using square brackets ("[" and "]") to separate the date in APA style, as well as to delineate the publication medium (e.g., "CD-ROM").

Inconsistencies also continue to exist in their presentation and examples of protocols. For instance, whereas the model shows "Available Protocol (e.g., HTTP):" as the basic structure of the format for citing Internet documents, their examples for APA style omit the protocol for "commercial supplier[s]." And their citation formats for Internet sites include unnecessary repetition of key elements, such as "http" (hypertext transfer protocol) in the citation as both the protocol and as part of the address, for example, "Available HTTP: http://whatever.edu." Further, they do not clearly delineate between "online" sources and those available from "commercial suppliers." If I access a full-text or full-image source online through the *MLA Bibliography*, using a telnet protocol included as a link from my university library home page, or through a portal such as GALILEO which my library home page uses to provide access to online databases such as ProQuest, do I cite the information retrieved as a database (a "commercial supplier"), as the Internet protocol I used to access it (the library's URL, the URL for the library's portal, or the URL for the online database), or as a telnet site? What if the *MLA Bibliography* links me to a home page on the WWW, or to an article published in an online journal such as *Kairos: A Journal for Teachers of Writing in Webbed Environments*? Should I cite the path from the library home page through the telnet portal to the database and back to the WWW? What if I further complicate the picture, and connect through a subscription provider such as America Online (AOL) to access a resource? For example, if I access an online encyclopedia through AOL, do I cite the address of the encyclopedia or of AOL? How do I include the AOL keywords, or do I need to? In order to adequately address the primary purpose of bibliographic citation of sources—to allow the researcher to access the source—it is essential to first understand the complexities of such access for electronically accessed sources. Li and Crane's models, like MLA's, fail this acid test. After all of this, Li and Crane have now decided to cede this work to others. "We have no plans to update it now," states Crane, adding, "Let everyone else figure it out."[15]

As with MLA, APA has again updated their style for citing electronic sources. Currently, this information is available only on their Web site.[16] For references to an entire Web site, APA now argues that listing the URL in the text is sufficient; they do not require a bibliographic entry at all. Of course, Web sites often move without notice. Without a bibliographic listing, it may not be possible to track down such a recalcitrant source. For references to articles in online serials, APA continues to add unnecessary complexity:

> Author's Name. (Date of publication). Title of article. *Title of Journal, Volume #,* pages. Retrieved [date], from the World Wide Web: http://address

This model, although it eliminates repetition of the protocol (http), is still redundant, and still does not address the absence of end punctuation. Note, too, that an online publication may not have "pages" in the sense that print publications do. That is, a Web page consists of *one* page, regardless of how many pieces of paper it would use if printed out. The format recommended for citing articles accessed through an online database is even more complex:

> APA's recommendations for citing electronic media have changed substantially since we published the fourth edition of the *Publication Manual.* For databases, rather than the "Available: File: Item:" statement specified in the *Publication Manual,* we now recommend a retrieval statement that identifies the date of retrieval (omitted for CD-ROMs) and the source (e.g., DIALOG, WESTLAW, SIRS, Electric Library), followed in parentheses by the name of the specific database used and any additional information needed to retrieve a particular item. For Web sources, a URL should be given that points to an "entry page" for the database.[17]

Both MLA and APA continue to try to get it right. MLA's latest recommendations are far simpler than their original recommendations. As a matter of fact, the only differences now between MLA's latest recommendations and Columbia Online Style are the placement of the date of access and the use of angle brackets, the two elements that make MLA's formats problematic. The fifth edition of the APA *Publication Manual,* includes examples for sixteen different types of electronic sources, following the same guidelines published on the APA Web site. However, the manual also argues that "the majority of the articles retrieved from online publications in psychology and the behavioral sciences are exact duplicates of those in their print versions"[18]; thus, APA argues that providing the electronic publication information is not necessary at all.

COLUMBIA ONLINE STYLE

The Columbia Guide to Online Style is an outgrowth of the "Walker/ ACW Style Sheet,"[19] developed by Janice R. Walker and endorsed by the Alliance for Computers and Writing. First published on the Web in 1995, it was later expanded to include formats for both author-date and humanities-style formats for citing electronically published and electronically accessed sources. The *Guide* uses an element approach that allows users to translate information for any bibliographic style, with specific examples for many different types of electronic and electronically accessed sources. The *Guide* also includes suggestions for authors producing work to help achieve these standards by ensuring that the elements necessary for adequate academic citation will be available for future scholars. This work is far from over. As a Task Force member of the Conference on College Composition and Communication Committee on Computers in Composition and Communication (commonly known as 7Cs),[20] I am involved in evaluating suggestions by MLA and others on formats for electronically published academic documents and considering how these suggestions will play out in these new publishing spaces. Obviously, this task requires a bit of omniscience, a crystal ball, and partnerships between those involved in writing, reading, publishing, and archiving academic work. But some guidelines are necessary if we are to "support the continuous, communal, and cross-generational process of knowledge building."[21]

By providing specific models for a wide variety of electronic and electronically accessed sources, *The Columbia Guide to Online Style* addresses the needs of researchers to cite whatever information they actually use—and not just the information that is considered academically reliable by MLA or APA, for instance. That is, while a personal home page or a video game might not be a credible academic source, it might provide important information for researchers in cultural studies, sociology, child psychology, or whatever. A researcher who needs to cite these sources needs models; COS is the only style that provides models for a wide variety of nonacademic as well as academic sources published or accessed electronically.

The library of the future will most likely rely more and more on the digital preservation of materials, electronic catalogs, and electronic distribution methods. But these changes may entail more than merely translating print features into their electronic counterparts. Changes in the technologies of reading, writing, research, and publishing may also prompt changes in our very conception of the text itself. The ease of self-publication, too, means that more information will be available, information that may need to be evaluated and perhaps cataloged as part of the scholarly conversation.[22]

This information needs consistent, logical, and economic ways to cite it, following five basic principles of citation style, including the principles of access, intellectual property, economy, standardization, and transparency.[23] The element approach used by COS ensures that researchers can interpret the necessary elements to cite any source following any style in a way that makes sense and that, unlike the MLA and APA models, adheres to these five principles.

Elements of citation used by all major styles include author's name, title of article, title of complete work, version, edition or volume numbers, and publication information. For electronically accessed sources, two additional elements are needed: the electronic address or path, and the date the source was accessed by the researcher. The general format for citing an article in an online journal in COS-humanities style begins by citing the journal just as for a print version. First, include the author's name, last name first, the title of the article enclosed in quotation marks, the title of the journal in italics, the volume number, the issue number, and the date of publication in parentheses followed by a period. For electronically accessed and electronic-only publications, however, this information needs to be followed by the electronic address or path and the date the site was last accessed by the researcher. For example, an online-only journal with volume and issue numbers would be cited as follows:

> Blais, Ellen. "O Brave New Net!" *Computer Mediated Communication Magazine* 3.8 (1996). http://www.december.com/cmc/mag/1996/aug/last.html (5 Aug. 1996).

An article in a journal published in print with an online analog that can be accessed with a unique URL would be cited thus:

> Herndl, Carl G. "Tactics and the Quotidian: Resistance and Professional Discourse." *JAC: A Journal of Composition Theory* 16.3 (1996): 455-70. *JAC Online.* http://jac.gsu.edu/jac/16.3/Articles/7.htm (28 Apr. 2001).

For articles with URLs that are created "on the fly," that is, URLs that include search paths and that cannot be used to directly access the source, cite the URL for the main page of the journal or database, along with any key words or links followed to access the article. For example, a full-text article retrieved through a university library database may return a URL that is not absolute, such as http://ehostvgw3.epnet.com/fulltext.asp?resultSetId=R00000000&hitNum=1&booleanTerm=emphysema&fuzzyTerm=#FullText.Trying to access this URL from a nonuniversity server will return only an error. Since, however, the article may be retrieved through any library server that subscribes to the database service by searching for the author's name or title, no additional information is required. For example, the article with the long, unwieldy, nonabsolute URL above can be cited as follows:

> Licking, Ellen F., ed. "Bionic Lungs Coming?" *Business Week* 14 May 2001: 121. Academic Search Premier at *EBSCOHost*.

Anyone with access to the full-text database can use this information to locate the article. Alternatively, the article can be located in print from the information provided, though it is important to include the information on the specific version of the work consulted (in this case, the electronic version) in case of errors or discrepancies. Note, too, that articles with long, unwieldy URLs, even if the URL can be used to directly access the source, may also be cited as links from a main page or search page instead, as long as the prime directive is achieved: providing a ready means of locating the source for future reference.

Author-date styles are similar to humanities styles, except that they usually include only the author's last name and initials, the placement of the date of publication is different, article titles are not enclosed in quotation marks, and only the first word and any proper nouns of article and book titles are capitalized. For example, COS-scientific style:

> Blais, E. (1996). O brave new Net! *Computer Mediated Communication Magazine, 3*(8). http://www.december.com/cmc/cmc/mag/1996/aug/last.html (5 Aug. 1996).

For styles that use footnotes, as in *The Chicago Manual of Style,* the same elements are included. For example:

> 1. John G. A. Pocock, "Classical and Civil History: The Transformation of Humanism," *Cromohs* 1 (1996): 1-34, http://www.unifi.it/riviste/cromohs/1_96/pocock.html (1 May 2000).

Full-text and full-image articles accessed through an online database sometimes pose additional problems. Many full-text articles do not include page numbers; however, online sources can be searched using browser features, so pagination can be omitted from the citation. In addition, it is necessary to cite the database that makes these sources available online in order to adhere to the principle of access. For example, a full-text news article retrieved from the Lexis-Nexis Academic Universe database (accessed through a university library portal or an individual or corporate subscription) would be cited in COS-humanities style as follows:

> Rorty, Richard. "The Unpatriotic Academy." *New York Times* 13 Feb. 1994: E15. *Lexis-Nexis Academic Universe.*

The example includes full print publication information, followed by information on the specific edition (i.e., the database) that the researcher used. Note that a date of access is not necessary for items retrieved through a database, since the database is not subject to the volatility of WWW sites. The URL for the database may be included if it can be accessed directly on the Web, but for most academic databases, researchers gain access through a library portal only available to students, faculty, and staff of the university. Including such local information could be confusing and it is unnecessary; researchers who want to access the specific electronic version from the database can check with their local library for instructions. The publication information provides sufficient information, then, to allow the researcher to locate the specific source. Why add complexity?

No single format exists for all of the different types of online serial publications. Print-based journals may offer online counterparts; however, electronic versions of journals may be substantially different from their print counterparts. Even the electronic address may be different depending on the route taken to access a given work. For example, searchable full-text databases may create document addresses based on a search path rather than a distinct document location.

The library has changed: sometimes it is hard to tell from the library catalog whether a given source is electronic or print—or both. It is easy to get lost in cyberspace, even when the point of access is the modern electronic library catalog. While MLA and others continue to privilege only those sources that have obvious scholarly credibility, determined by the imprimatur or site on which they are hosted, this, too, is not always as easy as it sounds. A Web publication on a university host may indeed be a credible source and may indeed be sponsored by the university; it may also be part of a student project. Web authors, even experienced ones, are often notoriously lax in citing their credentials or listing any publication information. Moreover, many scholars have opted to publish material on commercial sites, such as America Online or GeoCities home pages, rather than on their university sites, for intellectual property reasons. At any rate, as researchers follow links in otherwise credible sources, they may find themselves almost anywhere, sometimes without even realizing they have left the site where they began their journey. One easy answer, of course, is to require researchers to use only sources which we already know are reliable, i.e., traditional print sources collected in university collections—either online or onsite. Limiting researchers to only those sources that someone else has already decided are reliable is just not realistic. Ours has been dubbed the "Information Age," but what that seems to mean is that, although more information than ever before is available to us literally at the touch of a button, evaluating the information we find is more and more complicated, and figuring out how to ensure that we can locate a source again once we do find it requires knowing where we are in a "library" (the online world) with no systematic arrangement and design.

Columbia Online Style is the only style that applies the same logic to citation of electronic and electronically accessed sources as other styles do for more traditional sources. Thus, this type of element approach is the only approach to citing these sources that makes sense as we move into a new era of publishing. COS models allow researchers to present the information necessary to accomplish the purpose of bibliographic citations—to recognize authorship and to allow the reader to access the original material—in a way that is clear and concise. The formats are readable both in print and electronic publications (with a few minor modifications; i.e., hypertext documents do not usually follow the double-spacing and hanging indent formats used in print documents, and URLs—the WWW addresses—are usually hyperlinked). And they do not require any changes to the default settings of an author's software applications. They avoid the problems entailed by the use of such reserved characters as angle brackets, allow documents to be read online, retaining the functionality of links, and they avoid any possible confusion with punctuation in URLs and end punctuation used in bibliographic entries. COS has not changed its recommendations since they were first published on the WWW in 1995; both MLA and APA have changed with each new edition (and between editions with information presented only on their Web sites), and they still have not gotten it right. So we can continue to update our textbooks and handbooks and style guides every year or so to keep up with the recommendations of MLA, APA, and others, or we can settle on a style—COS—that continues to work without all those changes, and that promises to work with whatever changes in access to information the future may hold.

NOTES

1. Phyllis Franklin, Foreword, in *MLA Handbook for Writers of Research Papers,* Fourth Edition, by Joseph Gibaldi (New York: MLA, 1995), xv.
2. Joseph Gibaldi, *MLA Handbook for Writers of Research Papers*, Fourth Edition (New York: MLA, 1995), 165.
3. Franklin, Foreword, xvi.
4. Joseph Gibaldi, *MLA Handbook for Writers of Research Papers,* Fifth Edition. (New York: MLA, 1999).

5. Modern Language Association, "MLA Style: Frequently Asked Questions About MLA Style," updated 11 May 2001, http://www.mla.org/www_mla_org/style/styleFaq_index.asp (25 June 2001).

6. Ibid.

7. T. Berners-Lee, R. Fielding, U. C. Irvine, and L. Masinter, "Uniform Resource Identifiers (URI): Generic Syntax," Internet Engineering Task Force RFC 2396, August 1998, http://www.ietf.org/rfc/rfc2396.txt (23 April 2001).

8. Ibid.

9. Internet Engineering Task Force (IETF), "Overview of the IETF," http://www.ietf.org/overview.html (25 June 2001).

10. Janice R. Walker and Todd Taylor, *The Columbia Guide to Online Style* (New York: Columbia UP, 1998).

11. Gibaldi, *MLA Handbook,* Fifth Edition, 179.

12. Xia Li and Nancy Crane, *Electronic Style: A Guide to Citing Electronic Information* (Westport, CT: Meckler, 1993).

13. *Publication Manual of the American Psychological Association,* Fourth Edition (Washington, DC: APA, 1995), 219-220.

14. Xia Li and Nancy Crane, *Electronic Style: A Handbook for Citing Electronic Information,* Second Edition (Medford, NJ: Information Today, 1996).

15. Clive Thompson, "Good Citations," *Lingua Franca,* July/August 1999, 23.

16. American Psychological Association, "Electronic Reference Formats Recommended by the American Psychological Association," updated January 10, 2001, http://www.apastyle.org/elecref.html (25 June 2001).

17. Ibid., http://www.apastyle.org/elecref.html#Databases. This article is no longer available on the APA Web site. The site has now been updated to include information from the fifth edition of the APA *Publication Manual.* See http://www.apastyle.org/elecref.htm for more information.

18. *Publication Manual of the American Psychological Association,* Fifth Edition (Washington, DC: APA, 2001), 271.

19. Janice R. Walker, "Walker/ACW Style Sheet (Columbia Online Style): COS-Humanities Style (MLA-Style Citations of Electronic Sources)," Version 1.3, January 1995, Revised 1999, http://www.cas.usf.edu/english/walker/mla.htm (April 27, 2001).

20. Conference on College Composition and Communication Committee on Computers in Composition and Communication (7Cs), http://www.ncte.org/committees/7c/ (April 26, 2001).

21. Walker and Taylor, *The Columbia Guide,* xii.

22. Ibid., 183.

23. Ibid., 15.

Index

jake, 55, 232-233
Johns Hopkins University Press,
    Project MUSE, 172
*Journal of Interactive Media in
    Education,* 197-216
    discourse, 202-204
    peer review, 204-208
    technology, 211-214
Journal of Logic Programming, 85
Journal Web Site LLC, 54
JSTOR, 38, 168, 230

Lexis-Nexis, 18, 234
Liblicense, 59
Library Journal, 32
*Library Literature and Information
    Science,* 249-254
Library of Congress, 14n3, 134-135
licensing, 21-22, 23, 58-69, 100-102
    negotiation, 63-64, 81-82
    policies, 95
    and preservation, 184-185
    tracking, 65-71
LOCKSS (Lots of Copies Keep Stuff
    Safe), 182
Los Alamos National Laboratory,
    174-175, 187, 241
Loughborough University, 171

Mathematics Markup Language, 178
MathSciNet, 20
MDL, 25
Medline, 20
metadata, 9-12, 155-165, 211-212
    definition, 156-157
    for preservation, 182-183
Microsoft Internet Explorer, 267-268
Mind-It, 55
mirror sites, 4-5
MIT, 43, 44-53, 65-69, 72. *See also*
    DSpace
Modern Language Association, 275-279

NASA, 14n3
National Center for Supercomputing
    Applications, 13

National Endowment for the
    Humanities, 14n3
National Institutes of Health, 174, 241
National Library of Medicine, 14n3
National Science Foundation, 2, 14n3,
    218, 223
NEDLIB (Networked European
    Deposit Library), 178, 183
NEEDS (National Engineering
    Education Delivery System),
    161
NESLI, 172
Netscape Navigator, 267-268
New Zealand Digital Library, 2

OCLC, 56
    Electronic Collections Online, 34
OhioLINK, 36, 57-58, 75, 172
OPAC, 53, 56
Open Archival Information System,
    182-183, 247
Open Archives Initiative, 174, 243
Ovid, 33

PDF, 19, 173, 177, 178, 189
PEAK (Pricing for Electronic Access to
    Knowledge), 22
peer review, 204-208
Pennsylvania State University, 65
persistent identifiers, 6-9. *See also*
    DOI; Handle System;
    Uniform Resource Identifiers;
    Uniform Resource Names
Philosophical Transactions, 239
PostScript, 177
preservation, 167-195. *See also*
    archiving
    authenticity, 183-184
    data migration, 181-182
    definition, 168-169
    and legal deposit, 186-187
    and licensing, 184-185
    selection for, 188-189
    software emulation, 181
    technology, 179-180
    who is responsible, 185-188